PROPAGANDA AND NATIONALISM
IN WARTIME RUSSIA

The Jewish Antifascist Committee
in the USSR, 1941–1948

WITHDRAWN

SHIMON REDLICH

EAST EUROPEAN MONOGRAPHS, NO. CVIII

BURGESS
DS
135
.R92
R43
1982

c.1

BURG · carp
82- gift

To the memory of my father
Shlomo Redlich
and other members of my family
who perished in the Holocaust.

CONTENTS

ABBREVIATIONS

ACJWAS — Files of the American Committee of Jewish Writers, Artists and Scientists. The Centre for Research and Documentation of East European Jewry, The Hebrew University of Jerusalem.

E/A — Erlich-Alter File. The Bund Archives of Jewish Labor Movement, Atran Center for Jewish Culture, New York.

EMC — Alfred Einstein Microfilm Collection. Princeton University Library, Princeton, New Jersey.

FBI ARCHIVES — Archives of the Federal Bureau of Investigation, U.S. Department of Justice, Washington, D.C.

GOLDBERG PAPERS — Ben Zion Goldberg Papers. The Dropsie University Archives, Philadelphia, Pennsylvania.

GOLDSTEIN PAPERS — Israel Goldstein Papers, Jerusalem.

IHS — The Polish Institute and Sikorski Museum Archives, London.

INTERVIEW NO.   Interview deposited at the Oral History
                       Division of the Institute of Contemporary
                       Jewry, The Hebrew University of Jeru-
                       salem.

JDC/A   The American Jewish Joint Distribution
                       Committee Archives, New York.

MEISEL PAPERS   Nachman Meisel Papers, Kibbuts
                       Alonim.

NADB   U.S. National Archives, Diplomatic
                       Branch, Washington, D.C.

PGHI   Polish Government Collection. The
                       Hoover Institute on War, Revolution
                       and Peace Archives, Stanford University,
                       Stanford, California.

PEWHI   Polish Embassy in Washington Collec-
                       tion. The Hoover Institution on War,
                       Revolution and Peace Archives, Stanford
                       University, Stanford, California.

PRO   Public Records Office, London.

S/I YIVO   The Polish Institute and Sikorski Museum
                       Files at YIVO Institute for Jewish Re-
                       search, New York.

WISE PAPERS   Stephen S. Wise Papers. Archives of the
                       American Jewish Historical Society,
                       Brandeis University, Waltham, Massa-
                       chussetts.

WJC/R   Russian Files. World Jewish Congress
                       Archives, New York.

PREFACE

A graduate seminar conducted at the Hebrew University some twenty years ago generated my interest in Soviet Jewry. The present study is a result of this interest. Despite the many difficulties in researching this relatively unexplored area of contemporary history, I enjoyed filling in the pieces of what resembled a complicated jigsaw puzzle. Undoubtedly, some spaces still remain blank. I would like to thank all those who encouraged and assisted me during this arduous process.

I have discussed the issues and problems relating to this study more than once with my friend and colleague Prof. Mordechai Altshuler and benefited from presenting parts of it to his graduate seminar. Profs. Chimen Abramsky, Alexander Erlich, Shmuel Ettinger, Ezra Mendelsohn and Leonard Schapiro and Dr. Zeev Tsahor read parts of the manuscript and commented on them. Prof. John Armstrong read the entire manuscript and made valuable suggestions. The late Zosa Szajkowski of the YIVO Institute directed me towards significant archival collections in the U.S. as did my friend and colleague Dr. Yeshayahu Jelinek. Prof. Abraham I. Katsh enabled me to examine the B. Z. Goldberg Papers at Dropsie University. My friend Dr. Avigdor Shahan obtained relevant material for me in Mexico.

I appreciated the expertise and patience of the staffs of: the Centre for Documentation and Research of East European Jewry at the Hebrew University, the U.S. National Archives, the Hoover Institution Archives, the YIVO Institute Library and Archives, the Bund Archives, the Public Record Office, the Yad Vashem Library and

Archives, the World Jewish Congress New York Office, the JDC and
the American Jewish Committee Archives. I am particularly grateful
for the assistance extended to me by the Oral History Division of the
Institute of Contemporary Jewry at the Hebrew University in typing
my numerous interviews in various languages. I also appreciate the
cooperation and patience of my interviewees.

This study could have never been completed without the generous
financial assistance of the Faculty of Humanities & Social Sciences at
Ben Gurion University of the Negev, the American Council of Learned
Societies and the Kennan Institute for Advanced Russian Studies.
In the various stages of editing of the manuscript I was assisted by
Mrs. Ann K. Blumberg, Mrs. Haya Galai, Ms. Ina Friedman and
Mrs. Leah Pinhas. Mrs. Pinhas also helped me with the bibliography.
The final draft was typed excellently by Mrs. Tsila Barneis. And finally
many thanks to my cooperative editor, Prof. Stephen Fischer-Galati.

My wife, Judith, besides displaying patience and forbearance,
helped me in editing and indexing and my daughters Shlomit and
Efrat had to endure at times a "closed door" policy, for which I
apologize.

Omer, Israel, January, 1982

INTRODUCTION

This book attempts to examine the relationship between the Soviet Union and the Jews during what was a fateful period for both: the Second World War. Essentially, it traces Jewish responses to Soviet war propaganda. However, it also illuminates the crucial problem of Soviet policies and Jewish nationalism at that time. In order to understand the realities and implications of Soviet-Jewish relations during the War, it is necessary to review Soviet policies towards Jews and Jewish attitudes towards the USSR during the period between the Bolshevik Revolution and the outbreak of World War II.[1]

The theory and ideology of Bolshevism did not recognize the Jews as a nation. Both Lenin and Stalin believed that the Jews were in the process of shedding the last vestiges of national identity. However, for reasons of "realpolitik", the Bolsheviks both before, and (even more) after the Revolution, made certain concessions to Jewish nationalism. Basic theoretical premises were never abandoned, but day-to-day policies were adapted to circumstances.

The Soviet attitude to Jewish nationalism was usually governed by both general nationality policy and Jewish-oriented considerations. Whereas some "reactionary" aspects of Jewish nationalism were already being suppressed during the immediate post-Revolutionary years, other expressions of Jewish identity were allowed, and sometimes even encouraged, until well into the 1930's. Traditional Jewish communal life had come to an end by 1919 and the various Russian Jewish political parties ceased to exist. Jewish religious life was severely curtailed, but Zionism, although ideologically condemned, was tolerated for some time. The fact that most Zionist organizations, unlike other Jewish political groupings in Russia, were outward-oriented, and supposedly influenced Jewish public opinion abroad, alleviated Soviet anti-Zionist pressure during the first years of the Bolshevik regime. Hebrew culture, tolerated during the first half of the decade, was outlawed completely in the late 1920's. Nevertheless, Jewish national existence continued in the USSR, though not in its traditional sense. It assumed new forms, compatible with Soviet realities, and found its expression in the political, economic, administrative, and, above all, cultural spheres. For most of the 1920's the Soviets practiced a moderate policy towards the various nationalities in the USSR. The regime utilized national and ethnic politics for its own ends—namely to win internal support or recognition abroad. A policy of "Ukrainization", "Belorussification", or in our case, "Yiddishization" (i.e. concessions to certain nationalities in the administrative, cultural and other areas) was aimed at mobilizing the sympathy of various national elements inside the USSR and of their counterparts abroad.

The Evsektsiia, (the Jewish Sections of the Communist Party) was established for the purpose of modernizing and integrating Russia's Jewish population, and its main function was to eliminate the traditional structures of Jewish national life. But it also contained some nationally-conscious elements interested in the preservation of certain forms of Jewish national existence. The Evsektsiia also functioned as an official Soviet organ explicitly supporting Jewish economic and cultural ventures. In the economic sphere, official sanction was given to Jewish agricultural settlement in certain areas, such as the Ukraine, Belorusia, the Crimea and Birobidzhan, thus creating the possibility for a limited Jewish territorial base. The idea of Jewish Birobidzhan was also meant to compete with Palestine-oriented Zionism. Organizations promoting Jewish settlement, were established, and Jewish assistance from abroad for this objective was encouraged. This, in turn, resulted in the establishment of contacts with Jewish organizations outside the USSR. In the administrative sphere, local Jewish councils (Soviets) and Jewish national districts were allowed in territories with dense Jewish populations. Yiddish courts of justice also existed in those places. The possibilities for developing cultural nationalism within the communist framework, granted to various nationality groups, were, to some extent, also granted Soviet Jews. Thus, the 1920's witnessed the flourishing of Yiddish literature in the

USSR. Though this literature was communist-oriented and meant to Sovietize the predominantly Yiddish-speaking Jewish population it also abounded in elements of Jewish national identity. Some contacts were still being maintained with centers of Yiddish literature and culture abroad. There was a steady increase in the number of Soviet-Yiddish schools. They were established for the purpose of educating the young in the spirit of Soviet communism, but the fact that the language of instruction was Yiddish transformed them into focuses of Jewish national identity. Yiddish theatres, headed by Moscow's GOSET, became a significant component of Jewish cultural life in the USSR. Some Jewish scholarly institutions were also allowed. Besides serving the internal purposes, Soviet support for Yiddish culture in the USSR was used extensively for the mobilization of Jewish public opinion in the West.

The Jewish-oriented activities and structures, inspired by Soviet domestic and foreign policy considerations of the 1920's suffered a serious setback in the 1930's. Both socio-economic and cultural processes within the Soviet-Jewish population, and an increased tendency of the regime towards centralism and uniformity, significantly affected the various forms of Jewish national expression in the USSR. It is quite obvious that Soviet Jews, who lacked a substantial territorial base, suffered more than others, from the reversal in Soviet nationality policies. The Evsektsiia had played a role in the suppression of traditional Jewish nationalism, but its liquidation in 1930 also meant the disappearance of an official central Jewish structure in the USSR. The 1930's witnessed a decline in the distinctly Jewish agricultural settlements and the liquidation of organizations dealing specifically with Jewish agriculture. Jewish activities in Birobidzhan were seriously affected by the purges during the second half of the decade. The number of Jewish administrative units and Yiddish speaking judicial institutions which reached its height in the early thirties declined steadily afterwards.

Soviet-Yiddish culture suffered severe blows to both scope and content. The regimentation of Soviet literature in general in the early thirties, seriously curtailed the possibilities of national expression in Soviet-Yiddish literature. Certain topics and issues, were now taboo and a new Soviet orthography of the Yiddish language was enforced. The introduction of foreign elements into Yiddish literature was criticized and contacts with Yiddish literature and writers abroad came to a halt. There was also a steady decline in Yiddish publishing. Some

Yiddish theatres were closed down. All this spelled attrition for Jewish national culture inside the USSR, and total isolation from Jewish culture abroad.

Western Jewish attitudes towards communist Russia were largely affected by the treatment of Jews inside the USSR.[2] Criticism was directed at Soviet policies towards Jewish religion, culture and Zionism. But there were also expressions of appreciation of what seemed to be a solution to the perennial "Jewish problem" in Eastern Europe. The integration and advancement of Jews within Soviet society, support for Soviet-Yiddish culture, official Soviet criticism of antisemitism—all these evoked favorable responses, at least among some sectors of Jewish public opinion abroad. But even these pro-Soviet attitudes were gravely affected by the 1939 Molotov-Ribbentrop Agreement and the new image of Soviet Russia as Hitler's ally. On the eve of the Russo-German War, Jewish national existence inside the Soviet Union was on the decline and Russia's popularity among Jews abroad was at its nadir. It is our contention that the momentous events of World War II reversed this situation noticeably in both respects.

The addition of a two-million strong nationally conscious, Jewish population in territories annexed by the USSR in 1939–1940 had a significant impact on Soviet Jewry. Hundreds of thousands of Polish, Lithuanian, Latvian and Rumanian Jews spent the War years in the USSR. Of special importance were contacts established between Jewish refugee writers and artists and their Soviet-Jewish counterparts. Nazi policies towards Jews, had a profound effect on the Jewish population in the USSR. The reactions of the Soviet-Yiddish cultural elite, as well as numerous Russian-acculturated Jewish intellectuals assumed definite national overtones. Jewish consciousness and identity were also enhanced by the growth of antisemitism in the USSR. It was precisely at this time that, due to specific wartime considerations, the Soviet regime was obliged to formulate a moderate stand on a number of matters relating to domestic and foreign policies. Religious and national restrictions were relaxed considerably inside Russia and contacts with the outside world were now encouraged. A Soviet Jewish Antifascist Committee was founded at that unique meeting point of Soviet and Jewish realities. It was the most meaningful Jewish structure (on the All Union level) to emerge since the liquidation of the Evsektsiia. Although it was initially created in order to mobilize Jewish public opinion abroad, it was transformed in time into a focus of Jewish identity inside the USSR and of contacts with Jewish organizations and individuals abroad. The new realities of the wartime era were reflected to a considerable extent in the nature and history of this Committee.[3] This is precisely the reason why a study of the Jewish Antifascist Committe (JAC) can serve as a framework for examining Soviet-Jewish relations during the War in general.

The major issues to be examined in this study are: The nature of Soviet wartime propaganda; early Soviet attempts to organize a Jewish Anti-Hitlerite Committee in the USSR and their failure; the emergence of the Committee, its membership and structure; the Committee's activities and its meaningfulness for Soviet Jews; the emergence, nature and activities of pro-Soviet Jewish organizations abroad; contacts between the JAC and Jews outside the USSR; the attitudes of Jews abroad towards the Soviet Union; and finally the demise of the Jewish Antifascist Committee after the War.

The bulk of the material used in this book falls into the following categories:

a. Soviet publications, primarily those of the JAC itself, the most important source being the Committee's newspaper, *Eynikayt*.

b. Foreign Soviet-oriented Jewish publications.

c. Archival materials from the U.S. State Department, the British Foreign Office and the Polish Government in Exile.

d. Memoirs of persons associated with the JAC.

e. Interviews with individuals who were either close to the JAC in the USSR, or active within pro-Soviet Jewish organizations abroad.

These sources are mainly in Russian, Yiddish, Hebrew, Polish and English and were collected over a number of years in Israel, England and the U.S.

Perets Markish, David Bergelson, Solomon Mikhoels and Ilya Ehrenburg at one of the JAC meetings.

С. С. Михайлов читает свою речь на открытии с'езда.

S. S. Mikhailov speaking at the opening session of the V League Convention in Jerusalem, August 1942.

Mikhoels and Fefer at Shalom Aleichem's tombstone during their 1943 visit to the U.S. From left to right: B. Z. Goldberg, Solomon Mikhoels, Itsik Fefer, Mrs. Goldberg (Shalom Aleichem's daughter), the Goldbergs' son Mitchell. Courtesy of Dropsie University Archives.

Mikhoels and Fefer with Albert Einstein.

Mikhoels and Fefer during their 1943 visit to England. Courtesy of Joseph Leftwich.

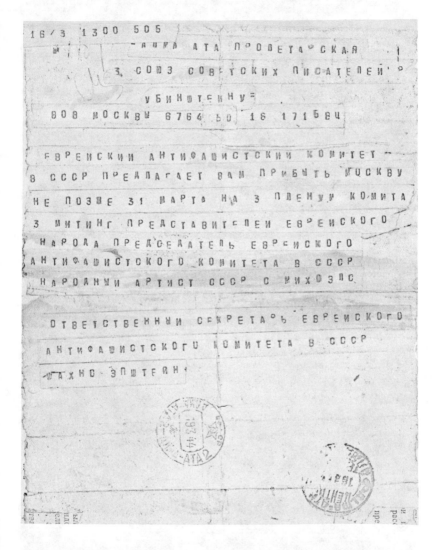

Telegram sent by the JAC to refugee poet from Poland, Joseph Rubinstein, inviting him to come to Moscow for the April 1944 JAC Plenary Session.

Ilya Ehrenburg surrounded by Jewish partisans in liberated Vilna in the summer of 1944. This photograph appeared in *Eynikayt* on July 27, 1944. Courtesy of Yad Vashem Archives.

B. Z. Goldberg during his 1946 visit to the Soviet Union as guest of the JAC. From left to right: poet Abraham Sutskever, unidentified, Ben Zion Goldberg, Prof. Lina Shtern, General Aaron Kats, poet Shmuel Halkin. Courtesy of Dropsie University Archives.

Paul Novick during his 1946 visit to the Soviet Union, at the JAC. From left to right: Paul Novick, Dr. Boris Shimelovich (standing), pilot Paulina Gelman, poet Shmuel Halkin, Ukrainiab poet Maksim Ryl'skii, Itsik Fefer, Solomon Mikhoels. Courtesy of Paul Novick.

At one of the Wednesday Evenings of the JAC at Kropotkina 10. From left to right: *Eynikayt* correspondent Solomon Rabinovich, Solomon Mikhoels, Paul Novick, Itsik Fefer. Courtesy of Paul Novick.

1

SOVIET WAR PROPAGANDA

The propaganda directed at Jews in the USSR and abroad during
World War II must be seen as part and parcel of overall Soviet war
propaganda strategies and techniques. Dissemination of propaganda
has always been a major instrument in Soviet domestic and foreign
policy. The two major facets of Soviet propaganda, in the 1920's and
1930's were the revolutionary Marxian themes on the one hand and the
emphasis on universalistic themes on the other. Whereas the former
preached international communism and revolution against the existing
order, the latter evoked general ideals of progress, humanitarianism
and enlightenment. A long-time student of Soviet propaganda has
rightly pointed out the Soviet ability to combine devotion to communist ideology with practical compromises of all sorts.[1] In 1935–1939 in
particular this approach was utilized, and under the slogan of a
"united" and "popular" front against Fascism and Nazism, the Soviet
Union attempted to rally public opinion in the bourgeois democracies
in the West. The "popular front" tactic emphasized the common interests of communists and non-communists in the face of the threat posed
by Mussolini's Italy, Hitler's Germany and Franco's Spain. In order to
understand Soviet wartime propaganda policies, one should recall that
it was under Stalin that its "tactical flexibility" was fully developed.
Though quite alien to Marxist ideology, national sentiments and issues
were also sometimes exploited for propaganda purposes at home and
abroad. The "popular front" approach was, of course, abandoned in
the wake of the Nazi-Soviet treaty, but after Hitler's attack on the
USSR, in June 1941, it re-emerged, adapted now to the particularities

1

of the war. The Soviet regime attempted to consolidate the support of the bulk of its domestic population for the war effort, and to mobilize public opinion abroad for its foreign policy objectives. It now encouraged expressions of national and religious sentiments at home, while, abroad, to a large extent, emphasis on the "universalistic" elements uniting the forces fighting Nazism, replaced communist-oriented propaganda. The dissolution of the Communist International (Comintern), a traditional focus of international revolutionary loyalties, was symptomatic of this new situation.

At Home: Issues and Structures

Inside Russia a tactical reconciliation took place between the Soviet regime and the Orthodox Church. The Church was apparently considered as a significant tool in the mobilization of Russian nationalism and as a means for shaping public opinion in the allied countries. The Soviets also hoped that a more favorable attitude to Christianity would help mitigate anti-Soviet attitudes in Eastern Europe and in the Balkans. In the first few months after the German attack anti-religious activities were severely curtailed in the USSR. Anti-religious propaganda ceased, the League of the Militant Godless was disbanded, and bans on religious instruction were relaxed. The new tacit concordat was symbolized by the fact that Stalin granted an audience to the head of the Russian Orthodox Church.[2] Although Orthodox Christianity was the main beneficiary of Stalin's new religious policy other religious groups, such as Jews and Moslems, were also granted certain concessions. Goodwill messages to Stalin from various religious communities were openly published in Soviet publications.[3] On one occasion the authorities sponsored a joint appeal by Soviet rabbis and refugee rabbis from Poland residing in the Soviet Union, urging the Jews of America and other countries to join the war effort.[4]

The Soviets, besides initiating an all-out appeal to Great-Russian patriotism also launched an impressive internal campaign to foster nationalist pride among non-Russian nationalities. A common technique of this campaign was the organization of meetings of "representatives" of various Soviet nationalities. Such activities were oriented toward both Soviet and foreign audiences. In early August 1941, for example, a meeting was held to rally Slav elements, not only inside the Soviet-ruled parts of the USSR, but also under Nazi rule and in the

West. The meeting of Jewish representatives which took place two weeks later, was directed at Jews outside the Soviet Union, mainly in the U.S. These meetings were a prelude to a series of similar gatherings, all following a similar pattern. At a gathering of Ukrainians, for example, which took place in late November 1941,[5] a carrot and stick approach was adopted. On the one hand, the regime proclaimed its support for Ukrainian national sentiments, and on the other hand, it threatened reprisals against those Ukrainian elements who collaborated with the Germans. Throughout 1942 and in the first half of 1943, the Soviet press published appeals to Ukrainians and articles on Ukrainian loyalty to the USSR.[6] Ukrainian-oriented propaganda was most intensive during the period of the German occupation of the Ukraine. Similarly, meetings of and appeals to the Belorussians and to the Baltic nationalities mainly took place in 1942.[7] Propaganda directed towards national and ethnic groups inhabiting the Caucasus region was stepped-up in July-November 1942, the most critical period of the German advance in that area. Soviet propagandists pointedly threatened those contemplating collaboration with the Germans, referring to the early period of Soviet rule in the Caucasus, when local elements had actively opposed Communism.[8] Rallies of Soviet Central Asia nationalities were also organized.[9] Party and Government officials constituted only a small percentage of the signatories to the various Soviet resolutions and appeals; the emphasis was clearly on representatives of national cultures. Among the signatories of the Ukrainian appeals were such personalities as O. O. Bogomolets, head of the Ukrainian Academy of Sciences, Pavlo Tychina, Mikola Bazhan and Maksim Ryl'skii, all nationally-known poets. The most prominent participants at the Jewish meeting were Solomon Mikhoels, director of the Moscow Jewish Theatre, such writers as Perets Markish and Ilya Ehrenburg, and a number of Jewish artists, actors and scientists. The campaign was extended to the Soviet Army.[10] The national and ethnic affiliation of numerous war heroes was highlighted by the Soviet press. Delegations representing national groups were dispatched to the front lines and appeals by members of various nationalities to their co-nationals in the Army were published in the national and local press and reprinted in Army newspapers. In addition, a growing number of broadsides in the languages of various nationalities were being printed and distributed on the fronts.

In order to increase the impact of the war propaganda, the Soviets frequently made use of specific population groups—women, young people or scientists for example. Meetings of "representatives" of these broad categories were organized in the early fall of 1941, soon after the first Slav and Jewish gatherings. An appeal by Soviet women to women abroad was signed by world famous figures, such as Dolores Ibarruri, the legendary leader of Republican Spain.[12] A mass youth rally was held in September;[13] in October Soviet scientists with world-wide reputations appeared at an anti-Nazi meeting.[14] Antifascist committees of Soviet women, youth and scientists were subsequently established.[15] These committees, drawn mainly from non-party elements maintained reciprocal contacts. Thus, the physicist Petr Kapitsa, a member of the Scientists' Committee, spoke at the first Jewish rally; the chemist Aleksandr Frumkin, served on both the Jewish and the Scientific committees. Academician, Lina Shtern, was a member of the Jewish, the Scientists' and the Soviet Women's Committees. In fact, all the committees were run by the Soviet Information Bureau (Sovinformburo), and their headquarters were located in the same building on Kropotkina street in Moscow.

The Sovinformburo, a branch of the Commissariat for Foreign Affairs, was responsible for a considerable part of Soviet wartime propaganda, for both domestic and foreign consumption. Stalin's use of the Sovinformburo and its various antifascist committees was con-committant with Soviet wartime emphasis on nationalism and statism and with the shrinking of Party influence in the ideological sphere.[16] This agency, set up during the first week of the Nazi-Soviet war, performed a wide variety of functions. It produced leaflets which were dropped behind enemy lines, issued official communiqués on the military situation and, most important supervised the flow of information and propaganda abroad. It supplied material for publication in Soviet embassy bulletins, (such as the *Information Bulletin* published in Washington, D.C. and *Soviet War News* published in London). By the end of the War, the Bureau was sending out about 7,000 words daily to American newspapers alone. During the summer and fall of 1941, the Sovinformburo sponsored special press conferences for foreign correspondents in the USSR, a total reversal of Soviet communication policy. Since the Bureau included special regional departments (most important were the US and British departments), it required a staff of experts. Journalists, editors and people with diplomatic experience were recruited to its staff. Solomon Lozovskii, Deputy Director and subsequently Director of the Sovinformburo, was one of the most sophisticated and Western conscious members of the Soviet elite.

Mikhail Borodin, Chief Editor of the Bureau, had served as Soviet advisor to the Kuomintang in the 1920s and had once been deputy director of TASS, the central USSR press agency. Stalin himself considered the work of the Sovinformburo to be extremely important for the war effort,[17] hence he . assigned Aleksandr Shcherbakov, one of his most powerful lieutenants and close confidantes to supervise it.[18] His early career had included a brief period as Gorky's secretary, (when the latter was Chairman of the Soviet Writers' Union); directorship of the Cultural Enlightment Section of the Party Central Committee, and service as Regional Party Secretary. He then became Secretary of the Central Committee and alternate member of the Politburo. During the War, in addition to running the Sovinformburo, he held an impressive number of posts, including that of chief Party boss in Moscow, Deputy Commissar of Defense, and Head of the Political Administration of the Army. Unlike most of the Bureau personnel, Shcherbakov was intellectually remote from foreign culture, and had never been abroad. He was in fact considered by Western observers to be one of the most chauvinistic, xenophobic and antisemitic members of Stalin's entourage and was believed to dislike America in particular. It seems that Stalin though aware that the Bureau needed foreign affairs experts and people familiar with Western culture, appointed a particularly trusty watchdog to supervise them.[19]

Abroad: Fronts and Fellow-Travelers

Soviet foreign war propaganda centered on the encouragement and manipulation of pro-Soviet groups and fronts abroad. Such groups ranged from those clearly identified with Communism to various amorphous Aid-to-Russia societies. Some of these organizations had ulterior motives of their own vis-à-vis the Soviet Union, so that each side hoped to gain dividends from wartime cooperation. Special Soviet efforts were directed towards cultural, religious and ethnic groups, for example Americans of East European origin, Orthodox Church believers, liberal intellectuals, and more vaguely-defined groups, i.e. youth, women and scientists. Individual writers, scientists etc. were also exploited, sometimes without their knowledge, for Soviet propaganda purposes. In addition, various old and newly founded pro-Soviet publications in several languages were utilized as platforms for

Soviet stands and policies. This massive Soviet public relations offensive culminated in visits abroad by non-political Soviet personalities: writers, artists, scientists, representatives of Soviet youth and women's organizations.

Soviet wartime propaganda methods were based on previous experience, acquired in operation of pro-communist international organizations established by the Comintern in the 1920's. Their propaganda had emphasized the fact that the Soviet Union, as the first socialist state in history, was the ally of all workers and liberal-minded people. The steady growth of fascist trends in Europe during the thirties greatly enhanced the credibility of such arguments. Refugee German intellectuals with leftwing sympathies influenced the shaping of public opinion in their host countries. Links with communist organizations became more acceptable in the West. Soviet Russia had always attempted to mobilize for its causes opinion leaders abroad, especially among Western intellectuals in both the cultural and scientific spheres. This may have reflected a characteristic Soviet tendency to foster close relations between the regime and its own intellectuals. The latters aid was also frequently enlisted to charm the foreigners. It became something of a Soviet tradition to invite prominent foreign writers and artists to visit the USSR and lavish on them official attention, such as they did not enjoy in their own countries. Publication of their books and staging of their plays was planned to coincide with the period of their visits. Official flattery included the bestowal of state decorations and, in some cases, interviews with the heads of state. Payment of royalties for works published by Soviet-government presses, (as a rule withheld from foreign authors), provided, in some cases, an additional incentive to admire the land of socialism. Some Western intellectuals were drawn to Soviet Russia by the very appeal of power, viewing the USSR as the ultimate winner in the historical process. Others, disappointed with the realities of bourgeois liberalism (especially with the worldwide economic crisis of the late twenties and early thirties) and with its culture, made their pilgrimage to Russia looking for inspiration and new ideals. The Soviets highly encouraged such foreign visitors, many of whom were sure to convey a positive image of the USSR among their audiences at home.[20] Intellectuals of this ilk were utilized extensively in Soviet propaganda campaigns outside the Soviet Union. Willi Muenzenberg, a top propaganda specialist of the Comintern, in the interwar years, recruited such people as Romain Rolland, G. B. Shaw, and Albert Einstein into the League Against War and Fascism, a prototype of the communist-sponsored anti-war organizations which mushroomed in the thirties. In the U.S., the League for Peace and Democracy, claimed more than a thousand affiliated organizations with two million members. In England there was a Society for Cultural Relations Between the British Commonwealth and the USSR and in France, Les Amis de l'URSS. Another such American organization was Friends of Soviet Russia or as it became known later—Friends of the Soviet Union.

In its war propaganda, as in its peacetime foreign propaganda the Soviet Union extensively exploited "fellow traveling" and "front organizations". A pro-Soviet "front" has been defined as resembling a steamship in which "the engine room was manned by communists . . . but both the admirals . . . parading the deck and the young ensigns enthusiastically hauling up the flags were fellow-travelers and sympathizers."[21] There are those who differentiate between degrees of pro-Soviet sentiment—moderate support of sympathizers and the greater involvement of true fellow-travelers. There is also some dispute as to whether those who 'hauled up the flags' were merely 'innocent dupes' or were involved by deliberate choice.[22] Perhaps the most important aspect of the 'front', vis-à-vis its usefulness to Soviet propaganda, was its ability to provide points of contact with non-communist sectors in the West. Numerous non-communists joined front organizations because they concurred with the communist core on certain issues. Another motive for joining was sometimes the wish to influence communist and Soviet policies in certain matters. A typical feature of a "front" was the internal division of functions and roles. Whereas the top ranking sponsors and officers were usually prominent non-communists who lent their names and prestige to the fronts' public activities, the effective posts were often manned by CP members, crypto-communists or trusted fellow-travelers. The president or chairman for example would be a prominent liberal, while the secretary and chief editor were loyal pro-communists. These "Hintermanner" quite often manipulated the unsuspecting and somewhat naive figureheads. Although the mechanics of directing and supervising the various fronts has never been fully revealed, it seems that both, the Moscow-controlled Comintern and Trade Union International (Profintern) performed a major role in it. The Soviet All-Union Society for Cultural Relations (VOKS) was also involved in "front" type activities. Though presented by the regime as a strictly non-Party organization, it was actually run by Party members and employed numerous GPU agents.[23]

The first two years of the Second World War were lean years for fellow-traveling and front organizations. Pro-communist and pro-Soviet sentiments were unpopular in the West, as a result of the Nazi-Soviet rapprochement. A considerable number of "fronts" became dormant or disappeared completely. The League for Peace and Democracy and the American Friends of the Soviet Union were dissolved. Communist party membership waned. But the image of Communist Russia which had been seriously damaged, was shortly to be restored under new circumstances. Hitler's attack on the USSR in June 1941 and the subsequent shift in world politics and alliances had an immediate and profound impact on attitudes towards the USSR. Now communists and communist sympathizers became more 'respectable' than ever before, they were accepted in political and public life inter alia in Great Britain and the United States. In the U.S. this acceptance was also a by-product of the sharp transition from isolationism to an intense involvement in nationally-accepted war aims. This new situation affected the communist movement as well. The CPUSA changed its name to The Cultural Association, and its membership peaked in 1943–1944.[24] Pro-Soviet Friendship Societies and other "front organizations" in the U.S. showed a dramatic resurgence from June 1941, and particularly from December, of the same year. The new situation promised the Communists more influence within the "fronts" and more political leverage in general. The activities of the pro-communist International Workers Order (IWO), and particularly of its ethnic divisions, expanded considerably. The membership of British "fronts" was also on the rise. One such organization, the Association of Scientific Workers, increased its membership from about 1,000 in the late thirties to some 17,000 after the War. The National Council for British-Soviet Unity, established during the War, had more than 300 local affiliates.[25] A leading specialist on Soviet Russia has remarked that "At the War's end Soviet Russia's standing in intellectual and artistic circles of the West was at its peak."[26]

The leading pro-Soviet organizations in the U.S. during the War years were the National Council of American Soviet Friendship (NCASF) and the Russian War Relief (RWR). The former was founded as the American Council on Soviet Relations in 1938 and lay dormant during the difficult period of the Ribbentrop-Molotov Pact. It was reactivated after June 1941.[27] Its Chairman, Corliss Lamont, was a typical, liberal-intellectual fellow-traveler. A graduate of Harvard, Columbia and Oxford, he was an author and lecturer in philosophy, politics and economics. The American Council on Soviet Relations, was founded after Lamont's visit to the Soviet Union, where he received the usual fellow-traveler, VIP treatment. Its core activists included such known Soviet sympathizers as Rockwell Kent and Paul Robeson, and among its sponsors was Joseph E. Davies, former U.S. Ambassador to the USSR, whose naive enthusiasm for Russia was effectively exploited by Soviet propaganda. The Congress of American-Soviet Friendship, organized by the Council in November 1942, solicited and won the sponsorship of numerous prominent personalities in American public life. Its activities culminated in a Madison Square Garden mass-rally chaired by Davies and Lamont, at which the chief speakers were Vice-President Wallace and Soviet Ambassador Litvinov. Friendship Congresses commemorating the Bolshevik Revolution became a tradition during the War years. The 1943 Congress was addressed by Harold Ickes, U.S. Secretary of the Interior. At the 1944 rally Davies acted as Honorary Chairman and among the chief speakers were Edward Stettinius and Andrei Gromyko. The leadership of the Council went out of their way to emphasize the non-political basis of the organization.[28] Indeed they succeeded in mobilizing the support of such people as Pearl S. Buck, Ernest Hemingway, Thomas Mann, Eugene O'Neill, Helen Keller, Edward G. Robinson and Aaron Copland. Among their Jewish sponsors were Joseph A. Rosen of the American Jewish Joint Distribution Committee (JDC) and Philip Klutznik of B'nai B'rith. The NCASF maintained close contacts with the CPUSA. Some of the Council's officers were even active members of the Party. It is worth noting, that the Council's Executive Secretary, Edwin Smith, often consulted Roy Hudson, Secretary of the Party's Political Committee;[29] and Avram Landy, CPUSA member in charge of nationalities, frequently participated in the Council's events. Contacts with CP functionaries took place on both local and national levels, and organizational and financial matters related to pro-Soviet activities were discussed during such meetings. Ties were also maintained between Council officers and Soviet diplomatic personnel. The Soviet diplomat in charge of propaganda on the East Coast involved in most public NCASF activities during the War was Eugene D. Kisselev, USSR Consul General in New York. His counterpart on the West Coast was Grigorii Kheifets, Soviet

Vice-Consul in San Francisco. The latter is also known to have been a Soviet intelligence agent.[30] It is quite possible, therefore, that the instruction and manipulation of "front organizations" were supervised by the Soviet intelligence and security apparatus.

The Russian War Relief, although originally established for the purpose of material assistance, often dealt with the dissemination of Soviet information and propaganda. It was quite common since the early twenties for Aid-to-Russia structures and campaigns to be used for propaganda purposes. The establishment of a voluntary public war fund to aid the Soviet Union had already been discussed in the U.S. in July 1941. This idea was also advocated by the American Council on Soviet Relations. The Russian Embassy made it clear that medical aid would be their first priority. An American Committee for Medical Aid to Russia was founded in August 1941, and changed its name in October to Russian War Relief. Edward C. Carter, Chairman of the RWR, like Corliss Lamont, was a liberal intellectual educated at Harvard. Active for many years in the YMCA, both in the U.S. and abroad, he was an officer of the American-Russian Institute for Cultural Relations[31] and Secretary of the American Institute for Pacific Relations. He visited the Soviet Union a number of times during the 1930's. The post of Secretary of the RWR, a crucial position in any "front" structure, was initially held by Harriet Lucy Moore, a known fellow-traveler. At one time she was Executive Secretary of the American-Russian Institute for Cultural Relations. A prolific writer, she specialized in defending Soviet foreign policy. Like many other fellow-travelers, she went on a pilgrimage to Russia in the 1930's and was then employed for some time by Edward Carter as his research assistant. She resigned the secretaryship of the RWR, after much criticism of her overtly pro-Soviet activities, but continued to exert her influence, even after Allen Wardwell, a New York attorney and banker, took over the job. Wardwell himself was sympathetic towards Russia, since he had been a member of the Red Cross mission to Russia in 1917. These declared pro-Soviet RWR leaders were counter balanced (in the best tradition of a "front organization,") by such people as Philip Murray of the CIO and William Green of the AFL, both of whom were on the Board of Directors. The Board members also included a number of Jewish public figures, such as Joseph A. Rosen, James N. Rosenberg and Stephen Wise.

The Ethnic Element

A blatant example of ethnic manipulation in Soviet war propaganda was the Slav movement. It was initiated in the USSR a few weeks after Hitler's attack on Russia, and grew, in time, into a worldwide network of organizations and societies.[32] Soviet Slav-oriented propaganda focused on such conceptions as common historical origin and culture of all Slav nationalities in the USSR and abroad. The common interests of all Slavs, headed by the Russians, were juxtaposed to Nazi War aims. The "Slav" propaganda campaign, directed by an All Slav Committee in the USSR, was part of an overall Soviet tactic of using ethnic elements for War propaganda. It was no coincidence, therefore, that the first Slav and Jewish appeals emanated from Moscow simultaneously and that the Slav and Jewish anti-fascist committees were organized and functioned in a similar manner.[33] The members of the All-Slav Committee were mostly cultural and military personalities. Aleksei Tolstoy, famous Soviet writer and playwright, was the chief spokesman at the first Slav meeting in August 1941, and later served on the Committee's Presidium, together with such literary personalities as Mikhail Sholokhov, Maksim Ryl'skii and Aleksandr Fadeev. Among the military leaders of the Committee were General Aleksandr Gundorov, the Chairman, and the famous partisan leader General S. A. Kovpak. Another important member was the Polish communist writer Wanda Wasilewska, whose husband the Ukrainian playwright and Vice Chairman of the Committee, Aleksandr Korniichuk, evidently played an important political role in the Committee. A member of the Ukrainian CP Central Committee and Ukrainian Foreign Minister at the end of the War he is believed to have been in charge of the whole Slav movement. Among the committee's functionaries were various people with diplomatic experience and specialists in propaganda.[34] It was for good reason that the key post of Committee Secretary was entrusted to Colonel V. V. Mochalov, of the security apparatus.[35] It was only natural for the Slav Committee, which maintained contacts with foreign nationals inside the USSR and with various organizations abroad, to be closely supervised. One should bear in mind that attempts to organize an international Jewish committee in the Soviet Union during the first months of the War were sponsored by Beria, head of the Soviet security police. Individuals connected with the security apparatus also performed a significant role within the Soviet Jewish Antifascist Committee which emerged in Spring 1942.[36]

The principal target of the Soviet-sponsored Slav movement during the War were North Americans of Slav origin (mainly in the USA).[37] This sector numbering several millions, was apparently considered by Soviet propaganda specialists as a powerful means of exerting pressure on U.S. public opinion, and consequently, on the Administration. The Soviet Union had already tried to become involved in U.S. "ethnic politics," in the late thirties but the Molotov-Ribbentrop Agreement severely impeded such plans. The outbreak of German-Soviet hostilities and Russia's alliance with America, however, created the first real opportunity for "Slav politics" to become effective in the U.S. The first Soviet appeal to American Slavs in early August 1941, came within a few weeks of the German attack on the USSR. Organizational efforts started in the U.S. in September, and a pro-Soviet publication, *The Slavonic Monthly,* was launched in November. A provisional Slav Committee to Aid the USSR was set up in Pittsburgh, and soon succeeded in organizing a network of similar committees, especially in such centers of American Slavs as New York, Detroit, Chicago, Cleveland, Milwaukee and Buffalo. A nationwide American Slav Congress (AMSC) was founded in Detroit in April 1942,[38] and soon established favorable relations with the majority of the Slav organizations throughout the country. The foreign-language press was also harnessed to this end. It is difficult to assess the degree of direct communist influence upon the AMSC; though, the composition of the organization's leadership may provide some clues. The President, Leo Krzycki, a native-born American of Polish ancestry, although not a declared Communist himself, seemed to be increasingly influenced by Soviet views. His pre-War visit to the USSR, and the warm reception he was granted there, must have influenced his attitudes.[39] His involvement in American left-wing politics intensified shortly after the War, when he became Chairman of the Progressive Party's Nationalities Division and member of the Party's Platform Committee. George Pirinsky, another Congress leader was clearly identified with Communism. A former editor of a Bulgarian communist weekly and a correspondent for the *Daily Worker,* he became Executive Secretary of the AMSC in mid-1944 and one of its principal spokesmen in the following year.[40] Vinko Vuk, the Croatian Treasurer of the AMSC, was known for his pro-communist sympathies, and Michael Tkach, one of its vice-presidents, was editor of a Ukrainian pro-communist daily. Beyond these personal links between American Communism and AMSC executives, a special department within the CPUSA, directed and supervised communist "Slav" policies and contacts with the Slav movement.[41] The Soviet All-Slav Committee, like other anti-fascist committees in the USSR was geared initially to Soviet war purposes, but was later exploited for postwar Soviet aims. Thus, using the existing propaganda structure, the Slav Committee embarked starting in 1943 on vicious campaigns against the Polish Government in Exile in London and against non-communist Yugoslav politicians. While East European territories were being liberated by the Red Army, Slav-oriented propaganda was being employed to consolidate Soviet and communist claims in the region. National Slav committees were established in Poland, Czechoslavakia and Bulgaria. A number of local Slav committees were also organized in Soviet republics with a majority of Slavs, such as the Ukraine and Belorussia. Yugoslavia was selected as the international post-War center of the Slav movement; but it was quite evident that orders and policy would stem from Moscow.

Though Soviet propaganda experts planned to continue exploiting the Slav movement to their own ends in the postwar era, the momentous developments both in Soviet-Western relations and inside the socialist block in the years 1945–1948, adversely affected such intentions. The Great Alliance started to disintegrate, even before the War ended, and a conflict of interests emerged between Soviet Russia and her wartime Allies. As a consequence Soviet foreign propaganda faced progressively greater complications and difficulties. The broad "universalistic" themes it propounded during the War and the unifying factors it stressed were gradually replaced by more controversial issues. Criticism of Britain and the U.S. was voiced, at first indirectly and later outright, in various Soviet information and propaganda channels. Western public opinion responded in kind to the new realities of postwar politics. The author of a detailed study of American public opinion at that time notes that "from March 1945 on, American goodwill toward Russia declined sharply"[42]. Anti-Soviet attitudes were reflected in public criticism and official action against "un-American" activity. The Moscow-directed Slav movement figured prominently on the blacklist. The American Slav Congress was eventually listed as a subversive agency in mid 1948. At that time the Slav movement suffered another severe blow as a result of the final breach between Yugoslavia and the USSR. The various pro-Soviet fronts retained their influence for some time, but by the end of the decade most of their wartime support and impact were lost for good.

THE ERLICH-ALTER AFFAIR

A typical example of Soviet initiative in the propaganda sphere during the first months of the war was the Soviet interest in a proposal to set up an international Jewish committee in the USSR. The proposal was made by Henryk Erlich and Wiktor Alter, two prominent leaders of the Jewish Socialist Bund, which had emerged as the strongest party among Polish Jews on the eve of World War II. The Bund had been under sharp attack from the Bolsheviks for decades. Furthermore both men were outspoken critics of Stalin's regime and of his deal with Nazi Germany.[1] They were imprisoned by the Soviets a short time after the annexation of Eastern Poland by the USSR, in 1939. A sudden reversal in the Soviet treatment of Erlich and Alter in the Fall of 1941 was caused not only by the recent change in Soviet-Polish relations, resulting from Hitler's attack on Russia and the emergence of the Grand Alliance, but first and foremost by Soviet foreign propaganda needs during the first crucial phase of the war. The Soviet-Jewish meeting organized in Moscow in August 1941 and Soviet interest in Erlich and Alter, indicate that the utilization of Jews and Jewish public opinion for war propaganda objectives, was under serious consideration by the Soviet leadership at that time. Still unresolved was the question of the organizational nature and scope to be granted to pro-Soviet Jewish propaganda emanating from the USSR.

Imprisonment and Release

Erlich and Alter were among the hundreds of thousands of refugees who escaped the German army as it advanced into Western and Central Poland in September 1939. The Central Committee of the Bund decided that all its members should relocate to the non-occupied part of the country, unaware that they would soon find themselves in the domain of another hostile regime. In fact, Bund activists were among the first to be detained by the NKVD in Soviet-occupied Eastern Poland. Immediately after the annexation of Eastern Poland, following the Molotov-kibbentrop agreement, Soviet security officers began to investigate the whereabouts of leading Bund members. Erlich, who was en route to Vilna, was arrested on October 4 at the railroad station of Brzesc (Brest-Litovsk). The fact that he was transferred to a Moscow prison within four days indicates the importance his captors attributed to him.

Wiktor Alter had been detained in the city of Kowel a week earlier. Together with other Polish Trade Union leaders, he drafted an appeal to the new Soviet authorities. It stressed the significance of cooperation in the common struggle against German Fascism, and the readiness of Polish socialists to assist the Soviets in re-establishing orderly life in Eastern Poland. The document also expressed the hope that the future of the Soviet-annexed territories would be decided according to the free wishes of their inhabitants. (Alter had categorically refused to go into hiding, arguing that it was his duty to express in public the utmost necessity of combating Fascism). It is not entirely clear from existing reports whether the appeal was actually delivered to the local Soviet authorities, but all its signatories were arrested by the NKVD. Alter was incarcerated locally for six weeks, spent some time in a prison in Lutsk, and was transferred to Moscow in early December.

A number of attempts were made to release the two. The Polish socialist and writer, Wanda Wasilewska, who was sympathetic to the Bund, and was on close terms with members of the Soviet regime, promised to do whatever she could. The only encouraging message she delivered, however was that the two Bund leaders were still alive. Outside the USSR, labor organizations such as the American Federation of Labor, also intervened on their behalf; and some efforts were made by the U.S. State Department, with no results.[2]

Alter and Erlich were kept apart during the two years of their imprisonment but were treated quite similarly. In a letter written shortly after his release, Erlich reported to his friends abroad that the main charges against him in his interrogation were: connections with the international bourgeoisie; cooperation (together with Alter) with the Polish counter-intelligence; and contacts with an illegal Bundist network inside the USSR, all directed towards subversive activities against the Soviet state.[3] His interrogators seems to have a comprehensive file on him, including copies of his articles and speeches. Interestingly enough, as time progressed, the NKVD interrogators seemed to stress foreign affairs issues, and by Spring, 1941 (according to an indirect source) were accusing Erlich of criticizing Stalin's pact with Hitler, and asking for his detailed criticism of German-oriented Soviet policy, as well as his opinions on the British and U.S. stands, should Soviet-German relations deteriorate. It is also highly significant that Lavrentii Pavlovich Beria himself was present during one such interrogation. The interrogations intensified immediately after the German attack on the Soviet Union, but at the end of June, Erlich was hastily transferred to Saratov. On July 30th he was informed of indictment, and on August 2nd his death sentence was announced to him. At the end of the month, however, this sentence was unexpectedly commuted to ten years of labor camps. In early September, Erlich was brought back to the Lubyanka prison in Moscow, where, he was visited several times by a high ranking NKVD functionary, Colonel Aron Arkadii Volkovyskii. In a friendly and relaxed atmosphere, Volkovyskii told him that he would shortly be released, and should start making plans for future activities. The actual release occurred between September 11–13.

Alter's treatment, seemed to be somewhat harsher than that of Erlich, and he protested it from the first. In his arguments with the NKVD personnel, Alter repeatedly brought up the necessity to stop the use of terror in the USSR. His death sentence was announced on July 20, and 10 days later was commuted to 10 years in labor camps. He too was released around September 13–14.[4]

Soviet Considerations

The underlying reason for the reversal in treatment of Erlich and Alter was the momentous change in Soviet foreign policy, resulting from Hitler's attack on Russia, the Soviet rapprochement with the British and the thaw in Polish-Soviet relations. A letter from the British Foreign Office to the British Embassy in Moscow listed Erlich and Alter among eight outstanding Polish socialists whose release was sought by the British "to strengthen General Sikorski's hand with his people", i.e. to bolster the moderate Poles. Numerous appeals, **urging** the newly established Polish mission to the USSR to intervene for the release of the two outstanding Bundists, were received from various trade-union and labor organizations in the U.S. and England. The Polish Embassy in the USSR asked the Soviet authorities in late August and early September to release Erlich and Alter on a priority basis. On September 14, the two men appeared at the Polish Embassy in Moscow and Ambassador Kot notified his superiors in London that they looked rather weak but were energetic and anxious to act. It is significant to mention at this point that an official Soviet note to the Polish Embassy, sent a few days after their release, referred explicitly to Erlich and Alter as Polish citizens.[5]

The subsequent events should be examined in the light of the general military and political situation in the USSR, and its impact on the Soviet leadership, and on Stalin in particular. The commuting of the death sentences was possibly due to the newly signed Polish-Soviet agreements and the Supreme Soviet Decree of amnesty to Polish citizens detained in the USSR. But late August and early September also witnessed drastic deterioration in the Soviet military position. In mid-September, the Germans penetrated the last lines of Soviet defenses around Leningrad, and Soviet forces suffered a total defeat in the Ukraine. According to one historian of the period, September 12, "can be reckoned as the low point in the fortunes of the Red Army for the whole war".[6] Stalin's remarks to Harry Hopkins, personal envoy of President Roosevelt, in Moscow, at the end of July, reflected his stresses and fears at the time. Stalin seemed to believe that the entrance of the U.S. into the war against Hitler would be not only a significant military contribution, but a moral and psychological one as well. Though he was probably trying to flatter his visitor, we know from other sources how much weight he ascribed in those days to American attitudes towards Russia and to public opinion in the U.S.[7] In mid-September, when the Russian situation looked extremely bleak, Stalin also requested Churchill to transport British soldiers either to the port of Arkhangelsk or (via Persia) to Southern USSR.[8] Such appeals acquire special meaning when one considers Stalin's utmost distrust of what he considered to be uncontrollable forces inside the USSR. Still another critical period for Stalin was mid-October 41. He is believed to have fled Moscow then, at the time, convinced that the capital was lost.[9] The brief 'idyll' between the Soviet authorities, particularly the NKVD, and the two Bundist leaders from Poland, was undoubtedly a result of the unusual circumstances, prevailing at the time.

The extant evidence suggests that Beria and the NKVD were directly involved in the planning of a Jewish propaganda agency in the fall of 1941, using the released Bundist leaders for this purpose. To understand Beria's involvement in what appeared a matter of Soviet foreign policy and propaganda, one should examine his position within the Soviet leadership. By the fall of 1941 Beria had been the head of the Soviet security establishment for three years and a candidate member of the Politburo for two. His powers, as well as his influence, grew impressively as a result of the War. He was appointed one of the five members of the State Defence Committee, established as the supreme emergency organ a week after the Nazi invasion. The Defence Committee is believed to have superceded all State and Party structures, including the Politburo (at least during the first crucial part of the War). Its members not only advised Stalin, (who was Chairman), on matters of high policy; they were also delegated as special plenipotentiaries to some of the most crucial areas of battle. During the War, Beria was also involved in security and economic affairs in the organizing of partisan warfare and supervised armaments and munition production. The NKVD dominated both the military and the civilian sphere in particular during the early months of the War.[10]

We may assume that as intelligence boss, Beria also had a hand in Soviet covert propaganda activities abroad, such as the subtle manipulation of pro-Soviet fronts. One clear case of his involvement was in Polish affairs in the USSR. Many of the Polish deportees and refugees, (including the future commander of the Polish Army in the Soviet Union, General Wladyslaw Anders) spent long months in Beria's domain. Beria is also known to have been involved in preparing a nucleus of Polish communists inside the USSR for postwar purposes. A high ranking official of the NKVD, Colonel Arkadii Volkovyskii, who played a central role in the Erligh-Alter case, functioned as liaison officer between the Soviet authorities and the Polish Army Command. Generals Zhukov and Fedotov, both active in Polish affairs, also participated in the planning of a Jewish committee to be headed by Erlich and Alter. At a conference of General Anders with Soviet high ranking officers, Volkovyskii stated that ". . .we, for our part [meaning obviously the NKVD] will support, in Moscow, the further organization of the Polish Army".[11] The NKVD was also active in the promotion of Soviet War propaganda objectives, exploiting the complex relationship between Poles and Polish Jewish refugees in the USSR.

Who really engendered the idea of a Jewish anti-Nazi committee in the USSR? Available information seems to indicate that both sides— the Soviet authorities and the two Bundists were interested in the scheme, each for its own reasons and objectives. The idea must have been discussed sometime before the release of Erlich and Alter. The opening line in a report they submitted to the Polish Embassy in early October read: "In connection with, as well as after, our release from prison, we had the opportunity to conduct a number of discussions with authoritative Soviet representatives (NKVD). The idea of forming the Jewish Anti-Hitlerite Committee (JAHC) emerged in the course of these discussions."[12] One should keep in mind that Erlich and Alter were the most prominent Polish Jewish refugees in the USSR. They were known to have been in the forefront of anti-fascist and anti-Hitlerite propaganda campaigns before the War, had attempted to form anti-Hitlerite committees in Poland and supported similar organizations abroad. They also had excellent contacts with socialist and labor establishments in the U.S. and England, countries which in the fall of 1941 were primary targets of the Soviet propaganda effort. Colonel Aaron Volkovyskii met the two men shortly after their release, when they were comfortably located in the Moscow Metropol Hotel. He urged them to consider the two years of imprisonment, as well as their death sentences, as "mistakes". "Now", he said, "we are involved in a common struggle against the mortal danger of Hitlerism and we must fight together . . ." He also suggested that they head a world Jewish committee to fight Fascism.[13] A Bundist friend of Erlich and Alter testified that he too was visited by Colonel Volkovyskii before he was released from prison, and told him that Erlich and Alter, as well as other Jewish socialists from Poland, had been freed, since they were to be partners in the Soviet struggle against Fascism. Erlich and Alter submitted a list of 75 other Bundists whose release from prison they requested. The impression at that time was that many more Bundists were being set free than members of other Jewish political parties.[14]

The Plan

Very little is known about the contacts between Erlich and Alter and those Soviet-Jewish personalities who participated in the "meeting of Jewish representatives", in Moscow on August 24. According to one source, the Bundist leaders, met future members of the Soviet Jewish

Antifascist Committee while in Moscow. Khazanovich of the NKVD apparently accompanied them to the apartment of the leading Yiddish Soviet poet, Perets Markish, (whom they knew from his sojourn in Poland in the twenties) where they met the Director of the Moscow Yiddish Theater, Solomon Mikhoels, and the poet Itskik Fefer. [15] We may thus assume that close cooperation between Soviet and non-Soviet Jewish leaders was being seriously considered at the time. Several documents dating from that period clearly mention Mikhoels as one of the three leading members of the planned committee. [16] The official proposal to organize a Jewish Anti-Hitlerite Committee in the USSR was submitted to Stalin sometime in early October, about three weeks after Erlich and Alter were released. (Shortly thereafter they left for Kuibyshev, together with Soviet and foreign officials temporarily evacuated from Moscow).

In a note addressed to Beria around that time Erlich and Alter stated: "Following our conversation with you, we conducted a number of discussions in order to work out in detail the principles on which we had agreed. As a result of these discussions, an appeal by the 'initiating group' concerning the formation of a Jewish Anti-Hitlerite Committee was addressed to the Chairman of the Council of People's Commissars requesting permission to organize such a Committee on the territory of the Soviet Union . . . We turn to you at the same time, honorable Lavrentii Pavlovich, and request your assistance to speed the matter towards a satisfactory solution." In the opening sentences of the letter to Stalin, Erlich and Alter emphasized the role played by the USSR in the struggle against Nazi Germany and its significance to the international labour movement. Hitler's extreme anti-Jewish policies called, for a special effort on the part of Jews everywhere. They went on to outline the basic credo of the committee planners: "All activities of the Jewish Anti-Hitlerite Committee, and particularly its propaganda, should stem from the conviction that (a). The liberation of the Jewish masses from suppression in any country, and from Hitlerite persecution in particular, is strongly tied up with the liberation of all nations . . . (b). The liberation of the Jewish masses from national oppression will be possible only when the state's existence is based on the principle of social justice and national liberation." Such widely defined principles of national and social justice could be interpreted as applying not only to Nazi Germany or postwar Poland. They may also have hinted at conditions prevailing in the Union of Socialist Republics.

The tasks of the Committee, in addition to waging anti-Nazi propaganda, were to include caring for Polish-Jewish refugees in the USSR. The Committee was also to encourage the mobilization of able bodied refugees into the armed forces, mainly the Polish Army being formed by General Anders, and establish cooperation with governments of all countries opposing Germany. The U.S.A. and American Jewry in particular, were to be a central target. The proclaimed objectives, as well as the envisaged structure of the Committee, point to its decisively international character. Erlich and Alter proposed that the core of the Committee consist of 10 members, 7 representing Nazi occupied countries, (mainly Poland) and one each from the USSR, U.S.A. and England. The Committee Presidium would consist of Erlich, chairman, Alter, secretary and a Soviet Jewish personality. A representative of the Soviet Government and the ambassadors of the USSR, the U.S.A. and Great Britain would be honorary members. Writers, scientists and artists from various countries would also participate. The Committee would send representatives to the various centers of Polish-Jewish refugees in the USSR, and to countries outside the Soviet Union. The proposed Committee would maintain contact with and obtain information on the Jewish population in Nazi-occupied Poland, and it would also try to send there its own representative. Erlich and Alter considered Polish Jewry, the largest Jewish community in Europe at that time, as the mainstay of their political, as well as moral, authority. They drafted an appeal to Polish Jews, stressing the international nature of the struggle against Hitler and the necessity for Jewish-Polish cooperation. In it, they promised Polish Jewry that "the task of the Jewish Anti-Hitlerite Committee is to stir the Jewish masses all over the world and urge them to assist you in this struggle".[17] In the U.S.A. the Committee would form a Jewish Legion to fight the Nazis within the framework of the Soviet Army. With the help of friends and sympathizers, Jewish antifascist committees would be formed in the U.S. and, if possible, in England as well. Erlich and Alter concluded by asking for an initial working staff of 20, to consist of Polish-Jewish refugees, and for a budgetary allocation, and housing for the Committee's offices and its members. Erlich and Alter envisioned a truly international Jewish organization, enjoying considerable power and prestige in the USSR and abroad.

How could the two Bundist leaders, who had been closely acquainted with Bolshevik tactics for decades, assume that their plans would meet with Soviet approval?

The reasoning behind the plan is reflected in a number of documents. In a letter to the Bund in New York, Erlich wrote, "Representatives of the NKVD wait attendance on us. The reason is, that they hope to be able to use our connections in America. We, for our part, want to make use of them in order to establish contacts with Poland".[18] To a memo to the Polish Ambassador, in the USSR, Erlich and Alter, appended the following semi-official note: "The emergence of the JAHC (Jewish Anti-Hitlerite Committee) would be the first break in Soviet practice banning socialists from participation in any public activities. The decisive influence in the JAHC would be exerted by socialists. The fact that the Soviet authorities now comply with this break, points to the great importance which they attribute to propaganda activities of the Committee in the U.S.A. promoting military support for the Soviet Union. We are of the opinion that our Party's relations with public organizations in the U.S.A. has managed to achieve certain positive results for the struggle against Hitlerism. . . . Moreover, the formation of the JAHC would facilitate activities for and among the refugees".[19] Alter, in a letter to Adam Ciolkosz, a Polish socialist residing in London, expressed hopes for a far-reaching change in one of the basic tenets of Stalin's regime "I met Citrine here [Sir Walter Citrine, a British Trade Union official then on a visit to the Soviet Union] and spoke to him about the amnesty. I am afraid that I did not succeed in convincing him of the need to act in this matter, since his approach is 'not to meddle' [in Soviet affairs]. It is therefore even more important that this issue be dealt with in the press. I know that you have excellent contacts and have no doubt that you will do whatever you can. Recent events point to the need for an immediate amnesty. Only a change of heart of the local population (if it is not already too late) can hamper Hitler's successes. An amnesty is an inevitable condition for such a change of moods".[20] Both men, and particularly Alter, apparently considered the Polish amnesty as the harbinger of the 'mellowing' of the Soviet regime. Alter had been active after the 1917 Revolution in attempts to build bridges between socialists and communists, and may have felt that the War could push the Soviet Union in such a direction. They also firmly believed that everything possible should be done to defeat Hitler, including temporary cooperation with Soviet security organs. The combination of these factors could explain their conduct at the time.

Dangerous Contacts

Erlich and Alter never considered themselves to be under the sole custody of the NKVD, and established contacts with foreign diplomats and journalists first in Moscow and then in Kuibyshev. Their closest connections were, naturally, with the staff of the Polish Embassy, and particularly with the Ambassador, Professor Stanislaw Kot. Less than two weeks after their release they submitted to him, both orally and in writing, a declaration of their beliefs and intentions. They made it explicitly clear that they considered themselves representatives of the largest Jewish political party in Poland, which as such, had an immense stake in Poland's future. In fact, they stressed triple allegiance to international socialism, to Poland and to its Jewish population. One focal point of the declaration was an appeal to Polish Jews in the USSR to join the Polish Army then being formed on Soviet soil. As for the future Polish state, they considered only the prospect of complete independence and true democracy. Although they spoke of the necessity for social reconstruction, and criticized the prewar capitalist Polish regime, they did not hint at any future Soviet influence. "The New Poland" they declared, "should become an active member of the community of nations which will shape the fate of the future Europe in the spirit of political freedom, social justice and national equality". The appeal ended on a more practical note: "We are starting our work in the USSR in the light of these assumptions. The lion's share will consist of recruiting Jewish refugees for the Polish Army and of welfare work among the civilian population".[21] In his written reply, Ambassador Kot stated that there was no need for assistance in recruiting for the Army, since there was already a steady flow of volunteers. He also assured Erlich and Alter that Jews were treated as equals, by both Polish soldiers and officers, including the Commander in Chief, General Anders. Kot promised not to allow any discrimination against Jews in material assistance provided by the Embassy to the Polish refugees throughout the country.[22] The relations of Erlich and Alter with the Soviet Ministry of Internal Affairs were also discussed on that occasion, and Kot subsequently reported to his superiors in London that "the Bund delegates told me that the Soviet Government (NKVD) asked their assistance in spreading propaganda, especially in America. They promised their help on condition that they would conduct [the propaganda] themselves, not as figureheads, and that it would be under the control of the [Polish] Ambassador". Kot asked them to be extremely careful not to let the NKVD turn Polish citizens against their own government. Initially he was less than enthusiastic about the idea that two outstanding Polish citizens were cooperating with the Soviet security apparatus, and advised them not to get involved in the planning of Soviet propaganda activities[23], but after discussing the matter with them he reported to London that although "they are occupied with the organization of a Jewish Anti-Hitlerite Committee, it is in full loyalty to the Polish Government".[24]

As the most prominent Polish-Jewish refugees in the USSR, Erlich and Alter, were consulted by Polish officials on Jewish affairs. Because of this, and since they themselves were interested in participating in the formulation of policies and decisions regarding Jews, they became involved with the question of Jewish recruitment into the Polish Army. Both Poles and the Soviets exploited this issue, each accusing the other of discriminating against Jewish volunteers. There were also divergent attitudes within the Polish circles in the USSR, particularly between the Ambassador and the Commander in Chief General Anders.[25] Erlich and Alter were anxious to solve this complex Jewish-Polish-Soviet problem, and tried to explain the situation and the inherent difficulties to Western diplomats and journalists.[26] Loyal to their concepts, they opposed any suggestion of separating Jewish soldiers from their Polish counterparts. Thus, when two Revisionist Zionists proposed the formation of a separate Jewish Legion in the Polish Army, Erlich and Alter argued fiercely against the idea.[27] Another crucial issue on which the Bundist leaders adopted an unequivocal stand was that of the Eastern Polish territories annexed by the USSR in 1939. Kot tried to use the Polish-Jewish refugees, particularly those from the annexed areas, for Polish propaganda purposes, since he considered them the most pro-Polish minority in those territories. The Polish Government in Exile also wanted to gain the support of public opinion outside the Soviet Union against any changes in the pre-1939 Polish-Soviet borders. U.S. and Western Jewish public opinion was considered by the Poles to be potentially helpful in this border dispute.[28] Alter was convinced that he and Erlich could significantly help the Polish campaign.[29] Erlich and Alter were also given official responsibilities within the framework of the Polish Government. Alter was initially supposed to become a Bund representative on the Polish National Council in London, while Erlich would be sent to the U.S. Subsequently, however, it was decided that Erlich too would join the Council. Alter was also appointed delegate in charge of the Sverdlovsk and Cheliabinsk regions. He was sent by the Polish Embassy to Sverd-lovsk for a short visit and planned a longer fact-finding tour of Polish refugee centers in the USSR sometime in December.[30] Both became involved in problems concerning material help to Polish refugees, and attempted to make contact with various centers of Jewish refugees. They also tried to convince the Polish Ambassador to nominate more Jews as delegates to the refugee centers throughout the USSR.

Erlich and Alter also made contact with British politicians and public figures. A British government official reported that "they [Erlich and Alter] have bombarded a number of prominent socialists with telegrams . . . and have been agitating very actively to obtain the release of Russian socialists . . . who were in prison in the USSR".[31] As a leading Polish Trade Unionist, and a delegate to the International Federation of Trade Unions, Alter had been in close contact with British Trade Unionists since his stay in England during the First World War. An excellent opportunity to renew these contacts presented itself when Sir Walter Citrine, (President of the International Federation of Trade Unions and General Secretary of the British Trade Unions Congress) arrived for an official visit in the Soviet Union. Citrine, an outspoken supporter of Soviet Russia at that time, traveled to the Soviet Union in connection with the founding of a joint Soviet-British Trade Union Committee. He reached Moscow in mid-October 1941 and was evacuated to Kuibyshev, together with Soviet and foreign officials. Alter happened to be traveling on the same train and told Citrine the story of his imprisonment.[32] Since Citrine spent a number of days in the same Kuibyshev hotel as the two Bundist leaders, it is quite possible that they had additional encounters. Erlich and Alter also met Sir Stafford Cripps, British Ambassador to the Soviet Union. In mid-November Erlich and Alter handed Cripps an appeal relating to the Jewish question in postwar Europe, in which they emphasized the role of the Bund in Poland. They also pointed out that the Bund had followers and supporters in other countries, especially within the U.S. labor movement. They asked Cripps "to communicate to your government that the Jewish workers movement wishes to be heard before any decision on the subject of the Jewish question is made . . ."[33] Contacts were also established with Jewish organizations abroad, and inter alia, with the largest Yiddish newspaper in America, the *New York Daily Forward*, and its influential editor Abe Cahan. A week after their release from prison, Alter and Erlich cabled Cahan: "We continue common struggle against Fascism for Socialism. Greet comrades, friends". Both were shortly appointed *Forward* correspondents in the USSR.[34] The ORT (an international Jewish organization for the promotion of skilled trades and agriculture, which had been active in the USSR until the late thirties) contemplated appointing Erlich as its representative in Russia, in the light of the new situation.[35]

Rearrest

Erlich and Alter were rearrested in the early hours of December 4 in a manner typical of the Soviet security apparatus. At noon, December 3, Khazanovich called the Kuibyshev hotel where they were staying, and left a message to the effect that an answer to their proposals had been received from Moscow. Another call, apparently also from Khazanovich, at half past midnight summoned the two for an urgent meeting, from which they never returned.

What was the reasoning behind the sudden arrest and what were the possible causes for the abrupt turnabout in Soviet attitudes toward Erlich and Alter?

A basic conflict between the Stalinist system and the Bund as well as personal attitudes of Erlich and Alter towards Soviet Russia doomed the efforts for a long-range cooperation from the outset. However, the extremely unusual circumstances of the fall of 1941 apparently led the Bundist leaders as well as some Soviet authorities to believe, that such a cooperation was possible. The Soviets were apparently mainly influenced by the military situation on the Russo-German front. According to an outstanding military historian, the end of November brought both the height of the crisis for the Soviet forces and the beginning of their counter-offensive. On November 29, Rostov was recaptured by the Soviet forces after a few days of fierce fighting. Zhukov, convinced that the Germans had spent their strength presented Stalin on November 30th, with plans for a Soviet counter-stroke. Soviet military commanders seemed to believe by the beginning of December that they had "won" the north-west, and although the overall Soviet offensive did not start until December 5th, Stalin's confidence must have risen during the first few days of the month[36] to the detriment of the Soviet-Bundist rapprochement. As to Beria, an analysis of his character in a different context by a veteran observer of the Soviet scene, could easily be applied to his behavior towards Erlich and Alter. "He [Beria] had not suddenly become a 'democrat' (i.e. after Stalin's death). It was because he remained what he had always been that he saw more clearly than others that the dictatorship had reached an impasse out of which it could be led only by a radical change of course." It was precisely because he was, "a kind of robot . . . capable of calculating with mathematical precision the consequences of highly complex police-political operations" that Beria suggested extraordinary steps both in 1953 and 1941.[37]

We may never know who actually took the final decision on Alter and Erlich but Stalin must have been involved. It would be inconceivable for Beria to have played the whole game by himself, risking Stalin's wrath in the event of a wrong move.[38] The evidence points to the fact that the NKVD considered the use of the Bundists for Soviet purposes as a calculated and closely-controlled risk. A seemingly insignificant detail indicates that from the very outset the NKVD viewed Erlich and Alter as hostages of a kind. Unlike other Polish ex-prisoners, Erlich and Alter were not issued documents on their release stating their Polish citizenship by the Soviet Ministry of Internal Affairs.[39] A Bundist friend of theirs (who was to assist in the formation of the Anti-Hitlerite Committee) was asked by Colonel Volkovyskii on the eve of his release from prison, "What would you do if it turns out that your friends Erlich and Alter are betraying the struggle against . . . Hitler? Would you inform us?"[40] Soviet attitudes toward Erlich and Alter were also linked to Soviet-Polish relations, particularly to the question of Eastern Poland and the future Soviet-Polish relations, particularly to the question of Eastern Poland and the future Soviet-Polish borders. Only during the extremely critical period of September-October '41 were Polish Jews treated by Soviet authorities as full-fledged Polish citizens. From December on Jewish camp inmates were detained, while the release of Polish non-Jews continued. Some of those Jews who had been previously set free were rearrested.[41] The London Poles became Russia's new allies, but Soviet suspicion of them never really abated. The Soviet authorities regarded the Poles on Soviet soil as a potential threat and source of trouble. The Polish Embassy maintained a network of representatives in nearly all centers of Polish refugee population in the USSR, which could and did collect information from various parts of the country. The Poles were repeatedly accused, from 1942 on, of spying against their host country. Soviet authorities were especially wary of Polish counter-intelligence, the "Second Department". There was also the case of Leon Kozlowski, a former Polish Prime Minister who escaped from the USSR and showed up in Berlin criticizing the Soviet Union publicly and speaking against Polish-Soviet cooperation.[42] Erlich and Alter were evidently considered by some members of Soviet security as part and parcel of the dangerous Polish element in their midst. It was known that they planned to meet with the Polish Prime Minister, Sikorski, who arrived in Russia in late November, and rumors had it that Erlich would leave the Soviet Union in Sikorski's airplane.[43] Their personal contacts with Cripps and Citrine must have also increased Soviet suspicions. It has also been suggested that the alleged refusal of the two Bundists to join the newly formed pro-Soviet Union of Polish Patriots in the USSR led to their arrest.[44] Another suggestion, very popular in Bundist circles, that Mikhoels, future chairman of the Soviet Jewish Antifascist Committee, acted as agent provocateur in the affair, seems far fetched. Mikhoels was himself a victim of Soviet manipulation.[45] While it is only speculation, one wonders whether a negative attitude towards Erlich and Alter in some Polish circles in the USSR played a role in the Soviet decision to remove them. Stalin, one imagines, had the impression that certain Polish officials, particularly army officers, were not keen to have Jews among them.[46] The personalities of Erlich and Alter may also have influenced the decision to arrest them. The dignified behavior of the Bundist leaders during their first imprisonment kept their NKVD supervisors on the alert. Certain remarks, particularly by Alter, might have sharpened Soviet suspicions. Alter, for example, stated Henry Shapiro, an American correspondent stationed in Kuibyshev, had told the Soviet authorities that he was still anti-communist but was prepared to cooperate in the common fight against fascism. Kot reported to London that Alter "behaved very tough while in prison and was not willing to accept easily the negative aspects of local life."[47] Differences in the personalities of the two, as seen by individuals who came into contact with them in Moscow and Kuibyshev, should also be mentioned. The two seemed to complement one another. Whereas Erlich appeared calm, withdrawn and somewhat lugubrious, Alter was dynamic and constantly anticipating and planning. Erlich seemed at times to moderate Alter's enthusiasm while Alter encouraged Erlich to play a more active role. A keen observer noted that neither seemed at all traumatized by their long stay in prison.[48]

Reactions to the Arrest

Several interventions on behalf of the imprisoned Bund leaders were made in the weeks following their re-arrest. Polish Embassy officials asked the Soviet Foreign Ministry for information on the whereabouts of the two Bundists. Here the immediate reaction was one of confusion, which suggests that the decision to arrest Erlich and Alter may have been sudden. Only in the afternoon of 5 December was the first Soviet official statement on the arrest issued. Ambassador Kot sought to convince Vyshinsky that the re-arrest of Erlich and Alter would be damaging both for the Soviet Union and Poland. He warned of the certain negative reaction of Jewish public opinion in the U.S., an argument he used again and again. Vyshinsky's reply was a total surprise to Kot—Erlich and Alter were accused of working on behalf of Germany, a version to which the Soviets would cling in the years ahead. Vyshinsky compared the two Bundists with Trotsky, who was also a "German agent".[49] These allegations sound particularly ominous when we bear in mind the eventual fate of the Jewish Anti-Fascist Committee in 1948, and of its leading members in 1952. The group of Bundists in Kuibyshev applied continuous pressure on the Polish Embassy, stressing that the Soviet treatment of Erlich and Alter would serve as a precedent in regard to their treatment of Polish citizens in general.[50]

The news of the arrest reached the West in mid-December and efforts on behalf of both Bundists were immediately initiated. Abe Cahan, editor of *Forward*, cabled the American Embassy in the USSR, requesting it to intervene in the release of his two correspondents. Emmanuel Nowogrodsky, of the Bund in New York, appealed to Kot. The Workmen's Circle (Arbeter Ring) appealed to the Soviet Government via the Soviet Ambassador to the U.S., Litvinov. William Green, President of the American Federation of Labor, wrote to U.S. Secretary of State, Cordell Hull. A delegation of the Jewish Labor Committee sought for several weeks an interview with the Soviet Ambassador in Washington. Only in January 1942 did Litvinov consent to meet one of the Committee's representatives, and then only to tell him that the arrest was a strictly internal Soviet matter.[51] Soviet responses abroad during the first few weeks after the arrest seem to indicate that no explicit explanation of the events of 4 December had been formulated. Some Soviet media, for example, denied the arrest two weeks after it had taken place. In late December Kot received a

Soviet note stating that the arrested were under interrogation.[52] The end of January saw a new twist in the official Soviet version. A Soviet Foreign Ministry note stated that Erlich was considered a Soviet citizen for all purposes, and his Polish passport was returned. The Soviet note of 1 December 1941 was quoted as proof for the citizenship argument.[53] It should be remembered that during the initial period after the arrest the only argument advanced was that of anti-Soviet activities.

The date of the execution of Erlich and Alter was never published in the USSR; both were and are treated as "un-persons". One may assume that it took place sometime in December 1941-January 1942. On 12 December a Polish Embassy official submitted parcels for the arrested Bundists. He was told by the former NKVD liaison Khazanovich who accepted the clothing but not the food, "They are better fed in there than you are". Lucjan Blit was ordered to leave Kuibyshev on 28 December. A Polish source in Kuibyshev informed Thurston of the US Embassy as late as 19 January that Erlich and Alter were "probably still in prison in Kuibyshev". The Yiddish communist paper in New York quoted 23 December as the date of the execution. It may also well be that the Bundists were murdered immediately after their arrest, without any formal procedures. Whatever the date, an official Soviet announcement of their execution was made only in February 1943.[54]

From January 1942 onwards, the arrest of Erlich and Alter became a test case for the Polish citizenship issue. The Soviets and the Polish Embassy reiterated their respective interpretations. The Poles referred constantly to the fact that Erlich and Alter had been released in September 1941 as Polish citizens, and that this was never questioned even in the first weeks after their arrest. The exchange of notes ended in April with a curt Soviet announcement that the Soviet Foreign Ministry considered the Erlich-Alter case "closed".[55] On the eve of his departure from the USSR in mid-1942 Kot attempted to convince Vyshinsky, somewhat naively, that the arrested should be allowed to leave the Soviet Union with him; Kot would assume responsibility for their behavior abroad. In reply to Kot's argument that there could be no question as to Erlich's and Alter's Polish citizenship, Vyshinsky remarked cynically, "Warsaw will get along without Erlich and Alter."[56]

The campaign on behalf of the arrested Bundists continued outside the USSR, mainly in the U.S.A. Labour leader W. Green continually requested the U.S. Government to intervene. The State Department considered, however, that the U.S. Embassy in the USSR should not concern itself with this matter. The only step taken at this time by the American Embassy was to consult the Polish Embassy in Kuibyshev. This resulted in a report to the Secretary of State that the Polish Ambassador had not pressed for Erlich's and Alter's release, "fearing that this might rebound rather to their disadvantage". Assistant Secretary of State Breckinridge Long, a specialist in the evacuation of U.S. nationals from war areas, promised Green that although it was an exception, in this one case he would intercede on behalf of Erlich an Alter, who were not American citizens. Long's efforts, however, proved futile.[57]

There were also direct appeals to the White House. Erlich's son, who arrived in the U.S. as a war refugee, wrote to Mrs. Roosevelt warning "the axe is about to fall". The letter reached President Roosevelt first, and he instructed Long to inform the First Lady how to handle the request. Long's advice was that American involvement in cases concerning non-American citizens would "detract from the effective help we could give the American citizens when they needed it".

A further attempt to approach the U.S. President was made in mid-1942. However, the White House replied that President Roosevelt "would not want to interfere personally".[58] Approaches were made to U.S. officials believed to have personal contacts with Soviet leaders. Norman Thomas, a former socialist candidate for the presidency who knew Erlich personally, sought to mobilize the assistance of Harry Hopkins and Wendell Willkie. A similar request was sent by Thomas to Assistant Secretary of State, Adolph Berle. Berle replied that it would "not be advisable to ask Mr. Willkie to plead the case of these two persons"; continued pressure "might react" against the two Bundists. Hopkins' attitude was similar.[59] Willkie left the U.S.A. in August 1942 to deliver a personal message from the President to Stalin. In Iran, en route to the USSR, Willkie was once again approached by well-wishers of Erlich and Alter—on this occasion it was their friends who had just left Russia together with other Polish evacuees. Willkie finally did raise the issue with Molotov and Stalin.[60]

In Great Britain too there was concern for Erlich and Alter. Shmuel (Arthur) Zygelboym, an outstanding Bundist leader and personal friend of the two, raised the question of their arrest in the Polish National Council, of which he was a member. He also sought to enlist the assistance of Jan Masaryk, foreign Minister in the Czech Government-in-Exile in London. Masaryk, then on good terms with the Russians, discussed the question with both Litvinov and Maisky, Soviet Ambassador to London. Appeals were also made to British Government officials. R. Niebuhr wrote to Stafford Cripps who, on his return from Russia, became Lord of the Privy Seal and was close to Churchill. Sir Walter Citrine corresponded with Foreign Secretary Eden, on whose directives the Foreign Office discussed the question with the Soviet Embassy in London.[61] Soviet responses were not encouraging. The impression given by the available documents is that the pressures applied on the Russians were weak and indecisive. Stanislaw Mikolajczyk, Deputy Prime Minister and later Prime Minister of the Polish Government-in-Exile, subsequently described the atmosphere prevailing at that time: "Nothing was to be said that might embarrass Stalin. We were told by the British to hold our peace . . ."[62]

Despite the official restraint, the pressure of public opinion mounted throughout 1942. In early 1943 an appeal by W. Green and Albert Einstein was sent to Molotov. In February of that year the Soviet Government admitted officially for the first time that Erlich and Alter had been executed. Litvinov conveyed to Green Molotov's message that the two Bundists had been guilty of hostile activities against the Soviet Union, and had appealed to Soviet troops to conclude peace with Germany.[63] The timing of Molotov's announcement was significant. The victory of Stalingrad in early 1943 marked not only a final military reversal on the Soviet-German front, but also the high point of pro-Soviet sympathy in public opinion around the world. The disclosure of the execution of the two outstanding Jewish socialists was but a minor link in the chain of Soviet assertiveness towards their allies.

Symptomatic of the prevailing pro-Soviet mood was the printing of the news of Erlich's and Alter's execution in American newspapers on the back page. Nevertheless, the Erlich-Alter case became the crux of a political and emotional controversy. A paid announcement by the Bund in the *New York Times* in early March marked its beginning. The main "in-fighting" took place in the Jewish, primarily Yiddish, press in New York. The principal actors were the socialist *Jewish Daily Forward* and the communist *Morgen Freiheit.*. In its first editorial on the Erlich-Alter execution the *Forward* announced that the "Bolsheviks have learned nothing and forgotten nothing . . . The Soviet leaders will never be able to wipe Erlich's and Alter's blood off their hands". The veteran Bundist and Menshevik leader, R. Abramovich, accused the Soviets of "cutting the heads off Jewish and Polish Social Democracy".[64] The *Forward* backed the public criticism of the execution both morally and financially. This was true primarily for the New York area, although articles were written and meetings convened with the *Forward's* support in other American cities.

The *Morgen Freiheit*, on the other hand, fully adopted the Soviet version and argued that the USSR was the best friend the Jews had. It hinted that the future of the Jews in Europe as well as in Palestine depended on Stalin's goodwill. The paper stressed the danger of disrupting the anti-Hitler alliance; any Jewish critic of Stalin's Russia, it claimed, was automatically a critic of Roosevelt's America. A popular communist theme was the accusation that Erlich and Alter had cooperated with Polish counter-intelligence. A number of "personal testimonies" of Jewish workers who had allegedly known the Bundist leaders while in Poland were printed in order to villify them in the eyes of the American Jewish reader. In one case, a certain Louis Ente, formerly a tailor in the city of Przemysl, testified that Erlich and Alter were "stooges for the *Forward* and the Polish government . . . and agents for intervention against the Soviet people". A frequent communist argument was that the pair must have been guilty "or they would not have been punished".[65]

The controversy was not limited to the press. Mass meetings were organized by both sides. A rally sponsored by Jewish and non-Jewish socialists was held in the Mecca Temple in New York, at which the main speakers were W. Green of the AFL, J. Carey of the CIO, David Dubinsky of the ILGWU, and *Forward* editor Abe Cahan. New York Senator J. M. Mead also participated.[66] To counteract the effect of this meeting the General Secretary of the American Communist Party, Earl Browder, intervened in the debate. His speech in Brooklyn on 1 April was subsequently printed in the communist press and as an advertisement in other newspapers. Browder claimed a conspiratorial link between Erlich and Alter inside the USSR and their friends abroad, whose purpose was the overthrow of the Soviet regime. The Polish connection was heavily stressed. Erlich and Alter were also said to be linked with Nazi Germany, along the lines of the original Soviet allegations.[67] A meeting was organized by the pro-Soviet Committee of Jewish Writers, Scientists and Artists, whose participants reflected the extensive coalition of Soviet sympathizers on the Jewish political arena at that time.[68] Threats and intimidations were employed by the communists on several occasions.[69] The Erlich-Alter controversy created clashes within the CIO.[70] Within Jewish circles it provided an outlet for traditional hatreds and deep-seated emotions. The *Forward* referred to the Yiddish communist daily as the "blood-thirsty wolf from Union Square"; the *Freiheit* in turn condemned the "Dubinsky-*Forward* clique". Some Jewish pro-Soviet, but not card-carrying communist circles, accepted the Soviet view. Joseph Brainin declared, in the newly established mouthpiece of the Committee of Jewish Writers, that Erlich and Alter—to whom the Soviet government "offered hospitality when the Nazis overran Poland"—had been legally executed; their friends in the U.S.A. were using the incident "in order to whip up anti-Soviet hysteria". Echoing Browder, he linked Cahan with the "Polish anti-Soviet schemers". Brainin warned that the Erlich-Alter campaign had been designed to "destroy American-Soviet collaboration". The Yiddish daily *Der Tog*, second only to the *Forward* in its circulation and whose editorial policies were influenced at that time by B. Z. Goldberg, a Soviet sympathizer and chairman of the Committee of Jewish Writers, omitted mention of the Erlich-Alter issue for over two weeks. While denying the veracity of the Soviet accusations *Der Tog* warned that the execution should not be turned into an anti-Soviet campaign. It scolded the Bund for seeking to speak in the name of the "whole Jewish community".[71]

Some liberal intellectuals found it difficult to define their stand on the matter, wavering between the Scylla of indignation at the Soviet accusations against the Bundist leaders and the Charybdis of their desire to maintain a unified anti-Nazi front. Albert Einstein, a signatory to a protest letter sent to the Soviet Government in early 1943 (see above), later cautioned against excessive anti-Soviet criticism; however, he admitted that the execution was a "fatal political error".[72] Oskar Lange, a Polish leftist intellectual, regarded the execution as an act of "criminal stupidity". Stefan Arski, New York representative of the Polish Socialist Party, and later a leading journalist and editor in communist Poland, described the execution as "murder".[73]

While it did not publicly take a stand, the Polish Government-in-Exile was also an interested party in the Erlich-Alter dispute. At about this time Soviet-Polish diplomatic relations were ruptured as a result of the Katyn affair. Polish diplomats in Washington initiated the discreet pubication of articles on the Erlich-Alter theme, highly critical of Soviet behaviour.[74]

It is sufficiently clear that the protests abroad against the executions of the two Bundist leaders, and their impact on public opinion, worried the Soviet leadership. No direct mention whatever was made of the execution of the two Bundist leaders in the general or Yidish Soviet press; Erlich and Alter remained "non-persons". Maxim Litvinov, in an encounter with the Soviet Jewish writer Ilya Ehrenburg, confided that Jewish protests in the U.S. were causing considerable damage to the Soviet war propaganda effort.[75] A major attempt to offset this damage was the Soviet-sponsored mission abroad of Solomon Mikhoels and Itsik Fefer, two leading personalities in the Soviet Jewish Anti-Fascist Committee, which emerged in Kuibyshev in the spring of 1942. The need to repulse Jewish criticism of the USSR was discussed in JAC circles in February-March 1943. In mid-March Mikhoels launched an attack on those American Jews who did not fully support the Soviet Union; *Eynikayt,* the organ of the Soviet Jewish Anti-Fascist Committee, severely criticized "disruptive elements" in American Jewry. In a Yiddish broadcast Mikhoels called upon American and British Jews to support the Soviet Union.[76] Official Soviet steps to arrange for the visit of Mikhoels and Fefer to the United States followed in April, and the two left Moscow in early May 1943. The importance attached by the Soviet leadership to the Mikhoels-Fefer mission can be inferred from the fact that Stalin and Kalinin came to bid them farewell and wish them success.[77]

What lessons can be learned from the Erlich-Alter episode?

The organization planned by Erlich and Alter was seen by important Soviet officials (e.g. Beria, and maybe even Stalin himself) as a possible structure useful in an emergency. Their expectation was based on the fact that Erlich and Alter had maintained excellent contacts in the inter-war period with Jewish and non-Jewish socialist and labour movements in England and the U.S.A., the two main targets of Soviet war propaganda since June 1941. These movements possessed considerable influence both in terms of public opinion and the respective governments. The Bund was also highly influential among Polish Jews, the largest Jewish community in Europe at that time. Erlich's and Alter's anti-Nazi commitment, the need they felt for a common war effort and the atmosphere which prevailed in Moscow and Kuibyshev in those days, may have blurred to some extent the realities of Stalin's Russia. Influenced by certain Soviet political moves and the approaches made to them by the powerful Soviet security establishment, Erlich and Alter apparently developed hopes for possible changes in the nature of the Soviet regime. However, as far as Stalin was concerned, there was a delicate balance between Erlich's and Alter's usefulness to the regime and the possible danger they posed for it. Whereas the scales seemed to tip towards the former case in September-October 1941, they shifted towards the latter case in early December.

3

THE JEWISH ANTIFASCIST
COMMITTEE AND SOVIET JEWRY

First Steps

The attempt to mobilize such outspoken critics of Stalin as Erlich and Alter for Soviet propaganda purposes was characteristic of the first crucial phase of the War. After the extreme danger to the regime seemed to have been averted, Jewish propaganda structures, though still deemed useful and necessary, were planned along more conventional Soviet lines. The Jewish Antifascist Committee (JAC) which emerged subsequently was envisaged as a completely loyal tool of Soviet war propaganda.

It is hard to pinpoint exactly when the JAC was founded. Soviet propaganda activities utilizing national and ethnic sentiments were initiated within a month of the German attack. The prevailing propaganda technique during this initial period was that of public meetings and radio broadcasts, officially described as meetings of "representatives" of the various Soviet nationalities. The rather modest beginnings developed in time into permanent institutional frameworks, known as Antifascist Committees. The speakers at the initial broadcasts usually later became leading members of these committees. The emergence of a Jewish committee was an integral part of this overall Soviet organizational and institutional pattern.[1] What is striking is the fact that the Jews were the only nationality singled out for the formation of a separate committee. Their assistance as a separate national group was requested as early as August 1941. Only three months later, for example, was the support of the Ukrainians solicited, in spite of the fact that they constituted the second largest nationality within the Union, and,like Soviet Jews, had co-nationals abroad. Khrushchev, (although inaccurate on details) seems to have conveyed correctly the principle Soviet consideration for the establishment of a separate Jewish committee in the USSR: "It was set up for gathering materials—positive materials naturally- . . . and for the distribution of these materials to the Western press, principally in America, where there is a large, influential circle of Jews . . . The Sovinformbureau and its Jewish-Antifascist Committee were considered indispensable to the interests of our State, our policies and our Communist party."[2] The first official Soviet announcement about the various antifascist committees was Lozovskii's statement to foreign correspondents in Kuibyshev, in April 1942. Lozovskii, Deputy Chairman of the Sovinformburo, said that "all these committees arose in connection with Hitler's treacherous attack on the USSR" and that "the Jews have created an antifascist committee to help the Soviet Union, Great Britain and the U.S."[3] The time lapse between the initial radio appeals during August-November 1941 and this announcement may have resulted from the relocation of Soviet government offices and agencies from Moscow to Kuibyshev. The interruption in the planning and implementation of Soviet propaganda structures stemmed also from this move.

The first meeting and radio broadcast by a group of Soviet-Jewish personalities in August 1941 could be regarded as the direct forerunner of the Jewish Committee. This event held in the Moscow Hall of Columns and publicized in the USSR and abroad was apparently modeled on similar past meetings. Protest rallies condemning Hitler's Germany in the wake of the Kristallnacht had been organized in Moscow, Leningrad, Kiev, Minsk, and other Soviet cities in November 1938. Speakers included leading members of Soviet intelligentsia such as playwright Aleksei Tolstoy and film director Aleksandr Dovzhenko. Solomon Mikhoels, Director of the Moscow Jewish Theatre spoke at the Moscow meeting and the Soviet-Yiddish poet Itsik Fefer spoke in Kiev. All emphasized the equality and well being of Soviet Jews as opposed to treatment of Jews by Nazi Germany.[4] However, the August 1941 meeting though it dwelt on some previous themes, was much more outspoken, in its emphasis on common Jewish interests.[5]

The underlying theme of the August 1941 meeting and subsequent Soviet-Jewish wartime events was Jewish unity, and the phrase— "brother Jews"—was often reiterated. Ideas, emotions and attitudes which for many years had been taboo in the Soviet Union suddenly received the blessings of the Party and Government. Reference was made at the 1941 meeting to the "burnt synagogues of Rotterdam," to Jewish martyrology and Jewish historical tradition. Jewish suffering from and resistance to the Nazis was highlighted. The meeting formulated a clearly defined set of objectives in such areas as propaganda, financial aid and resistance, and called for "overall agitation for solidarity and effective assistance for the Soviet Union."

The opening speech was by Solomon Mikhoels, who had become increasingly prominent in the Soviet Union during the 1930's and who had been selected to play a leading role in mobilizing the Jewish support for Soviet wartime propaganda. His appeal was directed particularly to Jewish communities in the U.S. and England. The speech of Perets Markish, the outstanding Soviet-Yiddish poet, was marked by Jewish traditional and historical overtones. David Bergelson, another leading Soviet Jewish writer warned that the very existence of the Jews was at stake and appealed in particular to U.S. Jewry. Samuil Marshak, a popular writer for children, delivered an extremely emotional report on the Nazi slaughter of Jewish children in the Polish town of Otwock. Ilya Ehrenburg, one of the most assimilated Soviet Jewish intellectuals, spoke about his national re-identification caused by the War. "I am a Russian writer . . . However, the Nazis reminded me of something else: that my mother's name was Hanna. I am a Jew, and I proudly state this fact." His remarks, too, were directed primarily at American Jewry. In his memoirs, published years later, Ehrenburg explicitly mentioned the importance which Stalin attributed at that time to U.S. public opinion. The speech of Shakhno Epshteyn, a communist Yiddish journalist and the future secretary of the JAC was particularly laudatory of the Soviet regime and its attitudes towards Jews. Some of the speakers followed up their appeals with personal messages. At the end of September Mikhoels addressed a highly emotional letter to Leon Feuchtwanger, the German-Jewish historical novelist, then residing in the U.S. Feuchtwanger had visited the Soviet Union in 1937, received VIP treatment—including an interview with Stalin himself—and subsequently wrote his book *Moscow, 1937*. In his letter Mikhoels reminded Feuchtwanger of his visit and urged him to deliver the message to "all our brethren living in America . . . to all those who came from Vilna, Kovno, Bialystok (and) Warsaw . . ." In November Leib Kvitko a popular Soviet Yiddish poet for children wrote to Hollywood to the German and Yiddish actor Alexander Granach, who had performed in Germany, Poland and Russia and had been in the U.S. since just before the war. Kvitko demanded in his letter that (Jewish) organizations, societies and *landsmanschaften* in the U.S. actively support Russia's war effort.[6]

Whereas the meeting and broadcast marked the initial stage in the mobilization of Soviet Jewish intellectuals, the actual founding of the JAC probably took place in Kuibyshev sometime after the re-arrest of Erlich and Alter, during the first half of 1942. The interim period was used for the twofold purpose of founding an active nucleus of Soviet-Yiddish writers in the USSR, and of establishing contacts with the Jewish press and Jewish organizations abroad.[7] The first JAC-sponsored activity was a Jewish meeting and radio broadcast in May, 1942, referred to as the "second meeting of the representatives of the Jewish people."[8] Its major theme was an appeal for resistance to. Hitler's army and a call for Soviet military victory in the summer of that year. The speakers urged Jewish soldiers and officers of the Red Army to volunteer for special duties and to join elite Soviet military detachments. Jews in Nazi-occupied territories were called upon to actively resist the enemy. Mikhoels, demanded "an eye for an eye and a tooth for a tooth." A number of Jewish officers and men of the Red Army among them the Yiddish poet Aaron Kushnirov, participated in this meeting. Soviet Jewry's loyalty to the regime and to Stalin was now emphasized much more than in August 1941. Mikhoels announced that Moscow "is the center of all Soviet peoples, and of the Jewish People as well." There were repeated references to "the great leader of the nations" (Stalin) and to "the Great Russian People." Some of the speakers emphatically denied the existence of any animosity toward Jews among Soviet nationalities, apparently responding to accusations inside the USSR and abroad. Mikhoels addressed himself primarily to Jews in the U.S., England and Palestine, while other speakers addressed specific groups of Jews outside the Soviet Union. A Jewish nurse from the Ukraine appealed to Jewish women abroad; Aleksandr Frumkin a member of the Soviet Academy of Sciences directed his remarks to Jewish scientists; and the Soviet-Jewish sculptor P. Sabsai to Jewish artists. The chairman of a Soviet-Jewish collective farm appealed to Jewish farmers in Argentina, Palestine and the U.S. The writer David Bergelson used a traditional Jewish figure of speech, urging Jews everywhere to bear out the belief in the survival of the Jewish People ("Am Yisrael Hai"). The broadcast also set a definite target for Jewish assistance to the Soviet Union proposing a campaign to finance a thousand tanks and 500 airplanes for the Soviet army.

Soviet military units sponsored by funds collected by Jews, were to be named after such Jewish historical personalities as Bar-Kokhba, Judah Halevi, Heinrich Heine, Shalom Aleichem and Yudah Leib Perets. No information exists about the implementation of these promises, despite the fact that large amounts of money were collected for this purpose among Soviet and American Jews. The theme of equality of Jews and their attainments within Soviet society was reiterated in the broadcast. Academician Frumkin pointed out the possibilities in education and research opened up to Soviet Jews. The Yiddish philologist Elia Spivak spoke of Jewish cultural activities and institutions in the USSR. The message to Jews abroad was clear; they should support the Soviet Union not only because of its participation in the struggle against Nazism, but also because of its treatment of the Jewish minority in the USSR. At the same time Jews abroad were not only asked and urged, but also warned and exhorted. This approach, stressed specifically by Epshteyn, was to be intensified in future Soviet appeals to world Jewry.

The Jewish Committee: What Should it Be?

The first officially recorded discussion of the goals and mode of operation of the JAC, took place during the first plenary session of the Committee in late May 1942.[9] These discussions reveal that from the inception of the JAC, differing, and sometimes opposing opinions on the functions and obligations of the Committee were openly stated. One can of course attribute this relative openness to the special conditions prevailing at that time and to the wartime relaxation of controls. Besides the official goals of aiding the USSR and its army, a number of aims of specifically Jewish interest were discussed during the session. Some participants stressed for example the need for collecting and publicizing materials on Jewish resistance to the Nazis. This was apparently in line with the pressing need to answer antisemitic allegations that Jews evade front-line duty and that they "are fighting in Tashkent." Isaac Nusinov, Yiddish literary critic and historian urged the Committee to publish material on the participation of Soviet Jews in the war effort. Yekhezkel Dobrushin, Yiddish literary critic and playwright, spoke along the same lines. He also suggested that the Committee organize mass meetings with the participation of Jewish cultural and military personalities in the major centers of the USSR.

Mikhoels stated rather vaguely that "fascism infiltrates along with antisemitism." possibly hinting at the connection between these two trends and the effects of Nazi propaganda on the non-Jewish Soviet population. Fefer and Epshteyn seemed to oppose the idea that the Committee should concern itself with the problem of antisemitism in the USSR. They maintained that the sole purpose of the JAC was to assist Soviet war propaganda. Epshteyn warned his colleagues that some of them tended to assign the Committee functions which had no direct bearing on the tasks set by the Soviet authorities. Thus, even in the earliest stages of the Committee's existence, there were conflicting views, on its very nature. Epshteyn and Fefer in particular adhered strictly to the official Soviet perception of the Committee. Among the initial JAC public activities were a series of meetings held in the summer of 1942 to promote fundraising for the Army. Local "initiative groups" were organized for this purpose at which Committee members spoke. The sculptor P. Sabsai was among the organizers of a Jewish fund-raising meeting in Baku; Mikhoels participated in a similar meeting in Tashkent; and the Soviet-Jewish General Yakov Kreyzer, and the writer David Hofshteyn, spoke at a meeting in Ufa.[10]

The second plenary session, convened on February 18–20, 1943, shortly after the Stalingrad victory, marked a new phase in the development of the Jewish Antifascist Committee. As a result of the westward advance of the Red Army and the commencement of resettlement in the newly-liberated territories, a number of major problems concerning Soviet Jews became pressing. Some Committee members began to urge that the JAC undertake specifically Jewish tasks and responsibilities, such as the resettling of Jewish war refugees, the reconstruction of Jewish culture in the liberated territories, the documentation of the Holocaust and the denunciation of antisemitism in the Soviet Union. The divergence of opinions on the future functions of the Committee were even more pronounced than in May 1942. On the eve of this gathering, Epshteyn published a programmatic article in which he re-emphasized the official tasks of the JAC.[11] He attacked strongly those Jews abroad who allegedly did not support the Soviet Union and maintained that the JAC was not satisfactorily "unmasking" Jewish enemies of the USSR abroad. Thus, the main theme for the next plenary session was formulated, to be repeated, ad nauseam, by Epshteyn, Fefer and others during the discussions. Particularly virulent were the attacks on the American-Jewish socialists centered around the Yiddish daily *Forward*. It should be recalled in this context that although there was an upsurge of admiration and sympathy for the USSR in the West at this time, in certain Jewish circles in the U.S. there was growing concern for the fate of Erlich and Alter, accompanied by strong anti-Soviet feelings.

The February 1943 debates must have been the most frank and overt exchange of views, ever held at the JAC. The fact that they were published in the Committee's newspaper *Eynikayt* only after a 3 weeks' delay, is perhaps indicative of the difficulty in deciding in what form they should be made public. We may also assume that the report was a watered down version of the heated and emotional discussions, which actually took place.[12]

The division seemed to be between those who demanded that the Committee confine itself to foreign propaganda and those who wanted to turn the JAC into a meaningful internally oriented Soviet-Jewish institution. The chief exponent of the former view was Shakhno Epshteyn, who stated in his concluding remarks that "the main task of the JAC was and remains to attract and activate the Jewish masses all over the world . . . The most important question is what impact does our work have abroad." He also criticized Soviet-Yiddish writers for not participating sufficiently in the propaganda activities of the Committee. In addition to Fefer (who kept repeating his old arguments) Kvitko joined Epshteyn's criticism. Others argued, however, that the most urgent task of the Committee was to assist Jewish refugees in the USSR and to rehabilitate Jewish repatriates to the western territories. Prof. Nusinov suggested that "the Committee should not limit [its work] to foreign propaganda. Its activities should also be felt within the country." Markish demanded that the Committee "become interested in the condition of the evacuees," and Hofshteyn maintained that the JAC "has to prepare for a massive, constructive job." Shchupak, the chairman of an evacuated Jewish collective farm, suggested that the JAC become involved in the rebuilding of Jewish collective farms. Still another speaker remarked that "the most significant fact is that a structure [the JAC] has been founded which might serve as a focus for Soviet-Jewish leadership in the USSR." Some specific suggestions were made for organization and maintenance of contacts between the Committee and the centers of Jewish population throughout the country. The writer Abraham Kahan suggested that the Committee maintain a network of direct representatives in various parts of the USSR. Dobrushin argued that it had not utilized to the full "the possibilities of the periphery" and urged that "the work of the Committee should

become familiar to every town and village." Even such staunch supporters of the official line as Epshteyn and Fefer seemed to succumb to
the prevailing atmosphere of hope, enthusiasm and belief in the JAC's
responsibility for the Jewish population in the USSR. Epshteyn mentioned the possibility that the Committee might appoint representatives in various localities, and Fefer conceded that although the
Committee's functions were limited, it could refer Jewish evacuee
problems to the appropriate Soviet authorities. A number of participants hinted at the ominous anti-Jewish attitudes and accusations prevailing among the Soviet population and sought ways to reverse this
trend. Ehrenburg, openly spoke about the urgent need to publish "a
book which would convincingly prove the participation of Jews in the
war," and said that the Committee should "tell the truth." The philologist Elya Falkovich complained that too little had been published in
the Soviet press on Jewish heroism in the war, and blamed the JAC for
this. The writer Ezra Fininberg urged similarly that more emphasis be
given to publications in Russian on Jewish themes. He suggested that
the JAC publish a bulletin in Russian on Jewish life inside the USSR
and abroad. The writers Shmuel Persov and Elya Gordon suggested
that the Committee meet with Jewish soldiers and partisans. There was
almost unanimous support for the notion that the Committee become
a center of documentation on Jewish suffering and resistance.
Mikhoels, in his closing remarks, adopted a middle-of-the-road
approach. He acknowledged the differences of opinion on the question
of the Committee's future functions and stated that "some people have
forgotten that the Committee is a militant organization and has a
single clearly defined purpose (that of foreign propaganda) . . .
However there is also some truth in the arguments that the Committee
has not yet turned into a living center for the Jewish population in our
country . . . The dispersed Jewish population is seeking an address
and we should not deny it to them."[12]

Eynikayt

The principal means of contact between the JAC and Soviet Jews
was the Committee's publication *Eynikayt*. As the sole Jewish publication representing the central Jewish structure in the USSR at that time
it naturally inspired expectation. *Eynikayt* began publication in
Kuibyshev in the summer of 1942 and appeared once every ten days.[13]

A year later, along with the Committee, it was transferred to Moscow, where it became a weekly. From early 1945 until the closing down of the JAC in late 1948, *Eynikayt* was published thrice weekly. When its Chief Editor, Shakhno Epshteyn died (shortly after the end of the war) he was replaced by G. Zhits, formerly Executive Editor of the *Minsker Shtern*. The Soviet Yiddish poet Shmuel Halkin was Secretary of the Editorial Board and another poet, Aaron Kushnirov was Deputy Editor. At one time Fefer, too, held this position. Although acculturation and the use of Russian had increased among Soviet Jews and the number of those who could read Yiddish had begun to decline before the War, there were still hundreds of thousands for whom a Yiddish periodical was meaningful. If we recall the large numbers of Yiddish-speaking deportees and refugees from the newly annexed territories in the West the demand for a publication like *Eynikayt* becomes logical.

From the start the JAC received a great deal of mail from *Eynikayt* readers. In just one year, from February 1942 to February 1943, the number of readers' letters exceeded 5,000 more than 1,000 of them dealing with questions concerning *Eynikayt* itself.[14] Letters arrived from the evacuation centers and from the front. The tone of the journal was Jewish nationalism. Such sections as "Our Sons and daughters," "Our Heroes" and "Our Scientists" underlined the specific Jewish contribution to the war against Nazi Germany, a theme hardly mentioned in the general Soviet press.[15] Letters were published from Jewish soldiers and officers serving in the Red Army who were filled with pride at the emergence of a Jewish institution, and a Jewish publication. *Eynikayt* was in demand among Jewish soldiers at the front. One of them reported: "My parents have recently sent me *Eynikayt.* This was an outstanding event for us. Jewish soldiers snatched it from each other." A Jewish Red Army officer who visited the JAC offices said: "In my company we have Russians, Uzbeks, Georgians, Ukrainians and Jews. We [Jews] translate *Eynikayt* to them and tell them what Jews are doing at War." Information on Jewish heroism published in *Eynikayt* was obviously used in this case to contradict antisemitic rumors among the soldiers. A Jew from Mozir in Belorussia told U.S. Embassy officials in Moscow that ". . . he likes to read it [*Eynikayt*] merely because it is printed in Yiddish."[16] *Eynikayt* must have been particularly in demand among the "zapadniki" (Jews from the territories annexed by the USSR along her western borders in 1939–1940).[17]

Repeated complaints about the scarcity and unavailability of the publication indicated the limited allocation of paper for its production, as well as difficulties in its distribution. It was extremely difficult to obtain copies not only in the Army, but also in the main towns.[18] Both, Halkin, Secretary of the Editorial Board, and Strongin, a Board member and Director of the *Der Emes* Publishing House, complained during the February 1943 plenary session about the difficulties faced by *Eynikayt*. Strongin pointed out the insufficient allocation of paper and complained that a disproportionate number of copies were earmarked for export. Only 2,000 copies of Eynikayt were actually available at that time for retail sale in the whole of the USSR. Strongin advised readers to demand an increase in the number of copies printed. Epshteyn, in his report on *Eynikayt* in April 1944, stated unequivocally that "the demand for the newspaper is enormous, and the limited circulation is completely insufficient to satisfy the growing need for a Jewish newspaper."[19] After the War *Eynikayt* was published in 10,000 copies, of which a considerable quantity were sent abroad. According to B. Z. Goldberg, an American Yiddish journalist who visited the Soviet Union after the War, the newspaper could then easily have sold about 50,000 copies inside the USSR alone.[20]

Eynikayt reporters were an important link between the Committee and some parts of the Jewish population in the USSR. As early as May 1942 the periodical had 100 reporters; by 1943 the figure had risen to 300. An examination of reports published in *Eynikayt* indicates that all the major centers of Jewish population in wartime Russia were "covered" by the JAC reporters' network.[21] In early 1943 Epshteyn spoke of the urgent need to send reporters to the western territories of the USSR, then being liberated,[22] and one of *Eynikayt's* veteran reporters testified that he had served in this capacity from the summer of 1942 until the Committee's liquidation in 1948. He travelled across the whole of the Soviet Union, and particularly in the Ukraine, Belorussia and Moldavia in search of Jewish survivors. He collected material on the Holocaust and on Jewish resistance to the Nazis.[23] After the war, the JAC also sent its reporters to cover the resumption of Jewish settlement in Birobidzhan.

The Committee established at its headquarters a special Jewish press agency [ISPA], directed by Z. Brikner, to collect material and send it abroad. The JAC actually sent more material to the U.S., England and elsewhere than it published in *Eynikayt*. Less than a year after its emergence, the JAC had sent abroad more than 8,000 pages of printed matter. The Committee maintained contacts with a wide range of Jewish newspapers and press agencies abroad, mostly in the U.S.[24] It also sponsored radio programs in Yiddish, Russian and English which were broadcast to the U.S. and England. These broadcasts were first launched from diverse localities such as Moscow, Kuibyshev and Tashkent. In September 1943, after the transfer of the JAC offices to Moscow, regular weekly broadcasts were sent out from the capital. Besides writers and poets, Soviet Jewish soldiers and partisans also participated in these programs.

The JAC and its information media were utilized for both specifically Jewish and general Soviet propaganda issues. One such issue was the rapid deterioration in Polish-Soviet relations. Thus, in the summer of 1942, barely a year after the Polish-Soviet agreement, a muted anti-Polish campaign was already launched in the USSR. The JAC attempted to persuade some Polish Jewish personalities living in the USSR to denounce the Polish Government in London.[25] *Eynikayt* openly disseminated anti-Polish propaganda after the rupture in Soviet-Polish relations in April 1943. The main aim of Soviet propaganda in this case was to point out anti-Jewish prejudices and anti-semitic behavior on the part of the Polish Government in Exile, and to contrast it with the friendly attitudes of the Moscow based Union of Polish Patriots and of the pro-communist Polish Army then being organized in the USSR.[26] The Warsaw Ghetto uprising was also used by Soviet propaganda, and the underground Polish Home Army (A.K.) in Nazi-occupied Poland, which was affiliated with the London Poles, was repeatedly accused by the JAC of denying assistance to the Jewish ghetto fighters in Poland.[27]

Cultural Activities

The initial home of the JAC was Kuibyshev. It was only in late August 1943 that the Committee, together with other Soviet antifascist committees, was transferred to Moscow. The JAC was housed with the other committees in an impressive two-story building on Kropotkina street, in the center of the capital. It occupied the whole of the first floor and part of the second. There were 80 Committee employees, more than half of them Yiddish writers. A number of subcommittees emerged now within the JAC framework, covering such functions as collection of data on Jewish participation in the War and collection of material on Nazi atrocities against Jews.[28] In Spring 1944 a committee was also established to deal with problems of rehabilitation of Jewish repatriates to the liberated territories.

The JAC soon beame the center of Yiddish literary activities in the USSR. The War had led to the almost total cessation of Soviet Yiddish printing and publication activities and the JAC tried to restore the prewar situation. By Summer 1942 it had contacted about 70 surviving Yiddish writers, all over the USSR, and had informed them that it would undertake the publication of their works. Yiddish writers who started to return to Moscow in the Summer of 1943 were now invited to participate in activities organized by the Committee. Already in October 1943 a number of meetings were held with repatriate writers, at which the groundwork for their participation in JAC's activities was laid.[29] *Der Emes*, the only surviving Soviet Yiddish publishing house, started functioning in Moscow, also under the auspices of the JAC. Before the War both the Ukraine and Belorussia had been centers of Yiddish literary and publishing activity, but they were now replaced by Moscow. A comparison of pre-war and wartime Soviet-Yiddish publications showed an increase in Jewish themes during the War. The sale of Yiddish books during that period also indicated an upsurge in interest in Jewish matters.[30]

The relationship between the Committee and the Yiddish writers was not always satisfactory,[31] but on the whole the JAC provided both material and cultural support during and after the War. In September 1943, it initiated "literary evenings," which became a permanent feature of the Moscow Jewish cultural community. Such events were attended not only by Jewish cultural personalities but also by Jewish soldiers and partisans and even by non-Jewish writers. In addition, the JAC became the focal point for the few remaining Jewish structures in the USSR, such as the *Der Emes* Publishing House, the Jewish sections of the Soviet Writers Union, the Moscow State Jewish Theatre and the Cabinet for Jewish Culture of the Ukrainian Academy of Sciences. In spite of the damage inflicted upon Soviet Jewish culture during the first two years of the War, late 1943 and early 1944 was a hopeful period. There was a growing feeling among the Soviet Jewish cultural elite that Jewish suffering, Soviet Jewry's loyalty to the regime and Jewish support abroad for the Soviet Union would result in far-reaching concessions to Jewish national interests in the USSR.

The April 1944 Meeting

Jewish hopes and expectations were voiced at the largest mass meeting ever organized by the Jewish Antifascist Committee, in the spring of 1944. Although the tragic dimensions of the Holocaust were already apparent at that time, there was hope for the revival of Jewish life in the USSR, and the JAC was looked upon as the leading Soviet Jewish institution working for the realization of these expectations. The JAC notified the Jewish Writers' Committee in New York in early March 1944 that a Jewish mass meeting was planned in Moscow. It was first publicized inside the USSR only a few days before the event.[32] In an article published on the eve of the meeting, Epshteyn wrote about the intensification of the Committee's activities during the preceding year, and its expanding contacts abroad and predicted that such activities would grow in the future. The American Jewish press, in the wake of information sent by the JAC, announced that a "meeting of all Soviet Jewry" was to take place in Moscow.[33] The April 2nd meeting took place in the Trade Union Hall of Columns, the largest and most prestigious Moscow auditorium, with the participation of about 3,000 people and was also broadcast by Moscow Radio. A visiting Canadian Jewish journalist was impressed by the fact that "the audience was Jewish, just as Jewish as the people who crowded the New York meeting to hear Mikhoels and Fefer."[34] The main speakers were Mikhoels, Epshteyn, Fefer and Ehrenburg. The crowd was impressed by the presence of Jewish military men and partisans. It was also for the first time that a Jewish religious leader was allowed to speak at a JAC public event.

The main theme of the meeting was the Holocaust and Mikhoels declared that "the most shameful crime of the Germans was that which they committed against the Jews."[35] Fefer declared, in a highly emotional tone that "the ashes of Babi Yar are searing our hearts," and Rabbi Schliefer of Moscow referred to such historical antecedents of Hitler as Amalek, Pharaoh and Haman. Abraham Sutskever, the young poet-partisan from Lithuania, spoke about the fate of Vilna Jews, of their suffering and resistance. Besides the twin issues of Jewish tragedy and heroism, some speakers, though in a muted tone, also pointed to the dangers of antisemitic attitudes within the Soviet population, especially when held by those who had been exposed to Nazi rule and propaganda. By the time of this 1944 Meeting, Jews had already started to return to their prewar homes in the western parts of the country, where the hostility of the local populace was overt and increasing. Ehrenburg, though less outspoken than in February 1943, warned in his speech of the "microbes of antisemitism" and the danger of "contamination." Fefer, too, mentioned this problem, referring to Stalin's condemnation of antisemitism in the early thirties. Ehrenburg and Rabbi Schliefer did however propound a view which was aimed at countering Jewish uneasiness about the attitudes of the Soviet non-Jewish population. Both spoke of the rescue of Jews by their non-Jewish neighbors, a phenomenon which was now inflated beyond its true scope. The *Pravda* account of the meeting highlighted this point in Ehrenburg's speech.[36]

In his report to a Plenary Session of the JAC which followed the mass meeting, Epshteyn cautioned those who criticized the resurgence of antisemitism in the USSR. He declared "even if the War had stirred up some abnormal phenomena . . . there is no reason whatsoever to generalize, to exaggerate and to blow up their implications and impact." He particularly condemned the "whiners" and "complainers" among the Soviet-Yiddish writers, and warned against excessive Jewish emotionalism in their writings. These and other warnings against "unhealthy nationalistic moods" were first signs of an official Soviet line, to be fully revealed after the War. Epshteyn also informed his audience that the censorship of materials sent abroad by the Committee had been stepped up. At the same time, he mentioned the continuing usefulness of the Committee for foreign propaganda purposes and spoke about the growing range of contacts between the JAC and Jewish organizations in the West. Mikhoels and Fefer reported mainly on their visit abroad and their successes. The gist of their speeches was that contacts and cooperation with world Jewry were beneficial to all concerned, and should be continued and expanded after the War.[37]

According to an *Eynikayt* report, "lively discussions," with the participation of numerous JAC members, took place in the wake of these reports. The prevailing view seemed to be that JAC activities should be expanded.[38] However, details of these discussions were never published.

Those in charge of the JAC clearly intended to use it after the War; in fact, new Committee members were co-opted during the April 1944 Plenary Session; a standing Committee Presidium was established and subsequently expanded during the summer.[39] Seventeen new members were co-opted to the JAC. Among them were the Soviet-Jewish writer and journalist Vassily Grossman, the poet-partisan Sutskever, the refugee-poet Chaim Grade and several Red Army officers and partisans. Among those co-opted to the Presidium was S. Bregman, Soviet Deputy Commissar of State Control, who was very active in the Committee in the postwar years. The others were L. Sheinin, a high-ranking official in the Ministry of Railroad Transportation; M. Gubelman (brother of Yemelyan Yaroslavsky, longtime Bolshevik and a major figure in Soviet journalism and propaganda), Chairman of the Trade Employees Union; and V. Briker, Head of the Film Workers Union.

Crimea and Birobidzhan

The discussions on drafting of a proposal for the settlement of Jews in the Crimea were symptomatic of the hopes and expectations within the Jewish Antifascist Committee in the spring and summer of 1944. Difficulties faced by Jewish repatriates to western Soviet territories, especially the Ukraine, and the fact that Soviet Jews served Soviet wartime causes loyally, led some JAC leaders to believe that Stalin would be willing to approve a massive postwar settlement of Jews on the Crimean Peninsula. Hopes for the establishment of an official national Jewish territory in that area were also nurtured in this context. Jewish settlements in the Crimea were something of an historical tradition, revived in the 1920's under the auspices of the Soviet regime, which backed agricultural settlement projects for Jews in that area. As a result, some 40,000 Jews lived in that region towards the end of the decade comprising more than 6% of the local population. On the eve of the War, Crimea's Jewish population reached 60,000 (7.4% of the total), of which a third lived in Jewish collective settlements. Five Jewish autonomous districts were founded there between 1929 and 1937, while the authorities were still approving plans for additional Jewish settlements. The continuing settling of Jews in the Crimea, on however modest a scale, evoked criticism and opposition among the Crimean Tatars, who considered it a threat to their national claims. The War seemed to have ended whatever Jewish hopes and plans existed for Crimea. The Crimean Jewish communities were either evacuated or annihilated. It should be recalled that Stalin was never enthusiastic about the emergence of a Jewish national territory in the Peninsula.

The Red Army's thrust into Crimea coincided with the April 1944 meetings of the JAC. Among the officers who participated in the Crimean campaign was General Yakov Kreizer, a leading member of the Committee. Thus it is possible that first-hand information concerning Soviet Crimean policies was forwarded by Kreizer to the JAC leadership. The JAC must have been influenced by word of the swift punitive measures taken by the regime against the Crimean Tatars, charged by Stalin with collaborating with the Germans. The bulk of the Tatars were deported in a single NKVD operation. The Crimean Autonomous Republic was subsequently abolished and transformed into the Crimean Province of the RSFSR; all traces of Tatar national existence in the region were eradicated.[40] After Stalin's death the Crimea became part of the Ukrainian Republic. Thus, from April-May 1944, the Crimea was apparently vied for by national groups such as the Ukrainians and, for a short while, the Jews.

The details and chronology of the JAC attempts to further the Crimean issue, are unknown, but sufficient evidence exists for an approximation of events. Several sources say that the Crimea was discussed, at least informally, during the JAC Plenary Session in April 1944. Israel Emiot, a refugee poet from Poland, who arrived in Moscow a few weeks before the Session, attended discussions of the Crimea within the Committee. Another poet from Poland, Joseph Rubinstein, was even inspired to write a poem about the future settlement of Jews in the Crimea. On one occasion, the Soviet-Yiddish writer, Bergelson, told Rubinstein that Jewish refugees from Poland would probably be the first to be settled in the Peninsula. Emiot heard similar assertions at the JAC.[41] According to still another source, the literary critic Prof. Nusinov suggested during one of the JAC meetings that Jewish repatriates should not be returned to the ruined towns in the Ukraine, but should rather be settled in the Crimea. Rumors of Mikhoels' appointment to head the future Jewish territory in the Crimea were also rife in the JAC and among Soviet Jewish writers. On one occasion at least Mihkoels hinted to the actors of the Moscow Jewish State Theatre that some future premiere might be held in the Crimea.[42]

A memorandum on the Crimea was drafted by the JAC leadership and submitted to the highest Soviet authorities, sometime during the summer of 1944. Khrushchev wrote in his memoirs: "Once the Ukraine had been liberated, a paper was drafted by the members of the Lozovsky Committee. It was addressed to Stalin and contained a proposal that the Crimea be made a Jewish Soviet Republic . . ."[43] Though there might be some inaccuracies in this description, the gist of the matter probably is correct. Khrushchev's testimony is corroborated by that of the poet Sutskever, who jotted down in his diary in July 1944 that a JAC delegation visited Maxim Litvinov and discussed with him the possibility of establishing a Jewish center in the Crimea.[44] Another name often mentioned in the context of the Crimean proposal is that of Molotov. It is possible that Molotov's Jewish wife, Zhemchuzhina, was instrumental in this regard. According to Khrushchev, "Apparently Zhemchuzhina had pulled him [Molotov] into it . . ."[45] B. Z. Goldberg's version of the events is similar to that of Khrushchev, i.e. that JAC leaders spoke first to Zhemchuzhina who arranged for a meeting with Molotov, who in turn suggested that a memo be drafted and sent to Stalin. A similar version is reported by Markish's widow.[46] Kaganovich was yet another political figure consulted on the Crimea. Fefer confided on one occasion that it was Kaganovich who urged him to submit a proposal for Jewish settlement in the Crimea to Stalin.[47] Lozovskii, the actual boss of the JAC, must have participated in such discussions, and there are some indications that, like Molotov, he favored the idea.[48]

Whether or not Mikhoels and Fefer discussed Crimea during their visit abroad in the summer of 1943 is not clear, but officials of the JDC (Joint Distribution Committee) certainly mentioned it in their correspondence with Soviet diplomats, following the visit.

Thousands of Jewish families had settled in the Crimea with JDC assistance between 1924 and 1928. More than one hundred Jewish agricultural settlements, aided by Agro-Joint, existed in the Crimea by the late twenties, some of them Zionist oriented and aimed at eventual settlement in Palestine.[49] It was J. N. Rosenberg of the JDC in particular who propagated the idea of Jewish re-settlement on the Peninsula during and after the War. The JDC submitted memos on assistance to Jewish repatriates to the Crimea to Soviet officials throughout 1945 with no tangible results.[50] There are hints in the *Eynikayt* that the Crimea continued to interest the JAC during the last stages of the War and in the immediate postwar years. The poet Kvitko visited the region in the early fall of 1944 and reported to his colleagues on the Committee about Jewish settlements there. Bergelson wrote to Sutskever in Vilna, possibly alluding to the Crimea proposal, "We are waiting for something good to happen."[51] A number of *Eynikayt* correspondents reported on Jewish re-settlement in the Crimea throughout 1945 and

1946. Subskever, was asked on the eve of his departure from the Soviet Union in May 1946, to try and involve Ehrenburg in the Crimean project and around that time Mikhoels urged B. Z. Goldberg to extend his stay in the USSR, since, "we expect news from the Kremlin about the Jews."[52] By 1946 the idea of Jewish settlement in Birobidzhan had been revived, but the Crimean Proposal had not yet been completely discarded. Jewish writers and *Eynikayt* correspondents continued to visit Jewish settlements in the region, and *Eynikayt* published their impressions. All this leads to the conclusion that, the Crimean Proposal lingered on at least until mid-1946.

It is very difficult to define the attitudes of the Committee and of Soviet Jewish literary circles to the Crimean Proposal. It is, clear, however, that while some of the Yiddish writers on the Committee supported the idea, Ehrenburg opposed it vehemently. In the course of a heated argument with Epshteyn, he said that, "the echelons (of Jewish repatriates) will go back to Zhitomir and Vinnitsa" (and not settle in the Crimea).[53] Another opponent was Perets Markish, who suggested the Volga territory (from which local German inhabitants had been deported in 1941) for Jewish postwar resettlement. Markish considered this to be an act of historical justice, in view of the Holocaust.[54] The Birobidzhan members of the Committee opposed the Crimean plan because of their own narrow interests, considering Jewish settlement in the Crimea as a threat to Jewish Birobidzhan. They also sought the help of President Kalinin on that matter.[55] As for the top Soviet leadership Molotov, Kaganovich and Lozovskii seem to have backed, or at least not opposed the idea. Khrushchev's memoirs and an interview he granted to a Canadian Jewish communist corroborate the fact that both Stalin *and* Khrushchev were basically opposed to the proposal. According to Khrushchev, "Stalin saw behind this proposal the hand of American Zionists, operating through the Sovinformburo [i.e. the JAC, run by the Sovinformburo], . . . "He, Khrushchev, agreed with Stalin that the Crimea, which was depopulated at the end of the war against Hitler, should not be designated a center for Jewish colonization, because in case of war it would be turned into a place d'armes [a base for attack] against the USSR."[56] Also opposed to the idea was Aleksandr Shcherbakov.[57] Soviet security agencies exploited the charge that the JAC plan to establish a Jewish national territory in the Crimea was a deliberate security threat to the Soviet regime in the course of arrests, interrogations and trials of the Committee's leading members in the years 1948–1952.[58] The "Crimean

Affair" surfaced again during the infamous "Doctors' Plot" in early 1953. Thus, JAC contacts with world Jewry and with such Jewish organizations as the JDC, as well as wartime plans for Jewish resettlement (which were quite legitimate, at the time) later became instrumental in the liquidation of the JAC and its leadership.

The JAC also became involved in the postwar effort to resettle Jews in the Jewish Autonomous Region of Birobidzhan. There were a number of possible reasons for the Soviet decision to revive the idea of Jewish Birobidzhan. First was the problem of Jewish repatriates in the Western territories, which could be partially solved by Jewish settlement in Birobidzhan. It would also counterbalance Zionist aspirations, and, last but not least serve as an impressive Soviet propaganda weapon abroad.[59] *Eynikayt*, had published articles on Birobidzhan since 1942, referring to Jewish "statehood" in the Far Eastern Soviet region.[60] Representatives of Jews from Birobidzhan also participated in the April 1944 Meeting organized by the Committee. More intensive involvement of the JAC in Birobidzhan affairs clearly started in 1946. At that time, *Eynikayt* began extensive coverage of Jewish postwar settlement in the area and actually became a part of a propaganda campaign to encourage Soviet Jews to emigrate to the region. A number of *Eynikayt* reporters became involved in this settlement campaign, either as permanent correspondents in Birobidzhan or as reporters on the "settlers' trains."[61] Trainloads of Birobidzhan settlers which happened to pass through Moscow were greeted by JAC leaders at the railroad station. Birobidzhan officials visited the JAC offices and consulted Committee personnel. A special subcommittee on Birobidzhan was established in the JAC.[62] It seems that the principal although somewhat unofficial liaison officer between the JAC and Birobidzhan was Israel Emiot, who had spent the war years in the Far East.[63] Another writer who became actively involved in Jewish culture in Birobidzhan was Der Nister. He joined one of the "settlers' trains" in the summer of 1947 and spent a number of weeks in Birobidzhan. Der Nister was welcomed by local Jewish intellectuals who apparently hoped that "somebody from Moscow" would be helpful in advancing local Jewish interests. Der Nister's national sentiments and hopes were quite clearly expressed in his reports on Birobidzhan. Upon his return to Moscow he spoke on Jewish culture there at an editorial board meeting of the *Eynikayt* and urged his colleagues to become more involved.[64] The JAC seems to have been regarded, both within the USSR and abroad, as an address in matters concerning Birobidzhan.

Thus, when a Canadian Jewish organization supporting Jewish settlement in Birobidzhan did not receive a reply to its correspondence with Birobidzhan officials, B. Z. Goldberg, Secretary of the Writers' Committee wrote to Mikhoels and Fefer: "if they (the Birobidzhan officials) are in doubt about anything, they should communicate with you."[65] Birobidzhan was used extensively for Soviet propaganda purposes. As late as the fall of 1948, Fefer wrote in reply to *Forward's* anti-Soviet criticism that "If (Jewish) migration to Birobidzhan continues at the present pace, within a few years we should have a Jewish Autonomous Soviet Socialist Republic in the Far East."[66]

The JAC As A Jewish Center

Soviet wartime nationality policies encouraged an upsurge of cultural nationalism among various nationality groups in the USSR. Ukrainian cultural nationalism for example was openly expressed as late as the spring of 1945. It is in this context of laxer attitudes to national expression that the role played by and demanded of the JAC should be considered.

Though its main official function was dissemination of propaganda, the Jewish Antifascist Committee became increasingly significant for Jews inside the Soviet Union. It served as the main address for Jewish requests and complaints, as well as a center of Soviet Jewish culture. Fefer wrote to B. Z. Goldberg late in the summer of 1944: "The activities of our Committee are growing and its prospects are increasingly encouraging." A Canadian Jewish journalist who visited the USSR in 1944–1945 reported that "at the center of all Jewish activity in the USSR . . . was the Antifascist Committee of Soviet Jews." B. Z. Goldberg, who was the Committee's guest during the first half of 1946, wrote home that he found the Jewish Antifascist Committee "a big undertaking" and that the impression that the JAC was just a committee of writers was false. While traveling with Fefer to various centers of Jewish population in the USSR, Goldberg saw how local Jews appealed to the JAC on various matters. Joseph Kerler, a young Yiddish writer who had served in the Army and arrived in Moscow towards the end of the War, testified that numerous letters from all over the country reached the Committee offices daily and that "Jews . . . looked upon the Committee as their representative vis-à-vis the government, and as the only Jewish address."[67] Leading JAC figures such as Mikhoels and Ehrenburg, were regarded by many Soviet Jews as their natural spokesmen.[68] *Eynikayt,* which published only a portion of the letters flooding the JAC offices, conceded, the special standing of the Committee among Soviet Jews.

JAC offices often served as a meeting place for Jewish soldiers and partisans. Although such contacts were initially established purely for Soviet propaganda purposes, they evolved into an outlet for Jewish national identity. In the light of antisemitic slanders, information on and records of Jewish resistance were particularly important for both the JAC leadership and Jews directly involved in anti-Nazi warfare. Jewish officers, soldiers and partisans were a common sight in the Committee offices during 1944/46. Besides Generals Kreizer and Katz, the Committee was visited by other high ranking officers such as Rear Admiral Pavel Trainin and Generals Cherniavsky and Rabinovich. Paulina Gelman, a young Jewish woman pilot and recipient of the Hero of the Soviet Union medal also used to visit the Committee. Partisans such as Sutskever, Smoliar and Oylitski also came.[69] A highly emotional encounter took place at the JAC in the early summer of 1945, involving Colonel David Dragunsky, a young tank unit commander who participated in the attack on Berlin and was twice awarded the Hero of the Soviet Union distinction. Dragunsky related how most of his family, had been killed by the Nazis, described his visit to Babi Yar and spoke of his special Jewish reckoning with the enemy. He also described the concentration camps he had seen and his visit to the ancient Prague synagogue.[70] The Committee and *Eynikayt* constantly received letters from Jewish soldiers, reporting their participation in the War. Some of them asked for books and materials dealing with Jewish history and culture.[71] *Eynikayt* continuously published articles on Soviet-Jewish war heroes and on Jewish participation in the War. The JAC was also behind the preparation of "Partisan Friendship," a collection of memoirs dealing with Jewish partisans, printed in book form, but never actually disseminated. In an interview in late 1947, Ehrenburg mentioned that a "Red Book" on Jewish resistance in ghettos and in the partisan movement was being prepared for publication. This book, too, was never published.[72]

A major concern of the JAC was the re-settlement and rehabilitation of Jewish repatriates to the Western territories of the USSR; a special sub-committee was set up to deal with that problem in the spring of 1944. The Committee collected data and prepared reports on Jewish survivors in all the territories liberated by the Soviets. Some of this information was obtained from Committee members who travelled to those territories. Thus, Ehrenburg, who spent some time in liberated Lithuania and Belorussia during the mid-summer of 1944, reported his impressions to the Committee. Another member of the JAC, the officer-poet Aaron Kushnirov, met with surviving Jewish partisans in Vilna. Committee members were sent on fact-finding missions to the Crimea, to Belorussia and to the Dnepropetrovsk Region in the Ukraine.[73] A few weeks after the liberation of Western Ukraine, JAC correspondents reached that area, and tried to recruit reporters for the Eynikayt among local Jewish survivors. Leading Moscow Yiddish writers, who were members of the Committee, continued visiting centers of Jewish population in the Western Soviet territories after the War. Markish visited Vilna in the spring of 1945 and Fefer visited the Western Ukraine in the spring of 1946.[74] It was only natural that the Committee and its cultural leadership should consider the western parts of the USSR a significant base for renewal of Jewish cultural activities. A number of Eynikayt articles referred to the responsibility of Soviet Jewish intelligentsia to assist in the revival of Jewish life in those territories.[75] It was also natural that those who attempted to organize relief and to reconstruct Jewish culture in the newly liberated territories turned to the JAC for guidance and help. When Eliezer Lidovsky, an ex-partisan from Rovno, arrived in Moscow in order to raise money for his fellow Jews in the Western Ukraine, he first turned to Mikhoels. The writer Shmerke Kaczerginsky, who tried to save and preserve Jewish archival and cultural materials in Vilna, also turned to the JAC. Hersh Smoliar, the veteran Jewish communist activist, and partisan leader from Belorussia, discussed the problem of postwar antisemitism in that republic with Fefer and Epshteyn. There were also numerous personal requests and appeals. A demobilized Jewish lawyer from Kiev for example tried to regain his prewar job with the assistance of the Committee, and a Jewish tailor from Zhitomir traveled to Moscow in order to complain at the JAC that his prewar apartment was now occupied by somebody else.[76]

The Committee made continuous efforts to promote Jewish cultural activities in postwar USSR, in spite of the obstacles and lack of substantial support by Soviet authorities. An Ey;nikayt editorial describing the almost complete ruin of Jewish culture in the Soviet Union, complained that "the dimensions of [the rehabilitation of Jewish culture] are far from satisfactory."[77] Though the difficulties were great, JAC leaders looked for hopeful omens. When, Mikhoels and his colleagues at the Moscow Jewish State Theatre were awarded the prestigious Stalin Prize in 1946, they wanted very much to believe that "this was an act of great political and public significance . . . a victory for Soviet-Jewish culture."[78] The modest Jewish cultural frameworks which existed in the Soviet Union at the end of the War, such as the Jewish Writers' Bureau, the Jewish theatres, the *Emes* Publishing House, the Jewish Section of the Ukrainian Academy of Sciences and the few Yiddish schools, all maintained close organizational and personal contacts with the Committee. The JAC "literary evenings" continued and became more frequent; art and music were added to the agenda. Jewish literary events in various Jewish centers were often reported in the *Eynikayt*.

In 1945/46 the Committee attempted to gain permission to turn *Eynikayt* into a daily with an increased circulation. One strategem was to publish in *Eynikayt* readers' letters complaining about the scarcity of the publication.[79] A similar tactic was used by the Committee in regard to the lamentable situation of Jewish books and libraries. At least during the first postwar months, the tone of the appeals published in *Eynikayt* was quite bold. One headline, for example, proclaimed: "The Demand for Yiddish Books Should be Satisfied." It was stressed, time and again, that requests and criticism were reaching the JAC from all parts of the USSR.[80] Committee members were also involved in the attempts to revive Yiddish literary periodicals. Attempts were made to import Jewish books from the U.S. B. Z. Goldberg suggested to Mikhoels that "Hebrew and Yiddish books, properly selected" should be sent via the Russian War Relief in America. Louis Levine (of the Jewish Council for Russian War Relief) informed Rosenberg of "a . . request (for Judaica books) made by the JAC."[81] It seems that Soviet authorities in charge of such matters were not overenthusiastic in extending their support, and if anything was done in that direction, it was negligible. Close cooperation existed between the JAC and the *Emes* Publishing House. The Committee also tried to assist in the rehabilitation of Yiddish printing plants elsewhere, but these efforts apparently bore no tangible results. A visitor to the USSR wrote in mid-1947 that "not a single Yiddish print shop now exists in the entire Ukrainian and White Russian Republics." Earlier that year, Mikhoels and Fefer asked a visiting Jewish journalist from Toronto to request that B. Z. Goldberg send printing equipment to the USSR for *Eynikayt* and *Emes*. The JAC also appealed to the "American Jewish Council to Aid Russian Rehabilitation," to raise money for printing equipment. Though the Soviet Consul-General in New York, supported this idea, nothing tangible came of it.[82]

The JAC was closely involved in the planning of numerous Soviet Jewish publications. At the February 1946 JAC Presidium Meeting, two major projects were discussed and approved. One was to be a "Book of Jewish Heroism" on Jewish participation in the War in Yiddish, Russian and English, and the other - "Moscow-New York", yearbooks, both to be joint ventures of the JAC and the Jewish Writers' Committee in New York. The editors of the prospective "Book of Jewish Heroism" included Mikhoels, Fefer, Grossman and General Katz. The Yearbook Committee, consisted besides Mikhoels and Fefer, of Leib Kvitko and Lina Shtern. Goldberg testified that both Mikhoels and Fefer were very interested in the Yearbook, the first issue of which was planned for early 1947, but it was then postponed for the fall of that year, and, in fact, never materialized.[83] As late as the summer of 1946, *Eynikayt* was audacious enough to openly criticize the situation in Jewish publishing, in an article entitled "Plans instead of Books." Goldberg was told, in early 1946, by his hosts at the JAC that the approval had been obtained for the publication of 350 Jewish books by the *Emes* Publishing House that year. In fact, only 18 were printed. Among those projects which never materialized were anthologies of the Bible, of Talmudic Literature, of Hebrew poetry in the Middle Ages, and histories of the Jews in Russia and of Yiddish Literature and Theatre.[84]

Jewish cultural nationalism in the USSR was influenced considerably by the close and intensive contacts maintained between the JAC, its Soviet Yiddish writers and Jewish refugee writers from Poland, Rumania and the Baltic States. The encounter began in 1939–1940, when the USSR annexed extensive territories, with large and nationally conscious Jewish populations.[85] For some Soviet-Jewish writers, like Fefer, this meeting was new and exciting while for others, like Markish, it was a reunion with longtime friends and colleagues. And although the official Soviet purpose behind this encounter was the Sovietization of Jewish culture in the newly annexed territories, it was only natural that the by product was revitalization of Jewish nationalism. the Holocaust had had a stunning impact on both Soviet and Jewish refugee writers. Already during the Molotov-Ribbentrop era, when anti-Nazi sentiment was taboo in the Soviet Union, writers from both groups expressed, (in unpublished verse), their identification with the tragedy of the Jews in German-occupied Europe. After 1941, when such literary themes were at least partially sanctioned by the regime, a significant trend developed in Soviet-Yiddish writing. Some Soviet Yiddish writers chose the wartime Polish-Jewish scene as background for their literary works. Thus, Der Nister, Markish, Halkin and even Fefer described at length the martyrdom and resistance of Polish Jews.[86] Most of these writers also extended everyday material assistance to their refugee colleagues. The refugees themselves made a considerable contribution to wartime Jewish cultural activities in the USSR. Their books were published by Soviet publishing houses, their literary writings and articles appeared in the *Eynikayt* and refugee actors appeared on the Soviet stage.

When the Jewish Antifascist Committee established contact with Jewish writers throughout the USSR it also approached the refugees from other countries. Some were invited to participate in the April 1944 Moscow meeting of the JAC, and remained in the Capital. Such was the case with Chaim Grade, Israel Emiot, Rachel Korn, Joseph Rubinstein, and the Polish-Yiddish actress Ida Kaminska. Close personal ties grew up between a number of refugee writers and their Soviet Yiddish colleagues. Thus, for example, Fefer became the confidant of Rachel Korn, and Markish of Ida Kaminska. A close relationship also developed between Grade and Bergelson.[87] Another refugee intellectual was the Polish-Jewish historian Ber Mark. Both he and his wife were brought to Kuibyshev in early 1943 and given assignments at the Sovinformburo, and at the JAC, where Mark dealt mainly with the documentation and research of the Holocaust.[88]

The relationship between Soviet-Yiddish intellectuals and their refugee counterparts was ambivalent. Though they were accepted as meaningful contributors to Jewish cultural life in the USSR they were also suspected of external loyalties. There was a strange mixture of proximity and aloofness in these ties, which were also affected by personal temperaments, attitudes and sentiments. On the whole, it seemed that the intimacy and trust was affected when it became apparent that the refugees would have the option to leave Russia after the War. Reactions varied: Fefer told Rachel Korn "We shall not let you leave" . . . Bergelson was deeply worried and warned that "[their departure] may hurt us." When the poet Joseph Rubinstein informed his Soviet colleagues of his intention to return to Poland, Markish exclaimed: "Are you going to those Polish roughnecks who are killing Jews?" His advice to Rachel Korn was: "Don't stay in Fascist Poland, go to Erets-Yisroel or America . . ." On the other hand, Der Nister, Dobrushin and Halkin encouraged the refugee writers to leave Russia and tell the West about the deteriorating situation of Jewish culture in the USSR.[89]

An "Organizational Committee of Polish Jews in the USSR" was founded in the summer of 1944, and made contact with the JAC. This Committee, sponsored and supervised by the Pro-Soviet Union of Polish Patriots in the USSR (UPP), was meant to perform a role similar to that of the JAC, i.e. to gather material and mobilize political support of Jewish communities in the West for the emergent pro-Soviet Polish Government in Lublin. Like the JAC, it consisted primarily of intellectuals, such as writers, journalists, actors and artists with no explicit political affiliations. Among its members were: Dr. Emil Sommerstein, a prewar Zionist leader and member of the Polish Sejm (Parliament), the writers Moshe Brodersohn, Joseph Rubinshteyn, Ephraim Kaganovski and Rachel Korn; the actress Ida Kaminska; and a number of rabbis. In fact, the Committee's activities were directed by a rather small communist group within it, which included such people as Dr. David Sfard and Shimon Zachariasz. They received their directives from Jacob Berman, one of the founders of the UPP and a leading figure in the postwar Polish-Communist Party.[90] Contacts between this Polish-Jewish Committee and the JAC started in early 1945 and continued until the repatriation of the majority of Polish Jews in the USSR was completed. During meetings held in February 1945 common objectives and possible cooperation were discussed. Fefer suggested joint cultural ventures for Soviet and Polish Jews, such as the publication of literary yearbooks, and he promised that *Eynikayt* would provide extensive coverage of the Jewish scene in postwar Poland. Epshteyn stressed the need for Polish and Soviet Jews to act jointly in the international Jewish arena. He also suggested the possibility of Soviet assistance in the revival of Jewish culture in postwar Poland and exchanges of Jewish writers, artists and scientists.[91] JAC representatives and Soviet-Yiddish writers regularly attended all public events held under the auspices of the "Organizational Committee." Thus in April 1945, when the second anniversary of the Warsaw Ghetto uprising was celebrated by the UPP and the "Organizational Committee of Polish Jews," Mikhoels, Epshteyn and General Katz were among the guests of honor.[92] JAC leaders actively participated in a three day conference of representatives of Polish Jews from all over Russia, which took place at the UPP offices in November of that year. Various aspects of the revival of Jewish cultural, and communal, life in

Poland were discussed, including Zionism and the teaching of Hebrew, subjects which were taboo in the USSR itself. The openness of the discussion and the explicit Jewish atmosphere must have made a deep impact on the Soviet-Yiddish intellectuals. Fefer announced that "we shall revive Jewish life" after the War; Bergelson spoke of the deep ties between Soviet and Polish Jews; and Markish praised "the rich national character of Polish Jewry." A particularly moving moment for the participants of the conference was Cantor Koussevitzki's prayer of *El Maleh Rahamim,* for the Jewish victims of the Holocaust.[93]

The overall relationship between the JAC and the Polish-Jewish Committee was characterized by the same measure of ambivalence as the ties between Soviet and Polish-Jewish intellectuals. The JAC, though interested in maintaining close ties with the Organizational Committee, regarded it a somewhat alien body, a part of another political entity. When the Committee ceased its activities and the Central Committee of the Jews in Poland became the main official organization representing Polish Jews, contacts with the JAC continued. They were expressed primarily in the publication of Soviet-Jewish literary and journalistic material in Polish-Jewish publications. The JAC also, at times, sought the advice of Jewish-communists in Poland on international Jewish affairs. At the same time, the continuing efforts of Polish-Jewish personalities to invite JAC representatives to visit Poland bore no results.[94]

The Black Book Project

During the War the Jewish Antifascist Committee became a major documentation center on Nazi atrocities against Jews. In the summer of 1942, an official Soviet publication stated that "the Committee resolved to make public materials . . . concerning the atrocities . . . against Jews." In December, *Eynikayt* quoted a World Jewish Congress report on the annihilation of Jews in German-occupied territories. Eyewitness accounts of mass murder in centers of Jewish population such as Kiev and Vilna were reported by the Committee. In an editorial, *Eynikayt* pointed out that ". . . . the Jewish people was afflicted . . . by the most acute pain and sorrow,"[95] a line which, as a rule, was not clearly presented in the non-Jewish Soviet press. The flood of information about the Holocaust increased with the liberation of the western Soviet territories. *Eynikayt* correspondents, Jewish Red

Army soldiers and survivors constantly sent the Committee documents and other materials relating to the fate of the Jewish population in the Nazi-occupied parts of the country. Thus, for example, material found by Soviet soldiers in the Shavli Ghetto in Lithuania were forwarded to the Committee.[96] Quite often people actually came to the JAC offices to deliver information and to share their sorrow with its members. Among those submitting information to the Committee were non-Jewish Soviet correspondents and writers as well. In addition, the JAC maintained close contacts with the Soviet State Committee for Investigating Nazi Crimes, from which it received German documentation. An impressive amount of material on Nazi atrocities against Jews, incomparably more than was published inside Russia by JAC's *Eynikayt,* was sent by the Committee to various Jewish organizations and publications abroad.[97]

The vicissitudes of the Black Book project reflected, the complexities and difficulties involved in the collecting and publication of Holocaust-related materials in wartime and postwar Russia, and shed some light on the relations between the JAC and Jewish organizations abroad. The idea of publishing a Black Book on Nazi atrocities against Jews first emerged in the summer of 1943, during Mikhoel's and Fefer's visit to the U.S. A few weeks after their arrival in America, *Eynikayt* informed its readers that "the Committee of Jewish Writers [in New York] approached us with a suggestion to publish jointly a Black Book on Nazi atrocities against Jews." A JAC sub-committee was soon established for this project. Among its members were Mikhoels, Fefer, Epshteyn, Kvitko, Markish, Halkin, Falkovich and Dr. Shimelovich. At the same time, *Eynikayt* appealed to its readers and to Yiddish writers in the Soviet Union to send any related material.[98] The project was apparently first discussed by Mikhoels and Fefer with B. Z. Goldberg of the Jewish Writers' Committee, a pro-Soviet Jewish front, and a decision was then reached to involve additional Jewish organizations. The Black Book project, besides recording Nazi policies towards Jews, was also part of the Soviet propaganda "unity" tactics intended to mobilize Jewish public opinion abroad. Mikhoels and Fefer suggested such a project at their meetings with World Jewish Congress (WJC) officials, who displayed an enthusiasm for cooperation with the JAC. They were, however, less than enthusiastic about having B.Z. Goldberg's Committee as a full-fledged partner in the project. The question of the participation of the Writer's Committee was still open as far as the WJC was concerned when Mikhoels and Fefer left the

U.S., in the fall of 1943. It seems that Mikhoels, Fefer and the Congress agreed among themselves that it would be a joint venture of the JAC, the WJC and the National Council (Vaad Leumi) in Palestine. The underlying idea was that each organization would collect and share out material relating to the Holocaust, which would then be published jointly in several languages. *Eynikayt,* in the meantime, stressed B. Z. Goldberg's participation, mentioning Sholem Asch, Joseph Brainin and Reuben Saltzman, all Soviet sympathizers and members of the Writers' Committee, as co-sponsors of the project.[99] The matter of the participation of the Writers' Committee was raised again in early 1944, a short while after Mikhoels and Fefer returned to Moscow. Dr. Nahum Goldmann of the WJC, in a cable to Mikhoels, argued that all previous discussions were based on a three-party agreement (i.e. the JAC, the WJC and the Vaad Leumi). JAC's reply was unequivocal: "Participation (of the Writers' Committee) (in the) publication (of the) Black Book (is) imperative."[100] The JAC stand on the matter was undoubtedly based on the fact that B. Z. Goldberg and his Committee were most trusted representatives of the JAC and of Soviet interests in the West.

The Black Book project went into high gear in Moscow in early 1944 when a working session of the Committee took up the plan. The main speakers at that session were Shakhno Epshteyn and Ilya Ehrenburg. Epshteyn reported on the Committee's ongoing efforts to collect documentation on the Holocaust while Ehrenburg quoted from materials already received and urged the further collection of information "on the terrible tragedy of the Jewish people." At that stage it seemed that Ehrenburg was the main figure behind the undertaking, and in Epshteyn's words, "one of the most active initiators of the Black Book."[101] A Black Book Literary Committee, headed by Ehrenburg, was established between January and April 1944. By the time the JAC Plenum was convened in April 1944 two new members had been added to this Committee: David Zaslavskii and David Bergelson. In his report to the Plenum, Epshteyn outlined the impressive scope of the planned book, announcing that it would be published in Russian, English, Yiddish, Hebrew, Spanish, German and other languages.[102] During the following months, Grossman, Bregman and Sutskever were co-opted to the Black Book Committee. By then, *Eynikayt* was already publishing parts of the collected materials. By September 1944, the JAC had sent B. Z. Goldberg over 500 pages of such material. Additional documents were handed over to a World Jewish Congress representative by the

Soviet Consul in New York.[103] Ehrenburg, who remained the "number one" man behind the Black Book project throughout 1944 and up to the spring of 1945, became deeply involved in the collecting of material on Jewish suffering and heroism. He considered the Black Book project a strong personal commitment. Some excerpts from the Black Book materials were published by Ehrenburg in Yiddish and in Russian in the years 1944–1945.[104] Then, in the spring of 1945, Lozovskii, Head of the Sovinformburo asked Ehrenburg to disband the Black Book Literary Committee which he headed, and to transfer the project in its entirety to the Jewish Antifascist Committee. It is quite possible that this step was taken in the wake of the changing Soviet conception in regard to Germany and the Germans. Ehrenburg's extremist approach, blaming all Germans for the misfortunes of the War, no longer fitted in with official Soviet ideology and propaganda which was becoming more moderate at that time.[105] Vassily Grossman replaced Ehrenburg as Head of the Black Book Editorial Committee, and within a year completed the preparation of the manuscript.

In the meantime, the preparation of the English version of the Black Book in New York had gone through several stages. By the fall of 1944, a Black Book Executive Committee existed, consisting of WJC and Writers' Committee representatives. Those most active in it were B. Z. Goldberg and Dr. Maurice Perlzweig of the WJC. The editorial staff was headed by Goldberg, Ursula Wasserman, a communist-affiliated journalist, and Valia Hirsch, a liberal-minded pro-Soviet Zionist. Preparation and publishing of the book were to be financed equally by the World Jewish Congress and the Writers' Committee. A public Black Book Committee, to sponsor and publicize the project, was also created. Among its members were Albert Einstein, Eleanor Roosevelt, Stephen Wise and Thomas Mann. It was Einstein, extremely sensitive on the issue of Nazi, anti-Jewish policies, who persuaded Eleanor Roosevelt to lend her name to the project.[106] The English version of the manuscript was completed by the early fall of 1945. It seemed, at that point, that the JAC's trust in B. Z. Goldberg was paying off. Goldberg sent a copy of the English manuscript to the Committee, stating that ". . . we can make all the changes you want" and asking "whether we can go ahead with publication." The English version however, contained only *some* of the Soviet material supplied by the JAC, and was not to the liking of the Soviet partners. A reply, signed by Mikhoels, Fefer and Grossman stated: "[we] deem it necessary to remind you how we formulated this task . . . (we) consider superfluous

these chapters on (the) history and (the) future of our people . . ."[107]
These remarks were probably directed at Einstein's planned introduction to the Black Book, in which as Honorary Chairman of the Writers' Committee, he demanded that the Jews be compensated for their
wartime suffering by being granted new opportunities for emigration
to Palestine, and settlement there. One should bear in mind that it was
only in the spring of 1947 that the Soviet Union formulated a clear cut
pro-Zionist policy on the issue of Palestine. Considerable pressure was
put on Einstein to alter his introduction for "ideological" reasons, and
apparently unwilling to create controversy, he wrote a second version,
which was also unacceptable. The Black Book was ultimately published without an introduction by this most illustrious member of the
Writers' Committee.[108] The English version of the Black Book was
launched at a mass rally in Madison Square Garden and published in
the spring of 1946. Though the JAC was urged by the Writers' Committee to sent its representative to the dedication ceremony, no representative arrived.[109]

By the time the English version of the Black Book appeared in print
in New York, its Russian counterpart was ready for the press. Fefer
announced in early 1946 that the Black Book would soon be published
in Russia, and Grossman reported to a JAC Presidium meeting in May
that: ". . . the whole book is already typeset in Russian and will shortly
be published." He also informed those present that copies of the Russian manuscript had been sent to a number of places abroad, among
them the U.S., England, Palestine and Rumania. Grossman, himself,
who was personally committed to the recording of Jewish resistance
during the War said that "In some circles the opinion has prevailed
that Jews did not resist and went as sheep to the slaughter . . . The
material collected in this book proves how wrong such opinions
are . . ."[110]

What were the actual contents of the Russian version of the Black
Book?[111] As stated by its Editor, Vassily Grossman, these materials
were of three major categories: (a) diaries, letters and testimonies of
victims and survivors of the Holocaust; (b) reports and essays by journalists and writers based on direct sources; (c) material submitted by
the Soviet State Committee on Nazi Atrocities. It was the clear intention of those who had prepared the book for publication to confront
the Russian reader with a picture of Jewish suffering and Jewish resistance. Grossman's preface was quite out of step with the general tone of
the Russian press and publications. In it he stated several times that the

Jews, as an ethnic and nationality group, had constituted a special target for the Nazis. When dealing with the problem of antisemitism, Grossman mentioned traditional Russian forms of Jew-hatred, and alluded to wartime collaboration of some segments of the Soviet population with the Nazis. He also quoted a 1931 statement by Stalin strongly condemning antisemitism. Following Ehrenburg's earlier urge to counteract prevailing charges of Jewish cowardice in wartime Russia, Grossman dealt quite extensively with the issue of Jewish resistance. He explained why Nazi policies towards Jews in the Eastern parts of occupied Russia had precluded any attempt at organized resistance, and dwelt on the numerous examples of Jewish resistance in the western territories of the USSR, mentioning the ghettos of Vilna, Minsk, Bialystok and Kovno. He wrote about the participation of the Jews in the partisan movement. Grossman also pointed out that there were other forms of resistance, mentioning, as an example, the underground cultural activities in the Vilna ghetto.[112] The various parts of the Black Book, compiled mostly by geographical areas, elaborated on Grossman's introductory statements. The most prolific contributor to the book was Ehrenburg. His reports incorporated numerous testimonies by Red Army soldiers and officers. Grossman wrote about the town of his birth, Berdichev where most of his close family were annihilated, Minsk and the Treblinka concentration camp. The official Soviet line was to point out the assistance of the Soviet non-Jewish population to the Jews under Nazi occupation. Some passages of the Black Book were however quite outspoken about the indifference and animosity. Thus, Grossman himself, writing about the fate of the Jews of Berdichev stated that "there were to be found wicked, criminal individuals . . . greedy for profit, waiting to get rich at the expense of innocent victims."[113] Leib Kvitko reported on the Crimea, and Ber Mark, wrote about the Warsaw Ghetto Uprising. Among the contributors were Russian poets and writers of Jewish origin, such as Pavel Antokolskii, Veniamin Kaverin, Margarita Aliger, Viktor Shklovskii, Vera Inber, Lev Ozerov and Vladimir Lidin. Their interest and participation in the Black Book obviously signified their wartime identification with Jewish national sentiments.

The Russian manuscript of the Black Book, forwarded to Rumania some time in 1946, was translated into Rumanian and published in part in Bucharest in 1947.[114] Besides the Editorial Committee listed in the Rumanian edition of the Black Book numbering almost forty members, the title page carried the names of Ehrenburg, Grossman,

Lidin and Ozerov. The last two, who wrote in Russian had participated in the Black Book project. Vladimir Lidin (whose real name was Gomberg), a novelist and journalist, was drafted in 1941 and served as a military correspondent during the War; he was a personal friend of Mikhoels. Lev Ozerov (whose real name was Goldberg), a poet, translator and editor, translated some of the Soviet-Yiddish poets into Russian; he also wrote one of the first poems on Babi Yar. Since the Rumanian edition mentioned that it was the first volume, we may assume that the publication of a second volume was planned at that time. There were also plans in Palestine to publish a Hebrew version of the Black Book, for which material was received from the JAC between 1944 and 1946.[115]

What happened meanwhile in the Soviet Union? It seems that the planned publication of the Black Book coincided with the onset of the conservative backlash and cultural restrictions known as the Zhdanovshchina. The changing atmosphere in the field of literature and publishing was already felt in the spring of 1946, and it became increasingly apparent that the relative freedom of the wartime years was being curtailed. The non-Russian, national sentiments that had been permitted and even encouraged during the War, were now being curbed. In August, 1946 the Central Committee of the Party issued its resolution on literature. The Zhdanovshchina also had its implications for the fields of Jewish literature and publishing. In the fall of 1946, *Eynikayt* began publishing a growing number of articles attacking Jewish nationalism. The Black Book was among the victims of this renewed phase of Soviet conservatism and censorship. In its typeset form, it was in limbo for more than two years, and when the JAC was liquidated in the fall of 1948, the fate of the Russian Black Book was finally sealed.[116]

4

THE JAC: A MEMBERSHIP PROFILE

The structure and membership of the Jewish Antifascist Committee in the USSR somewhat resembled that of pro-Soviet front organizations abroad. Officially it was always presented as an a-political institution. It consisted of a nucleus of activists, was headed by prominent personalities in the cultural world, and recruited a wide range of public figures for its activities. It acted under the auspices of the Sovinformburo of the Commissariat of Foreign Affairs and was not directly linked with any Party organs. There were differing degrees of membership of the JAC and not all members were equally involved. Hence we have chosen to describe the overall, "maximal" membership, on the basis of data on all those who signed JAC documents or participated in its activities at any time; and to analyze in-depth those people who were involved continuously and intensively in the Committe's functions. The number of JAC members had been on the rise throughout the War years, as revealed by the number of signatories to various JAC appeals. The Manifesto of the Jewish meeting of August 1941 carried 26 names. An appeal issued in mid 1942 had 54 signatures and an appeal issued at the April 1944 meeting contained 64 signatures. The overall number of persons who either signed JAC documents or directly participated in its activities passed the hundred mark.[1]

Intellectuals, Soldiers, Diplomats

The largest group in the JAC were literary personalities (35), and the other groups were considerably smaller. Thus, there were 15 artists (in such fields as music, painting and sculpture), 12 actors of theater and film, a similar number of scientists and scholars and 16 representatives of the military and the partisan movement. There were only 10 Government officials and 3 Party functionaries among the Committee's members. The composition of the JAC clearly reflected Soviet propaganda methods and techniques used during the War, as well as the state of the potential Jewish leadership in the USSR of the 1940's. Leading personalities in the Jewish political sphere, (including former activists of the Jewish Sections of the CPSU), had been purged in the late 30's. Moreover, it was felt that writers, actors and scientists were more suitable mouthpieces of Soviet propaganda goals vis-àvis the Jews of the U.S. and England than were Party apparatchiks. One should not forget that the Committee's mission was of international scope. All in all, "intellectuals" comprised three quarters of the total Committee membership.[2]

The theatre and film personalities, included besides Solomon Mikhoels, the leading Yiddish actor and theatre director in the USSR, such celebrities as S. Eisenstein, and F. Ermler. Eisenstein, although only a half-Jew (his father was Jewish), was apparently considered one of the "big" names on the JAC roster, as the best-known Soviet film director outside the USSR. Ermler, too, was one of the leading Soviet film directors at that time. A. Kapler was an actor and prolific script writer, who wrote the scripts for such popular Soviet war films as "A Day of War" and "She Defends Her Native Land." His successful career was cut short during the War because of his romantic relationship with Stalin's daughter, and his name disappeared accordingly from JAC publications. Another theatre personality affiliated with the Committee was Ida Kaminska, the leading Yiddish actress in prewar Poland who spent the War years in the Soviet Union.[3] A. Tairov (Kornblit), a personal friend of Mikhoels, was co-founder and Director of the Moscow Chamber Theatre. Besides his affiliation with the Jewish Committee he was also active in the Soviet Society for Cultural Relations with Foreign Countries (VOKS). Among the representatives of the arts in the JAC were the musicians David Oistrakh and Emil Gillels. The painter and sculptor Nathan Altman, another JAC member was very close to the Jewish cultural milieu in the USSR. His background, like that of many Jewish writers and artists in Russia, contained a mixture of Jewish, Russian and European elements. Born in the Ukraine, he studied in Paris and after the 1917 Bolshevik Revolution was appointed head of the Petrograd section of the Department of Fine

Arts. He used explicitly Jewish motifs in his art, and was stage designer for the Hebrew Theatre "Habimah" and for the Moscow Jewish State Theatre.

The outstanding scientists on the Committee were Lina Shtern and Aleksandr Frumkin. The former, a physiologist and the only female member of the Soviet Academy of Sciences, at that time, spent the early years of her career in Switzerland. She returned to Russia in 1925 and became a university professor in Moscow. During the 30's and 40's Lina Shtern was Director of the Moscow Physiology Institute.[4] Frumkin was educated at the University of Odessa and lectured at one time in the U.S. He became a member of the Soviet Academy of Sciences in the early thirties and was later appointed director of its Institute of Physical Chemistry. Like other outstanding Soviet scientists he was also active in the Antifascist Committee of Soviet Scientists. Dr. Boris Shimelovich, a son of a synagogue beadle from Riga, studied medicine in Voronezh and headed the medical services for Jewish victims of pogroms. He specialized in medical administration and from the early 1930's headed the prestigious Botkin Hospital in Moscow. Professor Miron Vovsi, who was destined to play a central role in the so-called "Doctors' Plot" in the early fifties, (and who was related to Mikhoels), was already a well-known name in the field of Soviet medicine during the War. Vovsi's career developed mostly in Moscow where he taught at the University and held leading positions at various medical institutes. Vovsi's reputation was enhanced during the War when he was appointed Chief Therapeutics Officer of the Army with the rank of Major General. He served as consultant to the Kremlin Board of Therapy and Health, thus having access to the highest Soviet political leadership, a fact later used against him.[5] among others recruited by the JAC was Z. G. Grinberg, a member of the Academy of Sciences, and lecturer at the Gorky Institute. Once a member of the Jewish Labor Bund, he filled a number of senior Soviet government posts in education after the revolution, and served as Deputy Commisar for Education under Lunacharskii. Grinberg was also involved in Jewish cultural activities in the twenties and was a member of the Jewish Section of the Soviet Commissariat for Nationalities.

The military men affiliated with the JAC were of various ranks. The two generals on the Committee were Yakov Kreyzer and Aaron Kats. Kreyzer, a recipient of the "Hero of the Soviet Union" award, had fought in the crucial battles for Moscow. Later, he served with the armies which liberated the Crimea and the Baltic region. He made a strongly nationalistic Jewish speech to a Jewish meeting in Ufa in 1942. In one of his meetings with the Committee leaders in the summer of 1944, he delivered a highly emotional report on Nazi atrocities in those areas where he had been fighting.[6] General Kats headed a department at the Stalin Military Academy and served as Deputy Commander of a Soviet motor corps. Those who met with him during the War testified that he identified strongly with Jewish matters. Lower-ranking officers and soldiers coopted to the Committee were mostly war-heroes, like I. Fisanovich, Commander of a submarine and eventually killed in action. Almost half the military on the Committee were recipients of the "Hero of the Soviet Union" award, the highest military distinction in the Soviet army. Among them was a recent newcomer to the USSR, a former Lithuanian Jew, Major Volf Vilensky. He was an officer in the newly formed Soviet Lithuanian Division, of which a considerable percentage was Jewish. The Committee Presidium, originally consisting of 15 members, and later expanded to 19, reflected the membership profile of the Committee as a whole; 6 representatives of literature, 2 of theatre, 2 of the military, 3 of government, 2 of administration and 2 scientists. There were no direct representatives of the Party. The Presidium included all leading JAC personalities such as Mikhoels, Fefer and Epshteyn, and the writers Bergelson, Halkin, Kvitko and Markish. Lina Shtern, Aleksandr Frumkin, and Dr. Shimelovich represented Science and Medicine. The military on the Presidium were General Yakov Kreyzer and Israel Fisanovich. Of the administrators on the Presidium, L. Gonor headed the Stalingrad "Barricades" factory and was a recipient of the Hero of Socialist Labor Award, and H. Nagler served as Department Head in a war industry plant.

Solomon Lozovskii, of the Sovinformburo supervised and guided the work of the Jewish Committee. The fact that he himself was Jewish had special implications for both the Committee and the man himself. Lozovskii was born in the Ekaterinoslav province and became a revolutionary at an early age. He joined the Russian Social Democrats in 1901 and from 1905 identified with the Bolshevik wing of the movement. He fled Russia in 1909 and lived in Geneva and Paris until 1917. While in Paris, Lozovskii became active in the French trade union movement, especially in its typically Jewish branches, such as the hatmakers, bakers and furriers.[7] After the February Revolution, Lozovskii returned to Russia where he became a central figure in the Bolshevik trade union movement. During the early stages of the Bolshevik regime Lozovskii quarreled with the Party leadership and as a result he was expelled from the Party. After being readmitted, he excelled as both organizer and theoretician of the Profintern—the communist oriented Trade Union International. He was also on the Comintern Executive Committee and maintained contacts with various pro-Soviet front organizations abroad. Lozovskii's career gained momentum on the eve of World War II, when he was elected a full member of the Party's Central Committee. From that year on he also held the post of Deputy Minister of Foreign Affairs. When the Soviet Information Bureau was founded, Lozovskii was made responsible for organizing and passing Soviet information and propaganda to the allies. As a specialist on the West in general and on workers movements there in particular, and as an expert on the mechanics of pro-Soviet fronts, Lozovskii was a perfect choice for this job. He was also regarded as a specialist on international Jewish affairs, and as such guided and supervised the activities of the JAC.[8] Those Western correspondents who met him during the War testified that Lozovskii, with his "old world" charm, his knowledge of several European languages and his noncommital witty manner of responding to journalists' queries, was well suited for his task. After Shcherbakov's death, Lozovskii was appointed head of the Sovinformburo. As late as 1947 he was active in matters of Soviet foreign policy, and received the Editor of the U.S. Communist *Daily Worker* to discuss with him policies and strategies of the American Community Party.[10]

The top leadership of the JAC consisted of Solomon Mikhoels, the Chairman and Shakhno Epshteyn, its Executive Secretary and Chief Editor of *Eynikayt*. The active nucleus consisted of Soviet Yiddish writers and poets, whose activities were occasionally supported by outstanding Soviet Jews in other fields.

The Chairman: Mikhoels

Solomon (Vovsi) Mikhoels, the central JAC figure, was a typical, Russian Jewish intellectual, deeply rooted in both Jewish and Russian culture. Even his personal history seemed to bear this out. Mikhoels' first wife, was the daughter of Judah Leib Kantor, a graduate of the Zhitomir Rabbinical Seminary and founder of the first Hebrew daily in tsarist Russia. His second wife, was a Russian scientist of Polish origin. It is possible that Mikhoels' fascination with Jewish historical personalities who existed on the fringe of two cultures, reflected his own feelings.[11] We may assume that the fusion of his two distinctively different backgrounds resulted at times in feelings of ambivalence and marginality. Mikhoels was born into a typical Jewish East European family. He received a traditional Jewish education, including Yiddish, Hebrew and Talmudic studies. His first encounter with the world of Yiddish theatre was that with the "purim-shpilers," groups of amateur actors. Mikhoels' career as an actor started rather late, when he was 28; but, within a number of years he rose to prominence and replaced Granovskii as director of the most prestigious Jewish theatre in the USSR, the GOSET (Moscow Jewish State Theatre). In the 1930's he took his place in the upper ranks of the Soviet cultural elite. Already then he showed considerable personal courage vis-àvis the regime, being one of the few people who extended financial aid to the ostracized poet Osip Mandelshtam. Luckily, this did not hurt his professional career.[12] Mikhoels was awarded the titles: People's Artist of the RSFSR and People's Artist of the USSR, and before the War, received the Lenin Award. In 1941 he was granted the academic title of professor and in 1945 he received a Stalin Prize. Mikhoels was active on various committees dealing with art: the Committee on Arts of the All-Union Council of Ministers, the Presidium of the All-Russian Theatre Association, and the Central Committee of the Art Workers Union. His membership of the Moscow City Council enabled him to wield some influence on non-cultural matters as well. Mikhoel's contacts with prominent Soviet personalities and intellectuals were extensive. He was a close friend of the famous Soviet pilot Valery Chkalov.

During the War years, Mikhoels became very intimate with the playwright and writer Aleskei Tolstoi. During the first two years of the War the two lived in Tashkent and often travelled together to the temporary administrative center in Kuibyshev. They also served together on the Committee on Stalin Prizes. The friendship between the Mikhoels' and Tolstoi families continued after their return to Moscow until Tolstoi's death in 1945.[13] Mikhoels' relationship with Ilya Ehrenburg must have become particularly close during the War as a result of their collaboration on the Jewish Committee. Both had a deep concern for Jewish suffering and heroism and protested against anti-semitism. These interests were expressed in long, heated discussions about the essence of Jewish culture and its survival. Although the solutions they propounded were often diametrically opposed, the War and the Holocaust created strong emotional ties between them. It was

Ehrenburg and Mikhoels, for example, who decided to suggest to the Soviet authorities that the young Jewish partisan-poet from Vilna, Abraham Sutskever, testify at the Nuremberg trial.[14] Mikhoels maintained friendly relations with non-Russian intellectuals, including the Ukrainian writer Aleksandr Korniichuk, who was appointed wartime Minister of Foreign Affairs of the Ukrainian Republic. Mikhoels naturally had numerous friends among the leading Russian theatre actors and directors. Among them were Yurii Zavadskii, Director of the Mossovet Theatre and Professor at the State Institute of Theatrical Art; Mikhail Klimov, a very popular comedy actor; Sergei Obraztsov, Director of the Moscow Central Puppet Theatre; and such senior personalities of the Soviet stage as Vasilii Kachalov, Mikhail Tarkhanov and Aleksandr Tairov. Mikhoels also cultivated a number of friends among the military. The closest among them was General A. A. Ignatiev, an ex-officer of the tsarist army who spent a number of years in Paris. Another was Paul Arman, a Red Army colonel who distinguished himself in the Spanish Civil War, was awarded the title of Hero of the Soviet Union and was eventually killed on the German front. In Tashkent, Mikhoels became friendly with General S. D. Trofimenko, who served after the War as Commander of the Belorussian Military District. Mikhoels also gained a number of friends and admirers among the Soviet scientific elite. Piotr Kapitsa, the outstanding Soviet physicist, was mobilized by Mikhoels for Jewish, anti-Nazi propaganda activities, as was Aleksandr Frumkin.

As a leading personality in the sphere of Jewish culture in the USSR, Mikhoels maintained a close relationship with most of the Yiddish writers and poets. After the liquidation of the Jewish sections of the CPSU and the purge of leading personalities in communist-Jewish politics, the Yiddish literary community became the sole center of Jewish activities in the USSR. Although disappointed, shocked and embittered by previous events, most of the Yiddish literati continued to nourish hopes for the preservation of Jewish culture in Soviet Russia. Mikhoels, too identified with their fears and hopes. He directed numerous plays by such writers as Perets Markish, David Bergelson and Shmuel Halkin. During the War he cooperated closely with Bergelson in the preparation of the latter's drama "Prince Reuveni" for stage. The play, (which incidentally was never produced), contained a clear analogy between the Spanish Inquisition and Nazi persecution of Jews. Mikhoels' relationship with Markish has been often described as that of "duelers." They were intimate because of their deep and sincere concern for art in general and for Jewish art and culture in particular. Their divergent views and stands stemmed from the different solutions they envisaged to various problems. Their endless discussions were quite often highly emotional. It has been suggested that, there were personal undertones in their relationship, especially on the part of Markish, who seemed to be losing his public image while Mikhoels as a result of his chairmanship of the JAC, gained prestige during the War years. Mikhoels' official cooperation with the poet Itsik Fefer, within the framework of the JAC, may also have deepened Markish's suspicions, since an open and well-known enmity existed between Markish and Fefer.[15]

The relationship between Mikhoels and Fefer was ambivalent. Their work in the JAC and particularly their wartime visit to the U.S. and other countries, as representatives of Soviet Jewry, tended to create an impression of understanding and cooperation between them. However, unspoken and unexpressed tensions prevailed. Fefer had hardly been a personal friend of Mikhoels in the pre-war years. They were both geographically and artistically far apart. Whereas Mikhoels' career flourished in Moscow, Fefer's domain was the Ukraine. Fefer was much more politically inclined than Mikhoels. Whereas Mikhoels never joined the Party, Fefer was a typical Party-line poet. There were even instances when Fefer, the proponent of official ideological attitudes, accused Mikhoels and other Jewish writers of nationalist Jewish "hysteria."[16] According to some sources, Mikhoels was quite uneasy when he was obliged to appear publicly with Fefer. Some of those who met them during their trip abroad in 1943, suspected that Fefer acted as Mikhoels' censor and supervisor. Fefer, although himself showing proof of growing national identity brought on by the events of the War, was usually regarded in Soviet-Jewish literary circles as the representative of the Party line. Mikhoels was much closer to "neutral" writers and to those with a traditionally strong identification with Jewish matters. This fact is borne out for example by Mikhoels' attachment to Der Nister (P. Kahanovich), perhaps the most a-political and nationally inclined member of the top-group of Jewish writers in the USSR.[17]

The War and his new position of Chairman to the only central Jewish structure which promoted contacts between Soviet Jews and Jews abroad, brought Mikhoels into the very forefront of Jewish activities. This was also accompanied by a growing feeling of Jewish communal responsibility. In the late thirties Mikhoels had already been a leading figure in Soviet anti-Nazi public activities, and was the main speaker at the first wartime Jewish meeting broadcast from Moscow two months after the Nazi attack on the USSR. When Soviet authorities discussed the possibility of organizing an international Jewish Anti Hitlerite Committee in the USSR in the Fall of 1941 with Erlich and Alter, Mikhoels was mentioned as the future representative of Soviet Jewry on that Committee. Various evidence indicates that Nazi, anti-Jewish policies and the Jewish War tragedy had a profound impact on Mikhoels. When Germany attacked the USSR, Mikhoels was in Kharkov with his theatre. His reaction to the outbreak of the War was highly emotional and instantaneous. His speeches and appeals as Chairman of the JAC abounded in anti-Nazi motifs. Such public and official utterances were closely linked to his innermost feelings. In an unpublished poem he strongly identified with the suffering of Jewish victims of the Nazis. During his visit abroad in 1943, he spoke out in extremely dramatic manner against Nazi atrocities. He was particularly sensitive to the issue of Jewish armed resistance, and the Warsaw Ghetto uprising greatly inspired him. He also took pride in Soviet-Jewish soldiers and partisans.[18] In witnesses to the Holocaust and to Jewish resistance, such as the poet Abraham Sutskever, who reached Moscow from Nazi-occupied Lithuania in early 1944, he saw the personification of the tragedy and heroism of the ghetto Jews. It was he who urged Sutskever to write a play about the Jewish underground in the Vilna Ghetto. When Eliezer Lidovski, a Jewish partisan from Rovno, met with Mikhoels in 1944 and told him about Jewish suffering under the Nazi occupation, Mikhoels "cried almost like a child."[19] The Nazis on their part explicitly used Mikhoels' name in their anti-Semitic propaganda.

Highly emotional encounters with Jews in the U.S., England, Canada and Mexico left a strong impression on Mikhoels. Some of these encounters were particularly complex since official identification with Jews abroad had to be kept within the permissible limits of Soviet war propaganda. Mikhoels was himself greatly concerned about the fate of Jews in general. He told his wife during the war that: " . . . At times it seems that I am responsible for my entire people . . ."[20] Mikhoels summed up his self image at that time as both a leading cultural figure and the spokesman for Soviet Jewry, when he told a friend that "an actor could become a tribune."[21] Although one can hardly define Mikhoels as a Zionist, he did display strong sentiments towards national-cultural aspects of the Jewish tradition. He had an adequate

knowledge of Hebrew and very often quoted Hebrew sources. Mikhoels must have also had a strong emotional attachment to the Land of
Israel and to the Jewish Yishuv in Palestine. He confessed privately on
more than one occasion that he was extremely moved when he flew
over Palestine during his wartime mission to the U.S. and when he
stopped over at Lydda airport on his way back.[22] Official Soviet pro-
Zionist policies in the postwar years encouraged Mikhoels to protest
openly against "the blood which is being spilled in the streets of Tel
Aviv, Haifa and Jerusalem." Mikhoels is also known to have reacted
very emotionally to Gromyko's speech at the U.N. supporting the
claim for an independent Jewish state in Palestine.[23]

During the War Mikhoels was known in Russia as "the number one
Jew." His stature, his contacts within the Soviet intellectual elite, his
chairmanship of the Jewish Antifascist Committee, his highly symbolic
mission to world Jewry, and most of all—the pressing needs of Soviet
Jews for a leader, made him the prime target of Jewish requests, complaints and appeals. For many he was the unofficial spokesman for the
Jewish Community in the USSR. Fefer testified shortly after Mikhoels'
death that "He used to receive letters by the hundreds; lots of people
came to see him, not only from Moscow, but from other cities of the
USSR as well . . ." Mikhoels kept a huge pile of such letters in the
GOSET library. Sutskever testified that Mikhoels' reception room was
always overflowing with visitors. These were "military, partisans, survivors of Nazi death camps, returning refugees . . . all were drawn to
the magic name: Mikhoels." The Yiddish actor Joseph Sheyn witnessed similar scenes. Ehrenburg related in his memoirs that "during
the War Mikhoels was the animating spirit of the Jewish Antifascist
Committee . . . When the War ended, thousands of people turned to
Mikhoels for help, because they saw him as a wise rabbi, the defender
of the oppressed."[24] His death in January 1948 revealed the tremendous popularity he had acquired among Soviet Jews. The official
mourning ceremonies and the funeral became a massive act of identification with Russia's "number one Jew." An official Soviet report has it
that "tens of thousands passed by Mikhoels' body." An eyewitness
related that "elderly Jewish women with children in their arms, old
people and students" were in the crowd which paid tribute to
Mikhoels."[25] As regards Mikhoels' relations and contacts with the top
political elite in the USSR, there are conflicting opinions. The oft-
repeated tale of Mikhoels' personal relationship with Stalin himself,
seems to be highly exaggerated. He seemed, however, to have been

on friendly terms with such high ranking Soviet personalities as President Mikhail Kalinin, and former Soviet Foreign Minister, Maxim Litvinov. He knew Lazar Kaganovich, the only Jewish member of Stalin's Politburo at that time. It is also possible that some contacts existed between Mikhoels and Molotov's Jewish wife, Paulina Zhemchuzhina.[26]

The Secretary: Epshteyn

The central political personality on the Committee, until his death in 1945, was Shakhno Epshteyn. Simultaneously, he held the posts of JAC Secretary, and Chief Editor of it's organ, *Eynikayt,* and was a member of the Editorial Board of *Der Emes,* the only Jewish publishing house in the Soviet Union at that time. Epshteyn, more than any other leading member of the Committee, had performed various functions for the Party and the Government in the past. In fact, he could be regarded as a blend of Soviet-Yiddish intellectual and Party apparatchik. Born in Lithuania into a rabbinical Jewish family, he left for Warsaw at the age of 16. His first attempts at writing were in Hebrew, and his earliest involvement in public life was connected with Zionism. Although initially ambitious for an artistic career, he became increasingly involved in socialist politics. Epshteyn joined the Jewish Labor Bund and became very active in its organization and propaganda. He also became increasingly involved in journalism and editing. Epshteyn arrived in Vienna prior to World War I, and served there for a while, as Secretary of the local branch of the Bund. Subsequently, he became the Secretary of the Bund Foreign Committee located in Switzerland. While still in Europe, Epshteyn made his first contacts with Jewish socialist circles in the U.S. by sending some of his articles for publication there. His subsequent career alternated between Russia and the U.S., which he visited for the first time in 1909. In the U.S., Epshteyn worked for the Bund, was co-founder of the Socialist Federation, and became an established name in the American Jewish socialist press. He served as Editorial Secretary for the *Tsukunft* and published in various Jewish and Russian-Socialist publications in the U.S. He was also active in the Jewish Workmen's Circle and was Editor of the Dressmakers Union weekly. His first stay in America ended in 1917, when, after the February Revolution, he returned to Russia with his wife and his American-born son.[27]

When the Bund split into factions, Epshteyn identified with the Bolshevik-oriented Kombund; he joined the Communist Party in 1919. In the years that followed he was among the leaders of the Jewish Sections of the CPSU. As a member of the Central Bureau of the Sections, Epshteyn was appointed, in summer of 1920, Executive Editor of the Moscow *Emes,* the central Communist-Yiddish newspaper in Russia. Less than a year after this appointment, he made a second appearance on the American scene, presumably as a Comintern organizer to American-Jewish Communists. Under the assumed name of "Berson," he became Co-editor of the leftist, American *Emes,* and when the leftist Yiddish newspaper *Freiheit* was founded in 1922, he was one of its two chief editors, representing the communist faction on the editorial board. During the early 1920's Epshteyn took part in the in-fighting which was going on within Jewish socialist circles in New York. (It was around that time that Abe Cahan of the *Forward* became disenchanted with the Soviet experiment.) After he returned to the Soviet Union, where he held a number of editing posts in the Yiddish and Russian press, Epshteyn maintained his contacts with America. During the 1930's he spent some time in Germany, France and Switzerland and visited the U.S. at least twice. He maintained close relations with B. Z. Goldberg, son in law of Shalom Aleichem and columnist for the *Tog,* a popular Yiddish New York daily. It is possible that this acquaintance dated from Goldberg's visit to Russia in 1934. Goldberg arranged for the publication in the *Tog* of several articles by Epshteyn (under the pseudonym Shmildner). Their author was described to the readers as "an objective Soviet journalist." In his daily column Goldberg used material supplied by Epshteyn to justify Stalin's purges of the late 30's.[28]

Besides his journalistic propaganda activities in Europe and the U.S., Epshteyn also assisted Soviet intelligence and security agencies abroad. He spent some time on a mission to Geneva, the seat of the League of Nations and assisted Soviet intelligence agents in the U.S. in the abduction of Juliet Poynts, a leading member of the American Communist Party.[29] He boasted to an American Jewish Communist that, "a medal was waiting for him in Moscow for his good work."[30] There must have been direct contact between Epshteyn and Beria (whom he knew from the days of the Civil War). It should also be recalled that Beria was personally involved in the Soviet effort to organize a Jewish Anti-Hitlerite Committee in the USSR in the fall of 1941.[31] Various references to Epshteyn's absolute loyalty to the Party, and the fact that he emerged unscathed from the purges of the late 30's seem to suggest that he enjoyed special protection.[32] Epshteyn's whole career, and especially his affiliation with Soviet intelligence indicate that he was the "watchdog" of the Soviet security establishment.[33]

The Poet-Politician: Fefer

The poet Itsik Fefer, a member of the JAC Presidium and of the *Eynikayt* Editorial Board, was the most political-minded personality among the group of Yiddish writers affiliated with the Committee. Like Epshteyn, he was an extremely devoted Communist, but unlike him, had hardly any former contacts with Jews abroad. His first extensive encounter with them was his wartime visit to the U.S. and England. Fefer was an exemplary product of the communist milieu in Russia. He had become a member of the Bolshevik Party at an early age, having been a member of the Bund for some time, and served as a volunteer in the Red Army during the Civil War. From the 20's on Fefer was both a Party activist and a militant communist Yiddish poet. His home territory, for many years, was the Ukraine and its capital, Kiev. Fefer was among the founders of the "Union of Revolutionary Jewish Writers in the Ukraine" and he headed the Jewish Section of the "All-Ukrainian Union of Proletarian Writers." He was also on the Presidium of the Union of Soviet Writers. A staunch opponent of individualism and symbolism, Fefer was considered the founder of "proletarian" Yiddish literature in the Soviet Union. Fefer took an active part in Soviet war propaganda. In the years 1939–1941, as an army officer, he was a major speaker at pro-Soviet Jewish mass meetings organized in the newly annexed territories.[34] Soviet propaganda fostered Fefer's image as a Soviet-Jewish soldier-poet. In the annexed territories, and later, during his mission to the U.S. and Canada, Fefer appeared in his Red Army Colonel's uniform.

The years of the Second World War and his affiliation with the JAC marked a significant change in Fefer's attitudes as well as in his status. The Jewish tragedy, his encounter with Jews abroad and the pressures on the JAC resulting from the postwar Soviet Jewish problems moderated and even changed some of Fefer's traditional convictions. His attitudes grew more complex and ambivalent as a result of the War and his new position in the midst of Jewish intellectuals on the Committee. Fefer had not been highly reputed by his fellow writers in the past. When he arrived in Moscow, the center of Yiddish culture in the USSR, and encountered literary personalities of the first rank, like Markish, he responded by nurturing even deeper animosity towards his critics, and, by trying to win the support and admiration of the lower-ranking, young and refugee writers. The hostility between Fefer and Markish reached its peak during those years. It is quite possible that Markish's withdrawal from JAC activities stemmed, at least partially, from the fact that Fefer was among its bosses.

Fefer's impeccable ideological credentials, were of great value to an intellectual propaganda establishment such as the JAC was meant to be. It is no wonder, therefore, that he was one of the trusted supervisors of the Committee's work. Whereas Mikhoels and Markish were supported primarily by Soviet cultural personalities, Fefer's benefactors were politicians. Thus, he seemed to have been on quite close terms with Solomon Lozovskii. Such relationships with those "higher up" were jealously guarded. When the young Vilna poet Abraham Sutskever visited Lozovskii without Fefer's blessing, the latter became highly suspicious, and his attitude toward Sutskever changed abruptly.[35] Fefer, more than others in the Yiddish literary group, used his outside contacts and political leverage in order to gain professional acceptance by his colleagues. Officially at least he held high rank in the JAC since he joined Mikhoels, on a mission to centers of Jewish population outside the USSR, and thereby enhanced his prestige as a poet and a public figure. However, he must have sensed that, despite the official honors heaped on him, he lacked the approval of his colleagues as an artist, and this helps explain his growing hostility toward Markish. In 1945–1948 Fefer gained ascendancy over Markish. Markish was eventually removed from such positions as Head of the Jewish Section of the Moscow Union of Writers, Editor of the *Heimland* journal, and of Soviet Yiddish radio transmissions abroad.

Fefer's wartime poetry reveals some of the changes in his attitudes toward Jewish culture and tradition. His writings became much less "proletarian," exhibiting a strong note of national identity with both his Jewish historical heritage and with his suffering fellow-Jews. In a poem entitled "I am a Jew," published in *Eynikayt* in 1942, (and subsequently translated into other languages) Fefer spoke of Jewish genius and kinship.[36] In one of his articles he expressed his pride in Jewish resistance to the Nazis and declared that the "Jewish people is alive."[37] In his play "Shadows of the Warsaw Ghetto," Fefer wrote with reverence and emotion about the very same Jewish religious objects and symbols which he had bitterly criticized in previous years. According to Rachel Korn, a Polish-Yiddish poetess whom he met in Lvov in 1941, Fefer remarked nostalgically while watching local Jews hurry to the synagogue for Friday evening prayers "in a year or two nothing will remain of it."[38] In early fall of 1942, while in Kuibyshev, Fefer visited the local synagogue and was deeply moved by the praying crowd. During the War he even started boasting of his rabbinical ancestry.[39] The impact of his emotional encounters with non-Soviet Jews, during his visit abroad, lingered long after his return to Russia. Fefer was deeply disillusioned by postwar attitudes towards Jews in his native Ukraine, and could not bring himself to return to Kiev. He became increasingly involved in JAC attempts to revive Jewish culture in the USSR, despite the political risks involved, and despite his political acumen. At the same time, he continued to perform his role in Soviet postwar propaganda, by writing vicious articles, against Jewish opponents of Soviet stands and policies.[40]

Markish and Der Nister

Perets Markish, for many years the outstanding Yiddish poet in the USSR, received a typical Orthodox Jewish education. His first poems, which he wrote in Russia at the age of 15 were distinctly Zionist, one of the central themes being his feelings of alienation in Tsarist Russia. As late as 1945, while celebrating the downfall of Nazi Germany, Markish reiterated a similar theme, maintaining that he had been no more than a "guest" among his fellow Russians.[41] At the same time however, like most of his colleagues, he wrote poems praising Stalin and his leadership. Like a number of other Jewish writers, Markish spent part of the 1920's abroad, in Warsaw, Berlin, Paris and London. In 1923 he visited Palestine and was highly enthusiastic about the Jewish settlements there. His return to the Soviet Union apparently brought disappointment and crisis. He even had contemplated leaving the USSR again, after he encountered Soviet literary realities.[42] Markish's writing was quite often criticized by both the officials of the Jewish Sections of the CPSU and by the proletarian Soviet Jewish writers. Fefer was one of the critics who accused him of excessive Jewish nationalism and of Zionism in disguise. Although artistically he ranked among the top Yiddish poets in the USSR and succeeded eventually in becoming a member of the Soviet intellectual elite, Markish remained doubtful and ambivalent in regard to his place and his future in the Soviet framework. What bothered him most was the growing isolation of Soviet-Yiddish culture. In this sense, the events of 1939–1941 and after, offered an outlet for his emotions. He could identify once more with non-Soviet Jewish writers and express some of his hidden feelings. In 1939–1941 Markish had identified with Jewish suffering under the Nazis,[43] but obviously such themes could not be published at that time because of the Soviet-Nazi alliance.

In the years following the outbreak of the Nazi-Soviet War, Markish wrote extensively about Jewish tragedy and heroism. Like many other Soviet-Yiddish writers, he focused on Polish Jewry. Markish's most impressive works of that period were "War", "The Ghetto Uprising" and "The March of Generations." His wartime writing abounded in historical and religious Jewish symbols. The wartime encounter with non-Soviet Jewish writers from the neighboring countries, was significant for all Soviet-Yiddish intellectuals, but had a special impact on Markish. It symbolized his physical and spiritual reunion with world Jewish culture. He was personally acquainted with some of the Jewish refugee writers from the Warsaw period, and many of them trusted Markish more than any other of their Soviet Yiddish colleagues. Like other Jewish refugees, particularly those from Poland, they turned to him for help and advice. Markish is also believed to have written poems "for the drawer" in which he strongly identified with the difficult lots of Polish Jewish refugees and deportees in the USSR. A most succinct expression of Markish's feelings and moods were his farewell words to one such refugee writer on the eve of his return to Poland after the War: "I am like a young newlywed girl whose parents are departing after the wedding ceremony and leaving her with strange in-laws."[44] Unlike Fefer, Markish was not very active in the political or public sense, although he joined the Communist Party during the War. He was a member of the JAC Presidium and of the *Eynikayt* editorial board, but his participation in the work of the Committee was limited, and his alienation from the Committee grew in the postwar years. He strongly criticized and opposed some of the plans for Soviet Jews suggested by the JAC leadership. His detachment from public affairs must have also increased as a result of his removal from various positions of responsibility after the War.

The most traditional and nationalistically-minded of the group of Soviet Jewish writers affiliated with the JAC was Der Niste "the concealed one"—pen name of Pinhas Kahanovich. From his youth in Berdichev in the Ukraine he was very close to Judaism and Zionism. He personally participated in the historical 1905 Poale Zion Conference, an event which influenced some of his later writing.[45] At the start of his career as a writer, he met with such outstanding Jewish literary figures as Perets and Bialik. During the early 1920's Der Nister lived outside Russia in such places as Kovno, Berlin and Hamburg. He returned to the Soviet Union in 1926, but was never a strict follower of the regime. "Proletarian" Jewish writers often criticized Der Nister for his individualism, symbolism and mysticism. Since he could hardly follow the prescribed line of writing, he evolved special forms of artistic creativity. Reconciling his integrity with the growing demands of the regime was a continuing problem and challenge. It is understandable, therefore, that the wartime atmosphere had a stimulating impact on Der Nister. His candor and courage during those years were unequalled. He made his personal statement on the Holocaust in a series of short stories dealing primarily with Polish Jewry. Most striking and typical in Der Nister's wartime writing was a particular juxtaposition of Jewish tragedy and survival. One of his main concerns and hopes was apparently for the younger generation of Jews, which would insure national survival and continuity in spite of the Holocaust. Those young Jews, who resisted the Nazis, particularly captured Der Nister's imagination. Thus, the central figure in his story "Flora" is a Jewish partisan girl from Poland who arrives in Moscow to celebrate the final victory over Hitler's Germany at the Jewish Antifascist Committee.[46] Der Nister published a most daring and revealing article in the summer of 1944 in which his preoccupation with the survival of European Jewry is linked with the revival of ancient Israel. In the article, a young Jewish partisan was portrayed as the future builder of the ruins of the "Mount," a transparent hint at the Mount of the Temple in Jerusalem.[47] The article was based on an actual encounter with a 16-year-old Jewish ex-partisan who arrived in Moscow in 1944, and, like the poet Sutskever, was seen there, a living symbol of Jewish suffering and heroism. He, too, had like Sutskever had tremendous appeal for the

Soviet Jewish intellectuals who gathered around the JAC.[48] Another Jewish partisan who met Der Nister around that time was Eliezer Lidovski, who came to Moscow from the Kovno region in the Western Ukraine. During a highly emotional night-long encounter, Der Nister urged him to tell all he knew about the Jewish plight under the Nazis. Some of this information was published in *Eynikayt*.[49] Der Nister was quite outspoken in his pessimism about the future of Jewish culture in the Soviet Union. He was perhaps the only one of the Soviet Yiddish writers, who openly advised his colleagues, Jewish refugee writers, to leave the USSR. It is possible that his ascetic approach to life, his natural modesty, and his lack of concern for the material aspects of life, made him less vulnerable to the pressures of the regime and, therefore, more open and daring. Der Nister advised the refugee writers that the best way to help Jewish culture survive in the USSR, was for Jews abroad to make continuous demands on the Soviet regime.[50] When Rachel Korn, was leaving Russia shortly after the War, Der Nister urged her to "tell the Jews that Yiddish culture here is on its way out."[51]

The Outsider: Ehrenburg

Ilya Ehrenburg was considered as one of the biggest names on the Committee's roster. Unlike Der Nister, Mikhoels, Fefer, Markish or Epshteyn, he was fairly remote from the Jewish cultural milieu in Soviet Russia, a striking example of an almost completely assimilated Russian-Jewish intellectual. Ehrenburg spent most of the prewar period outside Russia, and developed a strong kinship with and admiration for Western European culture. His first reaction to Bolshevism was not enthusiastic, and his subsequent relationship with the Soviet regime was rather ambiguous. Although at times a staunch supporter of the Soviet experiment, Ehrenburg was torn for years by inner conflict. He had experimented too much in his youth to accept the rather limited horizons which new Russia could offer him. At the same time, he could not tear himself away completely from his native land. In order to bridge the gap between his intellectual needs and the realities of Stalinist Russia, Ehrenburg developed and perfected the techniques of an intellectual acrobat, an extremely thin line at times. His life, as well as his work, abounded, therefore, in ambiguities. This was also true in respect to his Jewish identity. Although removed from Jewish tradition, he had displayed a certain preoccupation with Jewish themes in his early years. In a poem entitled "To the Jewish People," published in 1911, Ehrenburg revealed a strong sense of historical Jewish consciousness. One central theme was that of alienation, of the "diaspora condition," and of the highly negative attitudes of the Gentile world toward the Jew. The poem ended with a semi-prophetic call for a return to the ancient land of Israel.[52] The hero of one of his first novels was a pathetic Jewish tailor, Lazik Roytshvants. In spite of his nonconformist stands and opinions, Ehrenburg was apparently considered by Stalin an asset to the regime. His knowledge of the West, his contacts in the intellectual and artistic circles of Europe, his writing abilities and political acumen, all made him an effective tool of Soviet propaganda. Actually, Ehrenburg was not only a Soviet link to Western European sympathizers and fellow-travellers, but was himself, strangely enough, a special kind of "internal," Soviet fellow-traveller, an oddity deemed useful and necessary by the Soviets. According to some opinions, the fact that Ehrenburg had been granted highly unusual privileges by the regime, such as living abroad for extended periods, suggests that some kind of bargain was made between him and the Soviet security apparatus.[53]

Ehrenburg's inner conflicts and ambiguities seemed to disappear during the War years. It was a period in his career as writer and journalist when his personal attitudes seemed, at least for a while, to be congruous with official Soviet policies, the common denominator being anti-Nazism and anti-Germanism. The atmosphere prevailing during those years in Soviet Russia enabled Ehrenburg to express quite openly his diverse inclinations and interests: his anti-Fascist and anti-Nazi stand; his affinity to Western culture; his love for France; and not the least his renewed involvement with Jewish identity. For a number of years his state of mental conflict was replaced by basic certainties. Those years were Ehrenburg's finest, both as a writer and as a public figure. The War marked the apex of Ehrenburg's interest in and responsiveness to Jewish matters. As a leading correspondent of the *Red Star,* he followed in the wake of the military and was among the first to witness the unprecedented dimensions of Nazi atrocities against the Soviet Jewish population in Nazi-occupied territories. He also noted the increase in anti-Semitism among the non-Jewish population of these areas. Ehrenburg had a special interest in meeting Jewish soldiers and partisans. His encounter with a group of Jewish partisans in liberated Vilna, where most of the local Jews were murdered by

Nazis, had a particularly strong impact. In his preface to a book on Nazi atrocities against Jews, Ehrenburg wrote: "I was in Vilna during the battle for the city. There I saw Jews—partisans, men and women who burst out of the Vilna ghetto with weapons in their hands. In Ponar near Vilna the hangmen murdered about one hundred thousand Jews. Five hundred of them were saved and took part in the liberation of the city. I talked to girl students, workers, watchmenders and musicians. Their lives were dedicated to one aim—revenge!"[54] After the War Ehrenburg met with Jewish partisans in France and Yugoslavia.[55] His was one of the most popular names in wartime Russia, and when his identification with Jewish suffering and bravery became well known, increasing numbers of Jewish soldiers and civilians turned to him for advice and assistance. In a way, he, like Mikhoels, was an "address" for Jews in distress. His involvement found expression on the most personal level, when the Ehrenburgs adopted a 12 year old Jewish girl-partisan from Pinsk.[56] Ehrenburg's preoccupation with the Jewish tragedy was reflected in his writings. In 1940 when official Soviet policy was heavily influenced by the Molotov-Ribbentrop Agreement, he wrote a poem bewailing the fact that anti-Semitism had again reared its ugly head. He wrote one of the first poems commemorating the killings in Babi Yar. In another poem written during the War, Ehrenburg struck a rather pessimistic note, on the estrangement between Jews and non-Jews in Soviet Russia. At the same time however he could also write about the supposedly substantial assistance extended to Soviet Jews by the surrounding society. Ehrenburg did have the dubious talent of writing different things for different audiences at different times, but this was probably his solution to the perennial problem of reconciling one's convictions with the expectations of the regime in Stalin's Russia. The extermination of Kiev's Jews and the theme of annihilation camps in general were mentioned again in his famous novel *The Storm* completed and published after the War. Ehrenburg also started writing an historical novel about the martyrdom and heroism of Soviet Jews during the War, but it was never completed.[57] Ehrenburg was greatly concerned by the accusations by the non-Jewish population that there were Jews "who purchased their war medals in Tashkent." Ehrenburg urged the Jewish Antifascist Committee to publicly denounce such arguments by publishing material which would unequivocally refute these charges in a book in Russian on Jewish participation in the Soviet Army and in the partisan movement. Another of Ehrenburg's recurring themes was vengeance and retribution. "The Jewish bookkeeper from Chernigov," according to Ehrenburg's appeal to the JAC leadership, "marches westward as a representative of his people . . . to avenge (them) . . ."[58] The Warsaw Ghetto uprising made a deep impression on him. He wrote, pointing out the particular difficulties of Jewish resistance to the Nazis, "These people defended neither territory nor privileges . . ., but human dignity . . . saving their own and their people's honor."[59]

Ehrenburg's relations with the JAC and with its leading members were complex and problematic. Although he later denied any close contacts with the Committee, it remains a fact that he did participate in most of its official public affairs. Speaking at the August 1941 meeting, the first Jewish public appeal organized in the wake of the German-Soviet war, Ehrenburg declared "I am a Russian writer . . . however the Nazis reminded me of something else: My mother's name was Hanna. I am a Jew, and I state it with pride." The main theme of this speech was to emphasize Russian-Jewish friendship and it was probably meant to amend shock at the Molotov-Ribbentrop agreement, still fresh in the minds of Jews all over the world. He spoke again at the February 1943 Plenary Session of the Committee. Ehrenburg was one of the major speakers at the mass meeting organized by the JAC in April 1944. By then he witnessed the shocking dimensions of the Holocaust. His message this time was "There are no more Jews in Kiev, Warsaw, Prague or Amsterdam." He spoke of the Jews as a special target of Nazi policies, a point which was scarcely mentioned in the general Soviet press, and expressed his hope that the Nazis had not succeeded in contaminating the Soviet population with their anti-Semitism. At the same time he was very careful to emphasize Russian-Jewish friendship, and Russian humanism. On several occasions Ehrenburg also spoke to the JAC on Nazi atrocities against Jews. He urged the Committee to publicize these facts, and to collect all documentation concerning the Holocaust.[60] Ehrenburg differed significantly from those Soviet Jewish intellectuals who comprised the nucleus of the Committee. People like Mikhoels and the Soviet-Yiddish writers surrounding him nurtured a basically positive national identity, whereas Ehrenburg needed a war to remind him that he too was Jewish. The blatant revival of anti-Jewish feelings and expressions in wartime Russia violated one of the basic tenets of faith of this assimilationist Soviet Jew, who wanted to believe that the postrevolutionary social and political realities had succeeded in solving the problem of anti-Semitism. Ehrenburg strongly identified with another

Jewish intellectual, the Polish-Jewish poet Julian Tuwim, who like himself became aware of his Jewishness as a result of the War.[61] Unlike Ehrenburg, who was interested primarily in condemning contemporary anti-Semitism, such people as Mikhoels or Fefer, were also interested in the future preservation of Jewish culture in the USSR. Ehrenburg like the Soviet-Yiddish writers was mobilized by the regime to participate in JAC activities, and he identified with some of its premises, but he could never become an integral part of its Yiddishist millieu. Most of the "Yiddishists" on the Committee tended to look upon him as an "outsider." Fefer, for example told him openly that only those who write in Yiddish should be regarded as Jewish writers.

It was the Black Book project which brought Ehrenburg into head-on confrontation with the JAC. In his memoirs, Ehrenburg relates "at the end of the war, Vassily Grossman and I began to collect material relating to the mass extermination of Jews."[62] In a conversation with Smolar, a communist-Jewish partisan from Minsk, shortly after the War, Ehrenburg related how he together with the JAC leadership, decided to publish a Black Book on Nazi atrocities against Jews in the USSR. However, the material which he collected and submitted to the Committee, was wasted by sending it piecemeal to Jewish publications abroad.[63] Such accusations on the part of Ehrenburg smack of false naivete. He must have known that the Committee, even less than himself, hardly had a free hand in its decisions concerning publication of such materials, especially in Russian and for local consumption. The decision to disband Ehrenburg's Black Book literary committee, and to have the material transferred to the offices of the JAC, was clearly a political one. It was made sometime in the spring of 1945, after a *Pravda* article critical of Ehrenburg's extremist anti-German line (by G. Alexandrov, head of the Propaganda Section of the Party's Central Committee) marked an end of an era in Soviet propaganda.[64] Ehrenburg's criticism of the Committee's failure to act openly and decisively in this matter and the fact that his idea of a Jewish Black Book was allegedly "wasted" by the JAC, inspired in him a mixture of bitterness and cynicism, which he often expressed in private. He used to repeat that the Jewish Committee was actually an "anti-Jewish Committee." IIc also advised people that "there is no point in going there . . . there is nobody there who could speak up . . ."[65] Ehrenburg's personal relationships with the Yiddishist element within the Committee were limited to Markish and Mikhoels. In his memoirs, Ehrenburg related that "it was only during the war years that I really began to understand him (Mikhoels) and grew very attached to him." Besides their common concern for Jewish matters during that period, Mikhoels' artistic aspect must have also attracted Ehrenburg. In his memoirs, Ehrenburg portrayed him as a "wise rabbi" and a "defender of the oppressed." The friendship between the Ehrenburg and the Markish families was profound and endured the difficult postwar years, even after Markish's imprisonment and execution.[66] A particularly significant relationship was that between Ehrenburg and the young partisan-poet, Abraham Sutskever, who was coopted into the JAC after he had been flown to Moscow from Nazi-occupied Lithuania in the spring of 1944. Ehrenburg apparently regarded Sutskever as a combination and symbol of everything he admired at that time. Sutskever was a fighting Jew, an artist, and a survivor of the Holocaust. In an article about Sutskever, published in *Pravda,* Ehrenburg set out to disprove prevailing views on Jewish cowardice. For his part, Sutskever maintained that "He (Ehrenburg), became closer to me than all the Jewish and non-Jewish writers and artists I knew in Moscow."[67]

Sutskever was the embodiment of the suffering and courage of Nazi-persecuted Jewry in the eyes of many Soviet-Jewish intellectuals at that time. His writings on the ghetto preceded him to Moscow. The poet himself reached the Soviet capital in March 1944, and was one of the speakers at the JAC April 1944 meeting. He was also asked to broadcast in Yiddish to Jews in the U.S. and England. Though his public appearances were meant primarily for consumption abroad, his presence in Moscow had a dramatic and direct impact upon the Soviet-Jewish intellectuals, like Ehrenburg.

As we have seen, Ehrenburg's stand on Jewish matters was highly complex. He has often been accused of collaborating in the destruction of the JAC and the Jewish cultural leadership in the USSR during Stalin's last years. However no conclusive proof is available. Even his famous 1948 *Pravda* article condemning Jewish nationalism, could not serve as a clear cut indication of his allegedly anti-Jewish attitudes. It should be noted that a few months before the publication of this article Ehrenburg described himself in *Eynikayt* as "a Soviet citizen, a Russian writer and a Jew(!)"[68] Ehrenburg did indeed write some of the most servile pro-Stalin literary works, but he is also believed to have stood up to Stalin's plans for a large scale purge of Soviet Jews.[69] A succint conclusion on Ehrenburg's record, which can be applied to his Jewish aspects as well is that it is "too ambiguous and contradictory to yield either a blanket condemnation or a clean bill of health."[70]

Another "outsider" was the Russian-Jewish writer and journalist, Vassily Grossman. His close family had been annihilated by the Nazis in his hometown of Berdichev. Like Ehrenburg, Grossman was a correspondent for the *Red Star* and among the first to grasp the dimensions of the Jewish catastrophe. In a number of journalistic, as well as fictional, accounts, Grossman emphasized the specifically Jewish aspects of the War. The most moving were his "Treblinka Inferno," a report on the Treblinka extermination camp, and "Ukraine without Jews," an unfinished series published in the *Eynikayt*. Grossman collaborated with Ehrenburg in collecting documentary and other materials for the Black Book. In a preface to what was to comprise the Soviet Black Book, Grossman openly stressed the fact that Jews had been a special target for Nazi policies. He also hinted at the hostile attitudes and behaviour of the non-Jewish, Soviet population towards local Jews under Nazi occupation.[71]

Still another category of "outsiders" were people with political careers in the past. One such man was Solomon Shpigelglas. Never having belonged to the inner circle of Yiddish intellectuals, he nonetheless became a regular working member of the Committee in February 1945 and after Shakhno Epshteyn's death a few months later was even promoted to the position of Acting Secretary. Born in Warsaw, Shpigelglas had studied at Moscow University, joined the Party in 1919 and worked directly under Lenin. During the early twenties he was also active in the Trade Unions. From 1924 he worked in the Party apparatus, first in the Moscow Party Organization and then in the Central Committee of the CPSU and in the Central Committee of the Party in the Ukraine. Prior to the War, he worked in journalism and publishing. It is quite possible that Lozovskii knew Shpigelglas from his days as a Trade Union leader and Director of the State Literature Publishing House. Shpigelglas died in the Fall of 1946. Another "outsider," of a much lesser calibre was a man by the name of Kotliar, an ex-colleague of the veteran Soviet military leader Kliment Voroshilov.[72]

As we have seen already, it is impossible to grasp the essence of the Committee, without examining the personalities involved and the dynamics of the group. In fact, the most striking feature of that group of people, was the contrast between its heterogeneity and tension on the one hand and sense of cohesion and mission on the other. Prominent Jewish personalities from all walks of life were thrown together by the regime for wartime propaganda purposes. Besides the nucleus of Yiddish writers, poets and artists, there were Russian-acculturated individuals like Ehrenburg. Long time Party members rubbed shoulders with politically-uninvolved individuals. Intellectuals were balanced by soldiers and administrators. Within the inner circle of Yiddish writers there was a barrier, sometimes obscured but always present between the veteran Soviet Yiddish element and the new-comers from the western territories. There were also of course personal rivalries and competition, and in some circles within the Committee "cliques" formed, (for example around Mikhoels, Markish and Fefer). Various persons also enjoyed "outside" support which enhanced their prestige within the Committee. Such outside contacts existed between Markish and Fadeev, Mikhoels and Tolstoi, Fefer and Lozovskii. Attempts to resolve personal rivalries by political means and outside ties were not uncommon. However in spite of these dysfunctional reali-ties, the War atmosphere and its Jewish implications generated among the Committee members a feeling of a common fate and purpose. Many felt a deep sense of responsibility towards the Jewish community in the USSR and solidarity with Jews abroad. The expectations and pressures exerted by the Jewish public all over the country forced some of the JAC members to become semi-official leaders of the community. The Soviet practice of informal protektsiia and personal intervention with the authorities made this possible. Some of the most prominent personalities on the Committee like Mikhoels and Ehrenburg became, (or were rather forced by the circumstances to become), living symbols of Jewish identity in wartime Russia.

5

JEWISH RESPONSES

Jews in general and American Jews in particular were a central target for Soviet overseas propaganda during the War. Both as an ethnic group and as a liberal element, they were particularly receptive to anti-fascist and anti-Nazi motifs. In some cases separate Jewish organizations were set up and in others, Jewish sectors were established within pro-Soviet fronts. Like corresponding non-Jewish structures, Jewish fronts usually consisted of a core of communists and fellow-travelers and a wide range of sympathizers.

Before the War, Jewish supporters of Communism in the U.S. were mainly left-wing workers of Eastern European origin, mostly from the New York garment industry, and second-generation members of the liberal professions and intellectuals. They were won over by reports of Soviet stands on Nazi Germany and of the equality of Jews within the Soviet "family of nations." Such gatherings as the International Conference Against Anti-Semitism convened in Paris in 1936, were organized and supported by U.S. and European communists. Growing numbers of Jewish intellectuals, disappointed with the Western world's passive acceptance of Hitler's Germany, seemed to regard communism and the Soviet Union as the only serious opponents of Nazism. Many American-Jewish intellectuals joined such organizations as the American League for Peace and Democracy and the Hollywood Anti-Nazi League. American-Jewish communism also had great appeal as a supporter and promoter of Yiddish culture. The communist *Freiheit* (later *Morning Freiheit*), was, for many years, the most literary Yiddish daily in the U.S. It employed a number of first-rate Yiddish literary figures, who were not themselves communists, and cultivated a wide, non-Party readership. Its impact declined in the late twenties, partly because of its anti-Zionist stand on the events in Palestine. However, in the late 1930's, the Jewish section of the CPUSA and *Morning Freiheit* made a special effort to win back Jewish support via cultural activities sponsored primarily by fellow-traveling-type organizations. From circa 1937, the Party initiated a trend to recruit support on the basis of an appeal to group and ethnic allegiance (especially among Slavs and Jews) and this trend was strengthened during the War. A special attempt was made to attract the English-speaking second generation.[1] The unexpected Soviet-Nazi agreement of August 1939 was a serious blow to many communists and fellow-travelers, but it hit the Jews among them particularly hard. Those Yiddish intellectuals, like Leivick, Nadir and Opatoshu, who still maintained some contacts with pro-communist Jewish fronts, were now utterly alienated. *Morning Freiheit* tried to present the Molotov-Ribbentrop deal as "good for Jews," pointing out the improvement in the lot of Jews in the Soviet-annexed territories. However, news of Soviet activities, including the suppression of Jewish culture and religion and of Zionism in these territories soon reached America, and enhanced the dissilusionment of Jews there.[2]

American-Jewish Fronts

Hitler's attack on the Soviet Union and the subsequent realignment in world politics provided an opportunity for restoring the Soviet image in the West. Communist contacts with the mainstream of Jewish public opinion were stepped up. Russia's image as the principal enemy of Hitler and redeemer of Jews was now exploited intensively in Soviet propaganda. Reports of the Holocaust, of changing Soviet attitudes towards the Jewish Yishuv in Palestine, and of the anticipated role of the USSR in the postwar arrangements were all used by Jewish communists and fellow-travelers in order to influence Jewish public opinion. Thus, Alexander Bittelman, a leading member of the CPUSA and chief Jewish communist theoretician, spoke in 1943 of "a new form of Jewish national existence for the Jews living in Palestine." He suggested that Soviet support for Jewish interests in Palestine and the opportunities for contact with Soviet Jewry be considered a basis for a new policy of unity between world Jewry and Soviet Russia. These arguments were also cited by Jewish communists in order to combat anti-Soviet elements in Jewish public life. Using "unity" tactics and slogans, they emphasized their desire to become part and parcel of Jewish communal life.[3] Jewish fronts and fellow-travelers were exploited to gain the sympathies and support of the community. According to a leading Jewish communist ". . . the Jewish antifascists . . (should) organize such actions and movements . . . which will *stimulate and motivate other Jewish organizations* to do likewise, but on a greater scale and in a manner which will attract all the Jews of America . . ."[4] Among the leading "unity"-type Jewish front organizations were the Jewish Section of the International Workers Order, the Jewish Council for Russian War Relief and the Committee of Jewish Writers and Artists.

The Jewish front organization closest to the Communist Party was the Jewish Section of the International Workers Order (IWO). The IWO, founded as a mutual benefit society in 1930, dealt primarily with insurance plans, but gradually began to foster various social and cultural activities. It appealed primarily to ethnic groups and was organized in national sections. Its principal ethnic targets were Slavs and Jews. It attempted at times to disguise its communist nature, but leading members of the IWO such as Max Bedacht, a member of the CPUSA Political Committee, and Ruben Saltzman, its leading Jewish communist, exposed its true nature. The Jewish Section was the second largest section of the IWO, and many Jews also belonged to its English-speaking branches. With 35,000 members on the eve of the War, and rising to 50,000 in 1945, it served, with considerable success, as a means of disseminating communist and pro-Soviet sentiments to the Jewish public at large. To that end it was supposed to emphasize its Jewish character while dissociating itself, at least outwardly, from the communist main body. Hence, its assumption of a distinctive name—the Jewish Peoples Fraternal Order (JPFO). Its main goal was to gain the confidence of such mainstream Jewish structures as the American Jewish Congress and the American Jewish Conference, and although initially, it met with obstacles, in time it was accepted by both.[5] The JPFO was among the first Jewish organizations in the U.S. to be approached by the Soviet Jewish Antifascist Committee. The Order's Secretary, Ruben Saltzman, made continuous efforts to evoke pro-Soviet responses in various American Jewish organizations. His tactics and methods followed Bittelman's prescription for "unity" and "front" tactics. Saltzman also maintained Soviet contacts. Thus, he met Soviet

Ambassador Litvinov to discuss such issues as ethnic-based Soviet propaganda in the U.S. and power relations within the American Jewish community. Saltzman was also closely involved in the Mikhoels-Fefer visit to the U.S.[6]

Another Jewish front organization, less closely identified with communism than the JPFO, was the IKUF (World Alliance of Jewish Culture). Its aim was to use Jewish, and particularly Yiddish, culture in order to create a common framework for communist and progressive Jewish elements interested in the advancement of Yiddish culture. Its American Section became the most significant section of the IKUF following the outbreak of War. The leadership structure of the IKUF was typical of a pro-communist front. Its Chairman, Dr. A. Mukdoni, was a noted non-communist writer, and among its leading members were non-communist public and cultural figures such as Chaim Zhitlovsky, J. Opatoshu and H. Leivick; its Secretary, however was the poet Z. Weinper, a secret member of the Party. There were also a number of active Jewish communists in its ranks, such as M. Olgin, R. Saltzman, M. Katz and P. Novick. Nachman Meisel, a writer and editor who arrived in the U.S. from Poland shortly before the outbreak of the War, became the Editor of IKUF's mouthpiece, *Yiddishe Kultur*. B. Z. Goldberg, (the popular Yiddish columnist and son-in-law of Shalom Aleichem,) was also active in the American branch of the IKUF.[7] The 1939–1941 crisis in Jewish attitudes towards Russia had a devastating impact on the IKUF, and its outstanding members deserted. However, at least some of its former popularity was regained after Hitler's attack on Russia. The IKUF was among the first to respond to JAC appeals and maintained regular contacts with the Committee throughout and after the War.[8] About a third of the literary material published in *Yiddishe Kultur* during the War consisted of works of Soviet-Yiddish writers sent by the JAC. IKUF also published a number of books by Yiddish writers in the USSR. Additional pro-Soviet, Jewish organizations active primarily in the economic sphere were ICOR and Ambidzhan. ICOR (The Organization for Jewish Colonization in Russia), founded in the 1920's, was active during the War years both in fund raising, mainly to assist Birobidzhan, and in public propaganda in support of the Soviet Union. Among its leading members and sponsors were Ch. Zhitlovsky (Honorary President), B. Z. Goldberg, J. Brainin, R. Saltzman, A. Bittelman and B. Gold. Ambidzhan (The American Committee for the Settlement of Jews in Birobidzhan), founded in the mid-thirties, suspended activities in 1939 and resumed them only after the Nazi attack on the Soviet Union. Among its active members were Goldberg, Brainin and Opatoshu.[9]

The Jewish Section of the Russian War Relief, known as the Jewish Council for Russian War Relief (JCRWR), was founded in early 1942. It was supported from its inception by such pro-Soviet and fellow-traveling organizations as the Committee of Jewish Writers and the Jewish Section of the IWO. Most active in the establishment of the Council were Chaim Zhitlovsky, Abraham Goldberg[10] and B. Z. Goldberg. The latter argued that a distinct Jewish contribution to the Soviet war effort would "register in Soviet circles."[11] Varying attitudes existed for some time among and within the mainstream Jewish organizations in this regard. Both the American Jewish Congress and the World Jewish Congress ultimately accepted the idea of a pro-Soviet Jewish fund-raising institution, though not without some reservations. Stephen Wise of the World Jewish Congress (WJC) after initial hesitations, accepted the Honorary Chairmanship of the JCRWR (which he shared with Albert Einstein), but some of his colleagues had second thoughts about the nature and implications of a Jewish aid campaign for Russia. Strong reservations were also voiced by the American Jewish Joint Distribution Committee (JDC).[12]

In spite of the differing opinions on the need for a specifically Jewish aid campaign for Soviet Russia, the JCRWR succeeded in mobilizing support in various Jewish circles. Its chairman, Louis Levine was an observant Jewish businessman with socialist ideals. He was also active in the World Jewish Congress and the American Jewish Congress. Among its most active members were well known orthodox rabbis such as Joseph H. Lookstein of Kehilath Jeshurun in New York and President of the Rabbinical Council of America and Rabbi Ephraim Yolles of Philadelphia. Another prominent member of the JCRWR was Dr. Israel Goldstein, head of the Conservative B'nai Jeshurun Congregation in New York and president of the Zionist Organization of America. Goldstein became sympathetic to the Soviet experiment in the 1920's and early 1930's when he joined the League Against War and Fascism. His pro-Soviet enthusiasm must have been boosted by his visit to the USSR in 1932. Though he was later disenchanted with the communist regime in Russia, he remained convinced that the USSR would play a major role in the solution of Jewish related problems. Still another religious figure at the center of JCRWR activities was the controversial "Red" Rabbi Abraham Bik, a dedicated fellow-traveler at that time. The Council was actually run by its executive secretary

Moses I. Finkelstein. Though not an official member of the CPSU, he was very close to such American Jewish communist leaders as Reuben Saltzman. It is also not by chance that the communist sponsored JPFO had a decisive influence upon the Council.[13] The JCRWR succeeded in recruiting people influential in the shaping of significant parts of Jewish public opinion, such as William Edlin, Editor of the *Tog,* and D. L. Mekler of the *Morgen Zhornal.* Needless to say, P. Novick and his *Morning Freiheit* were more than enthusiastic supporters of any pro-Soviet activity. Among the Jewish intellectuals, who agreed during the War to appear on the Council's letterhead though never particularly active in Jewish affairs, were Howard Fast and Lillian Hellman.

As far as its financial goal was concerned, the Council succeeded in collecting over ten million dollars during the years 1942–1945, a significant portion of the overall sum collected by the Russian War Relief in the U.S. Nor should the public impact of the JCRWR be underestimated. Its first anniversary conference in February 1943 drew some 1,000 delegates from more than 500 Jewish organizations. The non-political nature of the organization was repeatedly stressed by the speakers, among whom was a Jewish Red Army officer. He went out of his way to underline the Jewish nature of his message to American Jews.[14] A select group of delegates to the 1944 JCRWR Conference were invited by Eugene Kisselev, Soviet Consul General in New York, to a showing of a Soviet film on the war in the Ukraine. It was at the 1944 Conference that concrete plans for aiding Soviet Jews in the liberated areas were discussed by Council leaders. It was then that the "regional" aid concept, advocated to Mikhoels and Fefer by JDC leaders, during the formers' visit to the U.S. in 1943,[15] was raised again and approved by Kisselev. JCRWR conferences became something of an annual tradition and continued even after the War, serving increasingly as a platform for the voicing of Soviet stands and policies.

The Writers' Committee

The American Committee of Jewish Writers, Artists and Scientists (ACJWAS) was a very special type of pro-Soviet front structure. Initiated by a small group, most of them Yiddishist intellectuals, headed by Dr. Chaim Zhitlovsky, it was meant primarily to provide an organizational response to the Moscow Jewish appeal of August 1941. The group met in early September at New York's Pennsylvania Hotel and issued an appeal to Jewish writers and intellectuals in the U.S. to join in U.S. Jewry's response to the Soviet Jewish appeal. Within a few weeks it had obtained the signatures and goodwill of about 200 prominent persons, among them Professor Albert Einstein, Rabbi Lookstein and Dr. Rosen of the JDC. A radio broadcast to Soviet Jewry in English and Yiddish followed on October 26. The leadership structure of the Committee emerged in mid-1942, when its Executive Committee was established. Dr. Chaim Zhitlovsky was Chairman, Menashe Unger—Secretary, and the other leading members were B. Z. Goldberg, Dr. R. Mahler, R. Saltzman and N. Meisel. The Committee, which considered itself a counterpart of the Jewish Antifascist Committee in the Soviet Union, declared its twofold purpose of assisting in the mobilization of material help for Russia and fostering pro-Soviet attitudes within the Jewish community in the U.S. It also pointed out the necessity for building bridges between the Jewish communities of the two countries.[16]

Though physically a modest enterprise (the Writers' Committee occupied four rented rooms on W. 109th Street in Manhattan), it succeeded in initiating and carrying out a number of impressive public events. The first, a mass meeting in Madison Square Garden on December 1941, drew a crowd of 20,000. Among those who addressed it were Czechoslovak Foreign Minister Jan Masaryk and the famous Yiddish writer Sholem Asch. The main speaker at the "Unity Congress" Rally organized by the Committee in November 1942 was Viktor Fediushin, Soviet Consul General in New York. Among the other speakers were B. Z. Goldberg, Dr. Israel Goldstein and Rabbi Lookstein. A greeting from Dr. Chaim Weizmann was also read out.

One of the Committee's principal functions was the dissemination of Soviet material, most of it sent by the JAC. It also started to publish its own periodicals, *Eynikayt* in Yiddish (named after its Soviet counterpart) and *New Currents* in English. Both publications were quite generous in their space allotment to pro-Soviet themes and views. Thus, some typical subjects were: criticism of the London Poles; the salvation of Jews by the USSR; and Jewish cultural achievement in the Soviet Union. *Eynikayt* and *New Currents* published materials by numerous Soviet-Jewish writers. Journalists writing for New York Yiddish newspapers such as *Tog Morgen Zhornal,* and *Morning Freiheit* also published in *Eynikayt.* The Writers' Committee was instrumental in organizing pro-Soviet support through its involvement in the founding of the Jewish Council of the Russian War Relief. It also stood behind the Mikhoels-Fefer visit in 1943. One of the main aims of the Committee was to involve the various American-Jewish organizations in pro-Soviet campaigns. Initial reactions of the American-Jewish establishment to the Committee's appeals were not too encouraging. As late as spring 1943, B. Z. Goldberg complained bitterly in his daily *Tog* column, that a lynch atmosphere was being created around his Committee.[17] This assessment was quite correct, especially in regard to such staunch anti-Soviet circles as the *Forward* and the Bund. The American Jewish Committee, for example, was hesitant to respond favorably lest such a response brand them fellow-travelers and communist sympathizers. The JDC showed some signs of cooperation during the Mikhoels-Fefer visit. It seems that the greatest success was scored by B. Z. Goldberg with the World Jewish Congress, which for its own reasons was interested in establishing permanent contacts with the USSR and its Jewish community. In an open letter to the World Jewish Congress Goldberg wrote: "The members of the Committee . . . appreciate the contribution of the WJC as a great instrument for the attainment of that unity on a world scale."[18] The Mikhoels-Fefer visit to the U.S. undoubtedly boosted the Committee's activities and prestige. Its leading members conferred at length with the Soviet-Jewish representatives and discussed future plans with them in detail. It was then decided to expand the Writers' Committee's publishing activities and to launch the Black Book project on Nazi atrocities against Jews.[19]

The Writers' Committee was, a close counterpart of the Jewish Antifascist Committee in the USSR, though on a smaller scale. Like the JAC, its membership was primarily of a cultural-scientific nature and its appeal was envisaged as non-political. As for its membership, it actually was "a mix of people" who joined for various reasons. One distinctive group consisted of those interested and active in Yiddish culture, such as Chaim Zhitlovsky, Sholem Asch and B. Z. Goldberg. Sh. Erdberg and William Edlin, also became active in the Committee. And although it did not win the favour of American Jewish liberals and leftists it did manage to recruit Howard Fast, Lillian Hellman, Arthur Miller and Leon Feuchtwanger. Artists on the Committee included Marc Chagall (he knew Mikhoels personally and had been designer for the Moscow Jewish Theatre in the early 20's); Maurice Schwartz, the leading Yiddish actor in America; and the Polish-Jewish artist and cartoonist Arthur Szyk. The Zionist contingent, mainly leftist was represented by the Polish-born historian Raphael Mahler.

Committee members who openly identified with communism or were declared Party members were Pesach Novick, editor of *Morning Freiheit,* Reuben Saltzman of the IWO, S. Almazov and Ursula Wasserman. Among the editors of *New Currents* were Abraham Chapman, a communist journalist who wrote for both the *Daily Worker* and the *Morning Freiheit;* Albert E. Kahn, affiliated with *Soviet Russia Today;* and H. M. Morais, a leftist history professor suspended from Brooklyn College for his communist activities.

B. Z. Goldberg

The founder and early leader of the Committee was Chaim Zhitlovsky, writer, philosopher and journalist. Born in Russia, he was connected in his youth, with the populists, Social Revolutionaries and the Bund. He settled in New York before the First World War, and became a spokesman for Yiddishism, socialism and Jewish national autonomy in the Diaspora. Zhitlovsky was an influencial figure in some segments of the Yiddish-speaking public in the U.S., for more than thirty years, inter alia through his articles in the *Tog.* Although originally not strongly pro-Bolshevik, he changed his views with the emergence of Hitler's Germany. He began to endorse Soviet solutions to the Jewish problem, praising such Soviet attainments as the productivization of the Jewish population, support for Yiddish culture, and the Birobidzhan settlement project. Even during the difficult years of the Nazi-Soviet pact, Zhitlovsky seemed to adhere to his pro-Soviet views. Hitler's attack on Russia and the subsequent realignment of attitudes and loyalties was a god-send to him. His reaction to the Soviet-Jewish appeal of August 1941 was highly emotional. He believed that it opened up new vistas for Jewish national existence in the USSR and ensured permanent ties between the two largest Jewish communities in the world.[20] In July 1941, he had issued a public appeal praising the USSR in its war against Nazi Germany. This was followed by pro-Soviet articles and by public activities, such as participation in the founding of the Writers' Committee, of the Jewish Council of Russian War Relief and in the planning of a visit of Soviet-Jewish delegates to the U.S. Zhitlovsky died while on a speaking tour shortly before the arrival of Mikhoels and Fefer, in the summer of 1943.

Whereas Zhitlovsky was the founding father of the Writers' Committee, Ben Zion Goldberg was the moving spirit behind it throughout its existence. Born Benjamin Goldberg at the turn of the century, he changed his name to Waife in the mid-1930's, retaining "Goldberg" as his *nom de plume,* but was widely known as "Bee Zee Goldberg" or just "Bee Zee". A fellow-traveler sui generis, and a controversial figure most of his life, he was the number one contact man of the JAC in America. Born into a Lithuanian Jewish family of rabbinical pedigree, Goldberg continued his religious education for a short while after arriving in New York in the early 1900's. His "Americanization" took place in the Mid West, where he attended local schools. Unlike those immigrant Jewish intellectuals whose cultural background was Eastern Europe, Goldberg was to a considerable extent influenced by both worlds. Besides being a supporter of Yiddishism and actively creative in Yiddish journalism in America, he also considered himself an American intellectual. He attended Columbia University and earned a Doctor's degree in psychology, but his main occupation was to be journalism. His affiliation with the Yiddish daily *Tog* started in the early 1920's and was to continue for most of his life.

Goldberg maintained that Jews could and should adapt their creative endeavors to the realities of the various societies and regimes within which they lived. He also believed in the continuity of Jewish culture in the Soviet Union in a communist-Yiddishist form. Goldberg's attachment to Yiddish culture had a personal significance as well. At the age of 20, after returning from the Mid West to New York, he became a frequent visitor in the house of Shalom Aleichem (Shalom Rabinovitz) and in 1917 he married the writer's youngest daughter Marie (Marusia). The connection with Shalom Aleichem was always a source of pride to Goldberg. It is quite possible that his first contacts with Bolshevik Russia were influenced by the special relationship between the writer and the Soviet regime. Shalom Aleichem was the most widely published and translated Yiddish author in the USSR, and his heirs were granted an exceptional privilege by Soviet standards: royalties on reprintings of his classic works. From the 1920's, (Shalom Aleichem died in 1916) the family maintained a continuous correspondence on this matter with official Soviet personalities, starting with Stalin and down to the officials of various Soviet publishing houses.[21] In a letter to Stalin in 1946, Goldberg wrote on his family's behalf " . . . thank you . . . for the kind interest you have taken in their (the family's) request with regard to the publication of their father's works . . . [for] your great personal humaneness, when twice you so generously replied to letters from their mother in time of great need. In the annals and hearts of the Shalom Aleichem family your name is inscribed with love."[22] Goldberg sounded quite sincere when he compared Stalin with George Washington or described him as "that quiet wise man in the Kremlin." Substantial payments were also made by the Soviets to the Shalom Aleichem family after the War, during Goldberg's visit to the USSR.[23]

Goldberg faced Soviet realities for the first time in 1934 on a typical semi-official tour of Russia during which sympathizers from abroad were shown what they expected to see and what the Soviets were interested in displaying. After returning home Goldberg became a member of the pro-Soviet Ambidzhan. He admitted years later that at that time he was a "Bourgeois liberal" and "an innocent abroad." What he regarded as the contrast between the capitalist "Humpty Dumpty" in America of the depression years and "the luminosity which was . . . rising in the East" helped to shape his political views. In the Soviet Union he saw hopeful signs for the future of Jewish cultural and communal life. On several occasions he even argued with Soviet Jews who were less enthusiastic than he about Jewish affairs in Russia.[24] Whatever the Soviets invested in this visiting journalist paid dividends. A series of pro-Soviet articles appeared in the *Tog* during and after the visit. As a columnist, sympathetic to the USSR but never officially linked with communism, Goldberg was the perfect progagandist as far as the Soviet Union was concerned.

An intriguing and somewhat obscure aspect of Goldberg's communist connection was his relationship with the future Secretary of the Jewish Antifascist Committee, Shakhno Epshteyn. According to a leading American-Jewish communist who became disenchanted with Soviet Russia following the Molotov-Ribbentrop agreement, Goldberg had met with Epshteyn even prior to his 1934 visit to Russia. The Goldberg-Epshteyn contact continued during the next few years, when Epshteyn spent time in Europe and in the U.S. The fact that Epshteyn did research on and admired Shalom Aleichem may also have affected their relationship. A person who knew both, remarked that "Shakhno used to speak of him [Goldberg] with unusual certitude."[25] It should be remembered that Epshteyn and Goldberg traveled abroad frequently, and could easily have met in Europe. Besides these ties, Goldberg maintained friendly relations with some American-Jewish communists, such as Pesach Novick and Kalman Marmor, both of the Yiddish *Morning Freiheit*. He was also close to the editors of such pro-communist English language publications as *The New Masses* and *Soviet Russia Today*.

Goldberg's controversiality was heightened during the strike of the *Tog* employees in 1941. The *Tog,* had a reputation for being liberal and pro-Zionist with relatively high literary and journalistic standards. Officially a bystander in the constant rivalry between the communist *Freiheit* and the socialist *Forward,* it succeeded in winning over some *Freiheit* readers when the latter took a clearly pro-communist and anti-Zionist stand in the late 1920's. The *Tog* had a tradition of intrigues and *coups* by persons aspiring to the editor's post. Various "outside elements" were also involved in this internecine warfare. The 1930's witnessed a growing cleavage between the conservative and left-wing factions on its staff, which finally led to a head-on confrontation. Goldberg sided with the left-wingers, and lost some of his influence on the editorial board as a result of accusations and insinuations that he was a communist agent. He was even brought before a "colleagues tribunal" and found guilty of some of the charges. Goldberg's dilemma was apparently solved when the *Tog* changed hands a few months after Hitler's attack on Russia. Both the new owner of the publication, Morris Weinberg, and his Chief Editor, William Edlin, who replaced Dr. Margoshes (a sharp critic of Goldberg's) seemed to back Goldberg and his views.[26] One should also recall the impact of the new wave of sympathy towards the USSR as a result of the War. For all these reasons Goldberg re-emerged as a central figure in the *Tog* establishment.

It was probably easier during the War than at any other time to use the *Tog* for pro-Soviet propaganda. Besides Goldberg's own daily column, the newspaper published Maurice Hindus' pro-Soviet book, *Mother Russia* in installments and gave extensive coverage to the Mikhoels-Fefer visit. Goldberg continued to wage untiring war against the *Forward.* Bitter recriminations were exchanged especially at the height of the Erlich-Alter affair and during the Mikhoels-Fefer visit to the U.S.[27] Goldberg's organizational involvement in pro-Soviet activities reached its peak during the War. Besides running the Committee of Jewish Writers he was also a leading member of the National Council of American-Soviet Friendship, of the JCRWR, IKUF, ICOR and of Ambidzhan. In addition, he lectured at the communist-oriented Jefferson School of Social Science. Goldberg was in frequent contact with Soviet diplomats in the U.S., and Central America, and especially with the Soviet consulate in New York. Some of his correspondence with the JAC was handled directly through the Soviet diplomatic bag.[28] As for his Zionist ties, he had established contacts with the American branch of the left-wing, Zionist Hashomer Hatsair movement in the late thirties. This relationship was strengthened during the War and in the postwar years. Hashomer Hatsair was perhaps the only group within the Zionist camp who were not scared by Goldberg's reputation. The fact that they themselves believed in the unique combination of Jewishness, socialism and support of the Soviet experiment, made such a match possible.

What kind of a fellow-traveler was Goldberg at this time? Although not a Party member, he was an important asset to Soviet propaganda, because of his access to a large non-communist, mainly Yiddish-speaking segment of U.S. Jewry. At the height of the War he declared: "Ideologically I am an opponent of communism,"[29] while at the same time admiring the USSR for what he believed to be its promotion of Jewish culture and condemnation of antisemitism. Goldberg was also extremely proud that Americans from all walks of life paid their tributes to Mikhoels and Fefer, whom he regarded as symbolizing Yiddish culture.[30] A close relationship developed between the two JAC delegates and Goldberg during their stay in America. The JAC thanked Goldberg profoundly for his efforts, and warm personal notes from Mikhoels and Fefer followed. Fefer wrote " . . . Here we keep telling . . . people about our friends [in the U.S.] and about you in particular."[31] It is difficult to ascertain to what extent Goldberg's praise for the Soviets was solely a matter of beliefs and ideals. The VIP treatment he received in Russia on his two visits there, as well as his view of himself as a prominent fellow-traveling Jewish intellectual, must also have been important to him. According to one critic, "he (Goldberg) wanted to become the Jewish Louis Fischer."[32] Goldberg prided himself on the fact that he was the first Jewish journalist to visit Birobidzhan in 1934 and hoped to be the first one to carry good news from Russia after the War. A loner and a non-conformist, he must have enjoyed the very fact of his controversiality. Like Corliss Lamont, his American counterpart, he considered himself a sort of maverick. And indeed, there were some reasons for it. Many people bought the *Tog* in order to read Goldberg's daily column, and he received an enormous mail from his readers.

Goldberg's two closest collaborators and confidants on the Writers' Committee were Joe Brainin and Menashe Unger. Brainin was one of those rare types who simultaneously supported Jewish culture, Zionism and Communist Russia. Those who knew him personally maintain that his opinions and attitudes were shaped to a great extent by his father, the Hebrew writer Reuben Brainin. The latter visited the Soviet Union in 1926 and again in 1930, became enthusiastic about the Soviet solution to the Jewish problem, and upon his return to the U.S., became active in Jewish pro-Soviet fronts. Joe Brainin met the prominent pro-Soviet journalist Louis Fischer during their service in the Jewish Legion in Palestine and became a fellow traveler sometime in the 1920's. As a specialist on advertising he was very useful to pro-Soviet wartime propaganda and was particularly helpful during the Mikhoels-Fefer visit. He was also among the guardians of the Rosenberg children, after their parents had been accused of espionage for Soviet Russia.[33] Menashe Unger, a writer and a journalist, was, like Goldberg, an ardent supporter of Jewish culture. His was also a rare combination of Hassidic tradition and pro-Zionist sentiments (himself a descendant of Hassidic rabbis in Galicia, he spent some time in Palestine) with pro-Soviet sympathies. During the War he wrote a number of pro-Soviet articles for the *Tog* and compiled a bibliography on the Mikhoels-Fefer visit in order to prove their popularity among American Jews.[34] The only prominent Yiddish literary figure whom Goldberg succeeded in enlisting for his Committee was Sholem Asch. Asch's willingness to support a pro-Soviet organization at that time could perhaps be attributed to the fact that he was shunned by the Yiddish literary establishment in America following the publication of his "Christian" trilogy.

Albert Einstein

The most illustrious name on the Committee's roster was that of its Honorary Chairman, Professor Albert Einstein. In order to understand Einstein's willingness to lend his support to the Writers' Committee and its pro-Soviet line, it is necessary to review the complex nature of Einstein's attitudes not only toward Soviet Russia, but also toward Fascism, Nazism and Jewish national existence. In the 1920's, when pro-Soviet societies were being founded in Weimar Germany, Einstein joined the Society of Friends of the New Russia. Willi Muenzenberg the Comintern specialist on propaganda also succeeded in installing him on the organizing committee of the League Against War and Fascism, another member of which was Maxim Gorky, whom Einstein greatly admired. Einstein's initial attitude towards Bolshevik Russia seemed to be one of simultaneous approval, hope and apprehension. Though he considered Lenin a great man and the Bolshevik Revolution a historical necessity, he wrote in 1932: "I certainly do not approve of much that is taking place in Russia." On another occasion he stated: "I am a convinced democrat . . . I am an adversary of Bolshevism just as much as of Fascism."[35] It seems, however, that in time, as the Nazi threat to democracy increased, Einstein assumed a militant anti-Nazi attitude, abandoning earlier pacifist notions. He believed that Soviet Russia was more sincere than others in her efforts to stop Hitler. In a speech delivered by telephone to a meeting of the JCRWR early in the War, he stated: " . . .The Russian Government has labored more honestly . . . to promote international security than any other great power."

The War doubtless had a strong impact on Einstein's opinions about Russia in general and its Jewish policies in particular. Like many of his contemporaries who witnessed the suffering and sacrifices of the Russians, Einstein argued that "without Russia, the German bloodhounds would have already achieved their goal."[36] At the same time, however, he was capable of making the distinction between the Soviet political system and the Russian people. To state that " . . . the heroic actions of the Red Army . . . blinded him [Einstein] to the facts of political life . . ."[37] seems too harsh a judgement. Ignorant, like most of his fellow Jews, of Soviet policies on Jewish evacuation during the War, he knew only that great numbers of Eastern European Jews *were* in fact saved by the USSR. Shortly after the end of the War, Einstein declared: "We must not forget that in those years of atrocious persecution of the Jewish people, Soviet Russia has been the only great nation who has saved hundreds of thousands of Jewish lives."[38] During the War he repeatedly expressed his belief in the equality enjoyed by Soviet Jews under the Soviet regime. In a letter to Judge Proskauer of the American Jewish Committee, urging him to lend a hand to the JCRWR, Einstein emphasized the humane and Jewish obligation to assist Soviet Russia and wrote that: ". . . . As Americans and more so as Jews, we have the very strongest reasons for giving our utmost to the struggle of the Russian People . . ."[39]

Einstein's stand on the Erlich-Alter affair was perhaps typical of the contradictions inherent in his attitude to Russia. Although he was among the signatories of appeals demanding their release, he refused to join the ranks of the critics when Erlich's and Alter's execution became a known fact. Though he condemned the murder, he warned against the misuse of the anti-Soviet campaign and the possible damage to the wartime alliance.[40] Einstein agreed to lend his name to both the Writers' Committee and the JCRWR. He rarely participated in any public event, and his greetings usually assumed the form of a letter or a telephone call, but those bodies (as well as their Soviet counterparts such as the JAC) were extremely eager to publicize their contacts with the world-famous Jewish scientist. Thus, for example, the Moscow *Eynikayt* boasted that " . . . He [Einstein] maintains close contacts with the Jewish Antifascist Committee."[41] Einstein did actually meet three prominent members of the JAC during and after the War. In his message to the gala meeting for Mikhoels and Fefer, Einstein pointed out the need "to preserve and cherish the solidarity of the Jewish people." Mikhoels and Fefer visited Einstein in Princeton. Since the two Soviet guests could by no means express themselves freely on antisemitism in the USSR, it remained for Einstein to remark somewhat skeptically, that the USSR was no exception to the rule that "wherever there is a Jew there must be antisemitism . . ." We do know that Mikhoels at least was very impressed by the encounter, and especially by Einstein's remark about antisemitism. As for Einstein himself, he expressed his appreciation in a message to the JAC representatives in which he stated: "You have strengthened our link with our Jewish brethren in the Soviet Union . . . and, therefore, also contributed to the creation of a favorable atmosphere for loyal cooperation between Russia and America." In a birthday greeting to the great scientist, Mikhoels and Fefer, wrote: " . . . We heartily greet the great son of our people . . ."[42] In the spring of 1946, Einstein met Ehrenburg; the two shared a profound hatred of Fascism and Nazism. Einstein seemed to believe that postwar cooperation between Russia and the West could still be possible. Ehrenburg showed Einstein some of the Black Book materials on Nazi atrocities against Jews which he and the JAC had been collecting. Einstein was still quite optimistic in regard to Russia and told his guest " . . ., I believe in Russia . . . He [Stalin] commands respect not only as a politician, but also as a man of high moral integrity."[43]

In spite of the increasing 'Cold War' atmosphere, Einstein continued to believe in the possibility and the necessity of cooperation between the West and Soviet Russia. He attempted, for example, to involve the Russians in his plan for a "World Government" and the elimination of the nuclear threat. He was rebuffed by Soviet scientists in the fall of 1947, but agreed to support the Soviet-sponsored Peace Movement and to send his greetings to the Peace Congress in Poland. At least one of his considerations was the necessity, as he saw it, to continue the contacts with Soviet Jewry established during the War. At one of the postwar conferences of the JCRWR, Einstein spoke of the necessity to "maintain comradeship between American and Russian branches of Jewry," and as late as the fall of 1948, he still believed that "it is of great importance for Jewry that the principle of mutual assistance be kept alive regardless of political antagonism existing in the non-Jewish world."[44]

The Black Book episode was symptomatic of Einstein's continuing hope for cooperation with the USSR and future contacts with Soviet Jews, in spite of antagonistic Soviet stands. As Honorary Chairman of the Black Book Committee, he was supposed to write the introduction to the book. However, the strongly Jewish nationalist tone of his preface was not to the liking of the Soviets. Einstein wrote in his preface of the particularity of the Jewish fate during the War, concluding that Jews should be compensated as a nation by being granted "a secure home in their ancient Palestinian country." Goldberg, who was in Moscow at that time, cabled Brainin in New York repeating what he had heard from the JAC leadership: Einstein's preface was "absolutely unacceptable." The Writers' Committee was not successful in its attempts to have Einstein rewrite it, and it was omitted from the book.[45] Einstein resigned from his membership on the Writers' Committee in September 1948, claiming that the Committee was becoming an ordinary "Jewish party organization."[46]

Mikhoels and Fefer in America

The Jewish Antifascist Committee stated clearly in its appeals that its prime aim was to create public opinion favorable to the USSR within Jewish communities in the West, particularly in the U.S. The visit of Mikhoels and Fefer to major centers of Jewish population during the second half of 1943, with its overwhelming emphasis on the U.S., was an expression of these intentions.[47] It aimed at mobilizing all possible shades of Jewish public opinion. *Eynikayt* wrote in a typical editorial: "It is utterly necessary that. . . every Jew. . . regardless of his stand, do all that is possible [for the Soviet Union]."[48] Behind this officially defined purpose, more complex aspects of the mission were to emerge in time. Soviet propaganda objectives in regard to the Mikhoels-Fefer visit to the U.S. and elsewhere were clearly defined; but some of its results and ramifications were apparently not anticipated. The encounter between these two Soviet-Jewish personalities, and the Jews in the West at that particular time, must have made a lasting impression on both sides. As we shall see, it also shaped to some extent future Soviet attitudes towards Jews.

Why did the Soviet Union plan the mission for that particular time? We can only guess at the motives, and at the general Soviet calculations and specifically Jewish considerations. Criticism of Soviet behavior had been voiced in March 1943 by the U.S. Ambassador in Moscow. In April, Soviet-Polish diplomatic relations were broken off with negative repercussions in the West, especially among Americans of Polish origin. A number of moves, aimed at placating Allied public opinion were initiated by the Soviet Union. Litvinov and the Soviet press praised the American Lend-Lease program. Soviet 1943 May Day slogans explicitly stressed the special relationship between the USSR and the Allies, and toward the end of the month, Moscow announced the closing of the Comintern. As far as Jewish public opinion in the West was concerned, it was obvious that the disillusionment caused by the Molotov-Ribbentrop agreement had not been dispelled. Jewish organizations were also involved in the "Polish question," since the fate of numerous Polish-Jewish refugees inside Russia would be influenced by its final outcome. Plans for an American-Jewish Conference, a representative organization of American Jewry which the Soviets hoped to influence, were also made around that time.

However, the specific reason for the timing of the mission was an urgent Soviet need to counter the highly critical reactions to the execution of Erlich and Alter. The execution was formally acknowledged by the USSR only in February 1943 and this sparked off an anti-Soviet campaign in Jewish circles, both in England and in the U.S. The strongest criticism emanated naturally from Jewish socialist circles, with the *Forward* as chief mouthpiece. In the course of discussions held at the JAC during the latter part of February, the need for more extensive foreign propaganda, was mentioned.[49] Although no word of the Erlich-Alter Affair ever appeared in Soviet media, criticism of "disruptive elements" within U.S. Jewry was from then on an integral part of Soviet propaganda meant for Jewish consumption abroad.[50] The first official Soviet steps regarding the Mikhoels-Fefer visit were taken in April, and the two left Moscow in early May 1943.[51] The importance attached to the mission can be inferred from the fact that they were instructed by Molotov himself on the eve of their departure and that Stalin with Kalinin came to bid them farewell and wish them success.[52]

Another significant question concerning the Mikhoels-Fefer visit was: how were various American-Jewish organizations involved in this Soviet propaganda initiative launched via the JAC? Bittelman, a leading American-Jewish communist related that "when the call for help.-. . came to us in America from the Jewish Antifascist Committee in Kuibyshev. . . the larger American-Jewish forces wavered and hesitated. Then, the Jewish antifascists, and among them, naturally, the Communists, convinced the Jewish organizations to which they belonged to take it upon themselves to answer the call. As a result, a number of unity movements got under way. For example, the Committee of Jewish Writers and Artists, the Jewish Council for Russian War Relief . . ."[53] According to an official JAC statement: "They [the JAC] were asked in early 1943 by the Committee of Jewish Writers and Scientists to send Mikhoels and Fefer to the U.S. to assist the Committee in its work."[54] According to B. Z. Goldberg, the idea of the delegation originated in the Soviet Union and was suggested to the JCRWR and to the Writers' Committee by Reuben Saltzman, the communist Secretary of IWO's Jewish Section. It was Saltzman according to Goldberg, who was representing Soviet interests. Though different suggestions were made in the U.S. as to who the representatives of Soviet Jewry should be, Saltzman made it abundantly clear that it would be either those suggested by the Soviets (i.e. Mikhoels and Fefer) or nobody.[55]

The official invitation was issued jointly by the JCRWR, and the Writers' Committee and both organized a National Reception Committee. The World Jewish Congress and Dr. Nahum Goldmann in particular were also instrumental in turning the visit into a success. Goldmann, diplomat par excellence of the WJC, discussed the Mikhoels-Fefer visit with U.S. State Department officials and briefed them on the subject. Goldmann's Soviet-oriented diplomacy became apparent at that time. He must have considered the Mikhoels-Fefer mission as a promising opener for a new era in the relations between world Jewry and the USSR, which would pay off, especially after the War. At the same time he wanted to dissociate the Soviet-Jewish delegates from American-Jewish communist groups and organizations. In order to create as much Soviet goodwill as possible, Goldmann adopted an explicitly pro-Soviet stand on the Erlich-Alter affair. In a memo on his meeting with the Head of the State Department's Russian

Division he wrote: "I also told him of our condition [for the Mikhoels-Fefer visit] that the Alter-Erlich murders be kept off the agenda."[56] The Reception Committee for Mikhoels and Fefer, which represented a wide spectrum of the Jewish community in the U.S., was headed by Albert Einstein. Members included such openly communist personalities as Reuben Saltzman and Ben Gold; fellow-travelers such as Corliss Lamont and B. Z. Goldberg; J. N. Rosenberg of the JDC; and Louis Levine of the Jewish Council of the Russian War Relief. Sholem Asch, Lion Feuchtwanger, Max Reinhardt, Lillian Hellman and Paul Muni represented Literature and the Arts; Wise and Goldmann represented the World Jewish Congress; Tamar de Sola Pool—Hadassah; Dr. Israel Goldstein—the Jewish National Fund, Louis Levinthal—the Zionist Organization of America, Henry Monsky—B'nai B'rith; and Rabbi Joseph Lookstein—the Zionist Mizrachi organization. Besides Jewish socialist elements such as the Jewish Labor Committee, the Bund and the *Forward,* all openly critical of the visit, other bodies such as the American-Jewish Committee refused to join the Reception Committee, arguing that they did not wish to appear on the same platform as such outspoken fellow-travelers as B. Z. Goldberg. There was also confusion on the local Jewish level as to the attitude to the Mikhoels-Fefer mission.

Mikhoels and Fefer arrived in the U.S. in mid-June 1943 and immediately commenced a series of public appearances. They were, of course, feted at official receptions by the Soviet Embassy in Washington and the Soviet Consulate General in New York (where, strictly kosher food was served). On June 22, the second anniversary of Germany's attack on the USSR, Mikhoels and Fefer issued an appeal to American Jewry, worded in strongly Jewish terms. The appeal to "brother Jews" became the main slogan of the mission. Another theme which was to be reiterated often was that of the Soviet Union as savior of Eastern European Jewry.[57] On July 4th, Mikhoels and Fefer, introduced by Helen Hayes, spoke over a nationwide Columbia network hookup of "We the People." During their stay in New York, the two men had several meetings with representatives of the World Jewish Congress and the JDC. They also visited Einstein and met Dr. Chaim Weizmann, President of the World Zionist Organization. Israel Meriminski [later Merom], a representative of the Histadrut Labor Union met with Mikhoels and invited Mikhoels and Fefer to visit the Yishuv on their way back to Russia.[58] A particularly moving encounter was that with Marc Chagall, who had once worked with Mikhoels. It was

not uncommon for Jewish intellectuals and artists of Russian background such as Chagall to re-identify strongly with their "old country,"
especially during the war years.[59] Together with B. Z. Goldberg and his
wife, Mikhoels and Fefer made a pilgrimage to the grave of Shalom
Aleichem.

The most impressive public event of the Mikhoels-Fefer visit was the
Polo Grounds mass rally of July 8th, attended by nearly 50,000 people.
The prevailing mood of that meeting reflected both enthusiasm for the
Allies and for Jewish national aspirations. The stadium was decorated
with American, Soviet and blue and white flags. Mikhoels and Fefer
spoke in Yiddish. The main theme of their speeches was unity among
the Allies and the urgent need to support Soviet Russia. They pointed
out time and again that the Soviet Union had saved Jews from sure
death, not only in Eastern Europe but in the Near East as well. The
implications were clear: any Jew, wherever he was, should regard himself as potentially saved and defended by the USSR. Similar views
were voiced by other speakers. Some speakers denounced American
critics of the Mikhoels-Fefer mission and Wise attacked the "Jewish
Trotskyites." Goldmann told the crowd that, despite of intimidations
and warnings, he had decided to speak out in favor of Mikhoels and
Fefer. Sholem Asch praised the USSR for being the first state to
destroy antisemitism, and J. N. Rosenberg claimed that "Russia has
given life, asylum, bread and shelter to a vast Jewish population." B. Z.
Goldberg spoke of "the great leader Marshal Stalin."[60] To conclude
the rally Paul Robeson sang Russian and Yiddish songs. The Polo
Grounds rally was considered a success by both local American organizers and the Moscow bosses of the JAC. *Pravda* carried reports on
the event in two successive issues, quoting Goldmann's assertion at the
rally that the visit would consolidate ties between Soviet and world
Jewry. The newspaper pointed out that the most powerful American-
Jewish organizations had been represented at the meeting, and that it
had been the most impressive pro-Soviet mass event ever in America.
In honor of that occasion *Eynikayt* featured a special appeal to U.S.
Jews, describing the Mikhoels-Fefer visit as a solidarity mission. The
necessity of establishing close contacts between the two largest Jewish
communities was also clearly stated.[61] A tet a tete encounter between
Mikhoels, Fefer and IKUF activists took place at Rappoport's restau-
rant on the Lower East Side, with the participation of such outspoken
Jewish communists as P. Novick and M. Katz. Mikhoels' and Fefer's
speeches on that occasion were of a distinctly national-Jewish flavor.[62]

Besides New York, Mikhoels and Fefer visited Philadelphia, Chicago, Pittsburgh, Detroit, Boston and other cities. Mass rallies were held in Los Angeles and San Francisco. While in Hollywood, they met with Thomas Mann, Lion Feuchtwanger, Theododre Dreiser, Upton Sinclair, Charlie Chaplin, and Edward G. Robinson. They also met Julian Tuwim, the outstanding Polish poet of Jewish origin, who had expressed his wartime national identity in his famous essay "We Polish Jews." Thought their mission was primarily of Jewish content, Mikhoels and Fefer appeared at non-Jewish gatherings as well. Meetings with American intellectuals and artists were arranged both on the East and West Coasts. There were also some encounters with Slav and Black groups.

In spite of their popularity and the highly emotional welcome they received from American Jews, there were also criticism and protest. The critics came from the Jewish Labor movement and such organizations as the Jewish Labor Committee, the Jewish Workmen's Circle and the Bund. Their chief mouthpiece was the *Forward,* a paper closely aligned with the Jewish Labor movement and the most popular Jewish daily in America. In the 1940's it constituted an influential force within American Jewry, primarily in the Eastern European immigrant population. Although the *Forward* was published in New York, its organizational network and influence extended into most major centers of Jewish population in the U.S. The Editor and guiding spirit of the newspaper, Abe Cahan, has been described as a man of "a highly personal intelligence and a rather grim and acrid temperament."[63] Though originally an enthusiastic supporter of the Bolshevik experiment, Cahan became disillusioned with the Soviet regime in the early twenties and thereafter was a consistent and unsparing critic of Stalinist Russia. He condemned the Purges of the 1930's, the Nazi-Soviet rapprochement of 1939 and the execution of Erlich and Alter, (they had been appointed *Forward* correspondents in the USSR shortly before their re-arrest and execution). In his treatment of the Mikhoels-Fefer visit, Cahan was faithful to his dictum that "one should not deal with the Soviets, one should ignore and condemn them." Cahan was supported in this campaign by his loyal assistants on the *Forward* staff Hillel Rogoff and Ben Zion Hoffman (Tsivion). Cahan vehemently attacked the choice of Fefer when he first heard of the planned mission. A few days after Mikhoels and Fefer arrived, the *Forward* attacked them again. This time Rogoff, quoted Fefer's poem written in the early 1930's, in which American Jews were described as "well-fed slaves." Mikhoels and Fefer were also accused of promoting a fake solidarity between American and Soviet Jews. Rogoff's article was subsequently translated into English and distributed throughout the U.S. Tsivion, in one of his articles, condemned the "Zionist diplomacy" of Wise and Goldmann, describing their behavior sarcastically as that of "di tsionistishe unterfirershaft oyf der komunistisher khasene" . . . (the Zionist best men at the communist wedding).[64]

The relations between the Soviet-Jewish guests and Yiddish literary circles in New York were also strained. While Asch supported the mission, others such as Leivick, Niger and Glatstein refused to be exploited publicly, for Soviet propaganda. Leivick proposed a meeting of the Yiddish Section of the PEN Club without the participation of local pro-Soviet elements. This was of course rejected by the Soviet guests, and the resentment and bitterness especially on Fefer's part, resulted in what was to become known as the Fefer-Leivick affair.[65] The Labor Zionists, were perhaps the only Zionist group in the U.S. to criticize the mission. Their organ, *Der Idisher Kemfer* edited by Chaim Greenberg, published a number of critical articles on Mikhoels, Fefer and the Soviet Union.[66] Polish officials in the U.S. also made efforts to influence Jewish public opinion in the U.S. and to reduce support for the Soviet-Jewish emissaries, citing the Erlich-Alter affair as a major anti-Soviet argument.[67] Mikhoels and Fefer visited Mexico City, then the center of pro-Soviet wartime propaganda in Central America, for a few days in mid-August. Mexican-Jewish organizations and personalities participated in the various Aid to Russia activities there.

A "Jewish Committee to Aid War Victims in the USSR" was formed in Mexico City as early as the Fall of 1941. It was headed by Mordechai (Marcos) Corona, businessman, writer and journalist with Labor-Zionist affiliations. Since, at that time, there was no Soviet legation in Mexico (Soviet-Mexican relations were reestablished only in 1943), Corona and his organization maintained contacts with Litvinov and the Soviet Embassy in Washington.[68] The main purpose of the Jewish-Committee which changed its name to "The League for the Soviet Union" in mid 1942 was to collect funds and goods. In time, it also started to disseminate pro-Soviet literature. The real boost to the League's activities was provided by the arrival of Konstantin Umanskii who was appointed Soviet Ambassador to Mexico in June 1943. Umanskii, himself of Jewish origin, became prominent in Soviet journalism and foreign affairs in the 1930's. At the age of 37, in 1939 he was appointed USSR Ambassador to the U.S., serving in that capacity until 1941, during a most difficult period for Soviet diplomacy. He was known for his wide erudition and fluency in languages. Umanskii was at home in Soviet literary and artistic circles and knew Mikhoels personally. During the War he proved to be a valuable asset to Soviet propaganda and maintained close relations with the various pro-Soviet campaigns and organizations in Central America. It was only natural therefore, that as a Soviet representative and as a Jew he should be intensively involved in the activities of the Jewish "League." Its head, Corona, now became a frequent guest of the Soviet diplomat, briefing him on general and local Jewish affairs, and consulting him. Umanskii seemed to be interested in the intricacies of the Zionist Movement and particularly in its various factions. Corona kept the Soviet diplomat continuously posted on the activities of his League and on local Jewish responses.[69]

Corona and Umanskii were the initiators of Mikhoels' and Fefer's visit to Mexico City. The details were worked out with the Soviet Embassy in Washington, and a Reception Committee was formed with Corona as Secretary. It consisted of both Mexican and Jewish community leaders. The League, like numerous other pro-Soviet fronts used "unity" tactics to mobilize the widest possible support within the Mexican Jewish community. Corona and Umanskii, seeking support among Zionist-oriented Jews, agreed for example that blue and white flags should be displayed at the airport during the arrival of the JAC representatives. Umanskii also suggested explicitly that the chief Rabbi of Mexico City's community and local Zionist leaders be actively involved in the visit.[70]

A significant event of the Mikhoels-Fefer mission to Mexico was a conference held by the local Central Jewish Committee. The guests, accompanied by Soviet Embassy officials and by Marcos Corona, were asked numerous questions on future contacts between Soviet and World Jewry, on Soviet attitudes toward Zionism and Palestine and on the functions of the Jewish Antifascist Committee inside the USSR. Mikhoels and Fefer were reluctant to discuss matters of high Soviet policy on Zionism and Jewish affairs. They stressed time and again the immediate wartime objectives of their mission. At the same time they made efforts not to antagonize Zionist-inclined Jews and to encourage future hope in that direction. The emphasis on the War needs of the USSR, according to Mikhoels, "does not mean that we have a negative attitude toward Zionism: On this question we have arrived at a complete understanding with Dr. Weizmann, Goldmann and Stephen

Wise. We do not talk about Zionism, but that does not mean that we take a stand against it." When Mikhoels was asked about the possibility of Jews in the USSR collaborating with Nazi Germany, [an allusion to Soviet accusations against Erlich and Alter] his reply was: " . . . With regard to [Jewish] refugees [in] Russia, there were certain individuals who, by their attitude, helped Nazism."[71] At the same time, both in public and closed meetings with Jews, Mikhoels stressed that the mission was not only a Soviet, but also a Jewish one. He told the Jewish Committee of Mexico: "We struggle in the battlefields as citizens of our country *and* as sons of the Jewish People." On another occasion, when speaking about the Jewish victims of Nazism, he expressed his belief that though the Jewish People had suffered immensely, it "would never die."[72] Since as a rule, the JAC's emphasis on national Jewish themes was more explicit abroad than at home, when Mikhoels and Fefer published an account of their visit to Mexico shortly after their return to Russia, the Jewish aspect was hardly mentioned.[73] Contacts between the Mexican Jewish League and the JAC were intensified as a result of the visit, and, at one point, Mikhoels even invited Corona to visit the USSR. The amount of information and propaganda material sent by the JAC and disseminated by the League in Mexico grew considerably. Just before their departure from the U.S. in early September 1943, Mikhoels and Fefer accompanied by Sholem Asch spent a few days in Canada.

The Mikhoels-Fefer mission to the Jews of the U.S., Mexico and Canada was a success. They reached various and divergent sectors of the Jewish public and numerous arbiters of Jewish public opinion. The encounter generated intensive feelings of national identity on the part of the hosts as well as of the visitors. Rabbi Israel Goldstein, in his farewell message to Mikhoels and Fefer assured them that their visit has occurred "on the crest of a high tide of goodwill to Soviet Russia." Another eye witness of the visit described it years later as "a sensational success."[74]

On their way back to Russia Mikhoels and Fefer spent a few weeks in England. Their visit there was sponsored by the Jewish Fund for Soviet Russia, affiliated with the Red Cross Aid to Russia Fund headed by Mrs. Churchill. The Jewish Fund like other pro-Soviet Jewish organizations had a politically mixed leadership. Although it consisted of such Jewish Communists as Prof. Hyman Levi and Alec Waterman, it was headed by Redcliffe N. Salaman, a scientist active in Jewish public affairs and a supporter of Zionism, by Lord Nathan and by the liberal Yiddish-oriented author and editor Joseph Leftwich. The Fund and its predecessors maintained contacts with the Jewish Antifascist Committee in the USSR and with Soviet diplomats in England. The messages delivered by Mikhoels and Fefer to British Jewry were similar to those voiced in the U.S. Besides open public events, Mikhoels and Fefer met in closed meetings with representatives of the Board of Deputies and with officials of the British Section of the World Jewish Congress. There were also unofficial conferences with the members of the CP Jewish Committee, during which the Soviet guests discussed such sensitive issues as the Erlich-Alter affair and the future of Palestine. A special concern of the two was the dissemination of materials sent by the JAC. Discussing the Jewish Antifascist Committee Mikhoels and Fefer underlined its significance for Soviet Jewry. They mentioned its impressive roster of members and pointed out that it was the central Jewish structure in their country and enjoyed a good rapport with the Soviet authorities. Similar views were voiced during a meeting with the Board of Deputies at which Mikhoels stated: "We speak to you as the representatives of the Jewish community of our country . . . we hope to establish a close and lasting cooperation with you."[75]

Mikhoels and Fefer returned to Moscow in early December 1943. An *Eynikayt* editorial summed up their visit abroad as a great success. It was praised for its impact on Jewish and general public opinion and on influential Jewish organizations. It was concluded that, following the Mikhoels-Fefer mission "the Committee [the JAC] became a [more] significant factor." Epshteyn, the JAC Secretary wrote: "The visit of our representatives [abroad] is a turning point in the Committee's activities."[76] As regards personal reactions, Mikhoels and Fefer had been overwhelmed by the dimensions and realities of a new world. "Like two paratroopers we landed in an unfamiliar world,"—Fefer explained after returning to Russia.[77] For many months both Mikhoels and Fefer repeated their impressions, both in public and in private. Mikhoels was overwhelmed by the expressions of Jewish unity and identification and described at length Jews and Jewish life in America.[78] Almost a year after the visit Fefer wrote to B. Z. Goldberg: "We are constantly talking about America."[79]

Mikhoels and Fefer delivered a number of official reports. A meeting with JAC members took place within a few days of their return. Another meeting was held at the Soviet Writers Union in early January 1944. Interest in what the two had to say must have been considerable, since, besides the Soviet-Yiddish writers, such writers as Fadeev, Tolstoy, Fedin, Marshak, Ehrenburg and Aliger were present at the meeting. The speakers presented their impressions of U.S. art and literature, mentioning their personal encounters with Einstein and Chagall. A differentiation was clearly made between the "good" and "bad" elements. Such pro-Soviet, American-Jewish organizations as the JCRWR and particularly the Committee of Jewish Writers were highly praised. At the same time, however, Mikhoels remarked that "the Americans were infected with racialism, made a cult of machinery and were not very far removed from Hitlerite ideas."[80] A few days later Fefer spoke at the JAC to an audience of writers, artists and soldiers about Jewish life abroad. Two accounts of the Mikhoels-Fefer mission were published in February in a central Soviet propaganda publication dealing with foreign affairs. It was perhaps significant that the Jewish aspect of the visit was hardly mentioned there. The U.S. was described in black and white. Progressive, pro-Soviet elements in the U.S. were juxtaposed with reactionary and anti-Soviet ones.[81] The Mikhoels-Fefer mission was a main topic of the speeches and reports presented during the meeting organized by the Committee in Moscow in April 1944 and during the discussions of the third plenary session of the JAC which followed. At the same time, an exhibit on the visit was displayed at the JAC offices. In the Moscow Hall of Columns Mikhoels delivered a lecture on "America in our Time," which evoked great public interest. A U.S. Embassy official reported that it was a "mixture of admiration and ridicule" and that the public reacted mainly to the positive points of the presentation.[82]

The World Jewish Congress and the JDC

While in the U.S. Mikhoels and Fefer met with representatives of various Jewish organizations. In the course of the contacts between these organizations and the JAC, it had become apparent that, despite of certain mutual interests, far-reaching differences existed regarding the nature of the cooperation and its objectives. A case in point was the relationships between the JAC and the World Jewish Congress (WJC) and the American Jewish Joint Distribution Committee (JDC).

At that time, the basic policies of the WJC were formulated by its President Dr. Stephen Wise and by Dr. Nahum Goldmann, Chairman of its Executive Board. Wise, an outstanding Zionist, who headed the

ZOA throughout the 1920's and 1930's, was also an American liberal. He was among the first American public figures to speak out against Fascism and Nazism. As for his attitudes toward the USSR and Soviet-Jewish policies, Wise seemed to grasp the seeming contradiction between early Soviet opposition to antisemitism and the gradual stifling of Jewish culture in Soviet Russia. His attitude was that of a pragmatist. He was among the supporters of diplomatic relations between the U.S. and Soviet Russia, his argument being that this was the only way to gain access to the country and to its society. His stand on Jewish-Soviet contacts was apparently similar. As early as 1936 Wise expressed his hopes for the participation of Soviet Jews in the World Jewish Congress and nourished the idea of influencing USSR Jewish policies.[83] Like many other Jewish leaders, he considered the outbreak of the Nazi-Soviet war an opportunity for improving relations with Soviet Russia. In a letter written shortly after Germany's attack on the USSR, Wise stated ". . . Weizmann and I have planned to see whether we cannot get a change in the attitude of the Soviet regime to Zionists."[84] Insight into Wise's attitude vis-à-vis the Soviet Union can be gained from his reply to Menahem Boraisha's criticism of Wise's Soviet-oriented policy. Boraisha, a pro-Soviet Yiddish poet and essayist, who visited the USSR in the 1920's, but broke with the Communists in 1929, accused Wise of lending his name to the Mikhoels-Fefer "hullabaloo." Wise in a personal note to Boraisha, explained that he had publicly supported the JAC delegates ". . . for purely political reasons, namely in the hope of getting Soviet help after the War, both for Palestine and the Diaspora . . ."[85] Wise maintained friendly contacts with pro-Soviet publications in the U.S., such as the *New Masses* and *Soviet Russia Today*. As late as 1946 he wrote: "I think I am a liberal . . . incapable of injustice to the Soviet Union."[86] It seems that Wise, like Einstein and other American liberal intellectuals, dreaded a postwar American-Soviet confrontation.[87] It was apparently his strong anti-Nazi commitment and his hopes for future Soviet assistance in Jewish matters that moved Wise to participate in various pro-Soviet activities during the War.

Most of the diplomatic attempts of the WJC vis-à-vis the Soviet Union were directed by Nahum Goldmann. In the early 1940's, he was already optimistic about the possibility of Soviet support for a Jewish political entity in Palestine. He also maintained that in order to establish contacts with Soviet Jews all avenues should be explored. During a press conference in 1944 Goldmann stated that "Though an official stand of the Soviet Government on Zionism does not exist yet, one should hope that it would be a favorable one (in the future)."[88] Even before the outbreak of Nazi-Soviet hostilities, Goldmann and Wise met with Umanskii, then Soviet Ambassador to the U.S., and raised the question of Jewish immigration to Palestine from the territories newly annexed by the USSR. The possibility of appointing a WJC representative in the USSR was also mentioned on that occasion.[89] Dr. Maurice Perlzweig, another WJC specialist on foreign relations, met with Umanskii less than a month after the Nazi attack on Russia, to discuss such issues as relief for Jewish refugees in the USSR, emigration, release of imprisoned Jews, and the future of Palestine. Soviet trends in regard to Jews and Jewish public opinion were clearly revealed by Umanskii's remark that he was in possession of a "thick file" on Jewish, anti-Soviet propaganda. Umanskii made it quite clear on that occasion that the Soviet Union would be willing to reward the Jews in the future in return for favorable attitudes towards Soviet policies and stands during the War.[90] In September 1941, a WJC memo was presented to Umanskii, in which the release of Jews imprisoned in the USSR was requested.[91] There was a subsequent meeting between Goldmann and Litvinov, who replaced Umanskii; and when Andrei Gromyko succeeded Litvinov as Soviet Ambassador to the U.S. in 1943, these contacts continued.

Whereas matters of high policy were discussed with Soviet diplomats, WJC efforts to establish and maintain contacts with Soviet Jewry were primarily directed towards the JAC. It was only natural, therefore, that the Mikhoels-Fefer mission raised high hopes for the future. Goldmann, himself a leading member of the "National Welcome Committee," in the U.S. was personally involved in smoothing out problems surrounding this visit. He also prodded the American-Jewish leadership into organizing a most impressive welcome for them. Both Goldmann and Wise were among the chief speakers at the Polo Grounds mass rally, and sharply criticized those American Jewish elements hostile to the JAC delegation. Goldmann linked Zionism and Russia distinctly by stating that ". . . I am here . . . not despite my being a Zionist . . . but because I am a Zionist."[92] Goldmann's contribution to the shaping of pro-Soviet Jewish public opinion in the West was highly appreciated by the Soviets. Thus, he was praised by Mikhoels and Fefer at a meeting with Jewish communists in England and at the April 1944 JAC meeting in Moscow.[93] Mikhoels and Fefer met WJC officials a number of times in New York. In a follow-up memo to these meetings, drafted on the eve of Mikhoels' and Fefer's departure, some of the questions previously discussed were raised: i.e. the possibility that the JAC act as a go-between with Soviet authorities; information on and relief for Jewish war refugees in the USSR; the emigration of some Jewish refugees from Russia; and Jewish POW's in Hungarian units taken prisoners by the Soviets. As far as relief for Jews was concerned, Mikhoels and Fefer were always very careful not to make any commitments and stressed the Soviet Union's nonsectarian principle on foreign assistance to Soviet population. On other issues they made no comment but merely listened. The WJC memo concluded: ". . . allow us to underline . . . how strongly we are interested in reserving future contacts with you and with the whole of Soviet Jewry."[94] Although the JAC could hardly be helpful in most of the requests presented by the WJC, it did, for example, send out partial lists of Jewish survivors in the liberated territories in the Western parts of the USSR.

Symptomatic of the relationship between the WJC and the JAC were attempts on the part of the Congress to establish permanent and meaningful contacts between the two organizations. One of the earliest attempts took place in September-October 1941 when the WJC tried to appoint Alex Easterman, a prominent British Jewish journalist, to be its semi-official representative in Moscow.[95] The tasks assigned to Easterman were "relief for Jews in the USSR; the release of imprisoned Zionists and permission for a WJC mission to the Soviet Union."[96] The WJC also attempted to appoint, as its representatives in the USSR, individuals who were officially employed by the Polish Embassy in Russia. These attempts came to an end when Soviet-Polish relations were broken off in the Spring of 1943. The WJC also tried to involve the JAC in plans for the rehabilitation of European Jewry. The most tangible attempt was the repeated invitation to Soviet-Jewish delegates to participate in WJC conferences. From December 1943, a number of invitations were extended to the JAC to participate in the Emergency Conference of the WJC, planned for 1944. At the same time, overtures were made to official Soviet representatives. Goldmann met with Gromyko, Soviet Ambassador to the U.S. in early January 1944 and reported that "he [Gromyko] thought that chances of delegates (to the WJC Conference) coming from Moscow were good . . ." Gromyko seemed to be very interested in assessing the "representative power" of the delegations from various countries. Goldmann's remark that representation at WJC conferences was not directly proportional to the Jewish population of a given country, and that if it had been so, "the Russian delegation would swallow the whole conference," obviously displeased the Soviet diplomat.[97] The JAC and its leaders were always extremely careful not to commit themselves in regard to their Committee's cooperation with the WJC. When Mikhoels was asked in London, in November 1943 about the possibility that his Committee would join the Congress, he answered that this was a tactical question to be decided in Moscow. When a spokesman for the WJC announced that Congress representatives were to participate in the JAC April 1944 meeting the JAC replied: "We do not know what conference their delegates propose to attend in the Soviet Union," and added: "The statement by the WJC British Section on the establishment of direct contact with the Jewish public in the Soviet Union has caused astonishment here."[98] JAC messages throughout 1944 indicated that, although Soviet attitudes to the WJC were unchanged, no clearcut decision had been taken on the question of direct Soviet-Jewish participation in WJC activities. Early in May 1944, the JAC notified the WJC that due to tasks connected with the liberation of Western Soviet territories, JAC representatives would not be able to participate in the planned WJC Emergency Conference. At the same time, the JAC Presidium expressed its hope that the collaboration between the two organizations would continue in postwar years.[99] In early September 1944 a JAC cable again requested details on the participants and the agenda of the conference. Later that month the WJC was finally notified that JAC delegates would not participate in the WJC Emergency Conference which, after a delay, finally took place in Atlantic City in the fall of 1944.[100] The next phase in the efforts of the WJC came before its 1945 European Conference in London. Y. Rosenberg, who was officially affiliated with the Czechoslovak Government in Exile, and was at the same time a WJC man, met with Fefer and Epshteyn in Moscow in December 1944 and cabled London that "they [the JAC] agreed to attend the conference on European Jewry." At further discussions with the JAC's Secretary Epshteyn in early January 1945, the JAC declared that its participation was conditional on a "fifty-fifty" formula: Epshteyn insisted that the number of Soviet delegates, and their representatives on all WJC bodies, should equal that of all the other organizations together. The JAC should also participate in drafting the conference agenda.[101] These negotiations ended with no tangible results.

Another major Jewish organization which maintained contacts with the USSR and the JAC during the War was the JDC, a traditional supporter of East European Jewry. The JDC had its representative in Russia during World War I and continued to extend help to Russian Jews after 1917, by special agreement with the Soviet government. It was active in the USSR through the Agro-Joint, which sponsored Jewish agricultural ventures and vocational training for Jewish youth. These activities, which reached their peak during the 1920's, became superfluous in the 1930's. The limitation of JDC activities and the final departure of its representative from Russia were also influenced by the political events of the latter part of the decade. Prevailing attitudes towards the Soviet Union in JDC circles remained favorable. An historian of the JDC stated that its leaders "were mostly men of rather limited social and political vision" and that there was an element of romanticism for some of the wealthy American Jews in transforming the Eastern European ghetto Jew into a peasant farmer.[102]

Some JDC philanthropists considered Russia a possible refuge for Jews of other Eastern European countries, particularly refugees from Polish anti-Semitism. James N. Rosenberg was a typical proponent of such sentiments. A wealthy lawyer and amateur painter from Pennsylvania, he was active in organizing and supervising JDC assistance to Eastern European Jewry following the First World War. He developed a deep commitment to the poor Jewish population of the region. In 1926, he visited Jewish Agro-Joint colonies in Soviet Russia, and wrote: "If we fail these Jews [of Russia] it will be a collapse of dreadful significance."[103] The visit itself was a "thrilling experience" for him, especially since he was received by Soviet dignitaries such as Vice-President Smidovich. It was only natural therefore that Rosenberg emerged as the main spokesman for Soviet-oriented policies within the JDC when the USSR became America's war ally. Like Dr. Goldmann, Rosenberg, foresaw decisive Russian influence on postwar arrangements. Rosenberg often stated that the only country which had behaved decently to Jews was the Soviet Union. He would often quote Soviet propaganda on the rescue of Jews from Nazis and on official Soviet attitudes to antisemitism. Rosenberg seriously considered the USSR, and particularly the Crimea, as a possible postwar haven for Jewish refugees from all over Europe.[104] He also pointed out his concern about competition from other Jewish agencies, which, to his mind, "had an eye on the whole field of postwar work in the USSR and the liberated countries."[105] Rosenberg's excessive pro-Soviet stand and his constant bombardment of the JDC with papers and memos to this effect worried the JDC leadership and caused concern lest "differences of opinion regarding Russian matters become a disruptive force in the top management [of the JDC]."[106]

The Mikhoels-Fefer visit to the U.S. lent impetus to Rosenberg's pro-Soviet activities. It was he who brought together the JAC representatives and JDC officials. A number of joint meetings took place in the latter part of September 1943. From the first, Mikhoels and Fefer were anxious to emphasize Soviet assistance to Jews. They pointed out that it was the USSR which had prevented Nazi Germany from occupying Palestine, and complained that Jewish institutions and public opinion in the U.S. were unappreciative of this fact. The central points of discussion emerged at the first conference: the Soviet-Jewish delegation was interested in mobilizing the JDC's economic support for Russia, and the all-Soviet, non-sectarian nature of such help was clearly indicated. The only compromise might be an arrangement whereby JDC aid would be distributed in those regions of the country where a large Jewish population had relocated during the War.[107] If an agreement were reached on this, Mikhoels and Fefer believed that the JDC would also receive permission to sent its representative to Russia. Soviet interest in re-establishing contacts with the JDC was clearly indicated by Mikhoels when he stated that "his government . . . was keenly appreciative of their (JDC) past activities, and would welcome their participation in some way both during and after the War."[108] Besides faithfully delivering the Soviet message to the JDC, Mikhoels and Fefer were also interested in impressing Soviet diplomats in the U.S. with their instrumentality in this particular instance of U.S. aid to Russia, and they must have conveyed this interest to Rosenberg. At a meeting with the participation of the Soviet Counsul General of New York and the representative of the Soviet Red Cross, Rosenberg spoke of "the great service these gentlemen had rendered" and advised that the JAC should be connected in the future, too, with any projects involving JDC help for the Soviet Union.[109] After their return to Moscow, Mikhoels and Fefer, cabled Rosenberg: "We and the JAC are ready (in) every way to cooperate with you."[110] Mikhoels and Fefer must have nourished hopes for future Soviet-JDC cooperation, at that time. A JAC report delivered at the April 1944 Moscow meeting stated: "Our (Mikhoels' and Fefer's) discussions (with the JDC) were very successful and would doubtlessly result in a more active participation of our brethren abroad in this unprecedented war, as well as in further cooperation in the postwar years."[111]

The initial amount of JDC "regional" assistance was half a million dollars, which was spent during 1944. JDC officials apparently nourished some hopes for the implementation of aid projects which would ensure maximum Jewish benefit from the goods. The Soviet stand on the question of "regional" distribution of foreign help to the Jewish population in the USSR was still flexible in early 1944, when Kisselev, Soviet Consul General in New York wrote to Louis Levine of the JCRWR ". . . we agree to your proposal that it be made possible for an organization . . . to send its supplies to a designated region . . ."[112] However, Soviet attitudes became more rigid as time went by. It also became evident that the JDC would not receive Soviet sanction for sending its representatives to supervise the distribution of its aid in specifically Jewish localities. Rosenberg continued pressuring the JDC for increased help to Russia, but JDC-Soviet relations took finally a turn for the worse in mid-1944.

Jewish responses to Soviet wartime propaganda overtures were colored by objectives and sentiments of organizations and individuals. Despite the Ribbentrop-Molotov accord, pro-Soviet attitudes lingered on within the Jewish community in the West. The image of the Soviet Union as a society which had found a solution to the perennial "Jewish problem", as Hitler's staunchest enemy, and as a saviour of Jews, generated goodwill among Jews in the U.S. and elsewhere. Jewish Communists and Jewish communist organizations and publications, like the *JPFO* and the *Morgen Freiheit* were the most outspoken supporters of the USSR. Pro-Soviet Jewish front organizations, like the Committee of Writers, presented a more complex picture. They consisted of a varied assortment of people, attitudes and objectives. Nevertheless, they were extremely useful from the Soviet point of view, since they constituted a bridge to the Jewish community as a whole. Some of their leaders, like B. Z. Goldberg, supported Soviet Russia out of a strange combination of public interests and personal motivations. Goldberg considered Russia as a world center of Jewish (Yiddish) culture and a defender of Jewish interests, but was undoubtedly also flattered by the fact that he, a Yiddish journalist from America, was regarded by officials of a world power as an important and useful ally. The Shalom Aleichem family contacts with the Soviet establishment and the special treatment accorded them by Stalin also influenced Goldberg's attitudes towards the USSR. Another set of considerations were those of some mainstream Jewish organizations such as the World Jewish Congress and the JDC. They too had their share of genuine pro-Soviet enthusiasts, like the JDC's Rosenberg; their central objectives, however, were utilitarian. Wartime circumstances and postwar prospects made cooperation with the USSR feasible and even desirable in their eyes. An outstanding proponent of this approach was the WJC's top "diplomat"—Dr. Nahum Goldmann. His objective was twofold: to mobilize Soviet support for Zionist and Jewish policies in the international arena and to initiate regular contacts between Soviet and world Jewry. The JDC's leadership was interested in extending economic assistance to the war-stricken Jews of Eastern Europe.

6

THE JEWISH YISHUV IN PALESTINE

Public opinion within the Jewish community in Palestine (the Yishuv) was ostensibly peripheral to Jewish-oriented Russian war progaganda. But the Soviets considered it a valuable instrument for transfer of pro-Soviet sentiments, particularly to Zionist-minded Jews in the U.S. The USSR-Yishuv relationship was more complex than ties with any other Jewish community in the West. It was heavily affected by Soviet attitudes and policies towards Zionism on the one hand and by Zionist reactions and expectations on the other. One should consider primarily the attitudes prevailing within the Zionist-Socialist parties in Palestine, the dominant force of the Yishuv.

Zionist-Soviet Contacts

Though Bolshevik attitudes towards Zionism remained traditionally hostile, limited Zionist activities inside the USSR, and limited emigration of Soviet Jews to Palestine had been allowed during most of the 1920's. Some Zionist-Socialist elements within the Yishuv hoped that the tougher line adopted by the Soviet regime in the 1930's, could be reversed. The attitude of the Zionist-Socialist movement as a whole, towards the Bolsheviks and the October Revolution were highly complex and ambiguous. Whereas day-to-day Bolshevik policies and tactics were increasingly criticized, the response to and the enthusiasm for the Bolshevik Revolution as an historical event were enormous. Many Zionist pioneers also felt a strong cultural affinity with the Soviet Union, because of their personal and political education. Even such a moderate socialist as David Ben Gurion is believed to have admired Lenin in the 1920's. Strong Pro-Bolshevik sentiments emerged within Gedud Ha-Avodah (The Labor Battalion—a commune of Jewish workers) and some of its members, disenchanted with the prospects for socialism in Palestine, returned to the USSR. Pro-Soviet leanings were displayed not only by small splinter groups. Hakibbutz Ha-meuhad, a significant sector within the dominant Mapai party (the Palestine Labor Party) also nurtured pro-Soviet sentiments. Yitzhak Tabenkin, chief ideologist of Hakibbutz Ha-meuhad, following the Soviet definition, considered the first stage of World War II (up to June 1941) as an "imperialist" War and justified Stalin's invasion of Finland.[1] Growing anti-British moods on the eve of the War also helped to foster pro-Soviet attitudes within Mapai. To the left of Mapai was Hashomer Hatzair, initially a Zionist-Socialist youth movement in Eastern Europe, which established a network of communal settlements (kibbutzim) in Palestine, and was transformed into a conventional political force only in the 1940's. Hashomer Hatzair tried to reconcile a strictly Marxist terminology with Zionist activity. Further left than Hashomer Hatzair was a relatively insignificant splinter group known as "the left Poalei Zion," which adhered to Marxist views. Zionists of all shades of opinion took a considerable interest in Soviet Jewry, considered by all a potential source for Jewish migration to Palestine. When the idea of a Jewish State in Palestine, started to appear feasible during the War, some Zionist leaders began to consider the USSR as a potential supporter in the international arena. Though most Zionist leaders were critical of Stalin's Russia, they tried to maintain avenues of contact. These attempts were stepped up in spite of, or perhaps due to, the Molotov-Ribbentrop Pact and its consequences. The fact that the considerable Jewish population of the territories now annexed by the USSR (including hundreds of thousands of Jewish refugees from Nazi-occupied Poland), found themselves under Soviet rule, impelled Jewish Zionist organizations to attempt to assist them. Weizmann, Wise and Goldmann met with Soviet diplomats in England and America, and a special Committee on the USSR was established at the Jewish Agency in Palestine.

Hitler's invasion of Russia in the summer of 1941 seemed to herald a new era in the relations between the Yishuv and the Soviet Union. The Soviets were interested now, perhaps more than ever before, in arousing Jewish public opinion in the West. Zionist leaders, some out of self-interest, others out of naive enthusiasm, actually expected the

Soviet Union to change its traditional attitudes toward Zionism. David Ben Gurion, had condemned the USSR shortly before the War as a "dictatorship of one man," but nevertheless considered it a significant factor in international politics, whose support for the Zionist cause in Palestine should be sought. Many years later he wrote: "Knowing the strength and value of Russia . . . I sought ways of meeting her emissaries." At the height of wartime enthusiasm for the USSR, he repeated his condemnation of the Soviet regime but at the same time stated pragmatically: "Where there is no democracy, we have one chance only: to gain the rulers' favor."[2] Some Socialist-Zionist leaders, were carried away by the prospects of genuine ideological and emotional accord between the Yishuv and the USSR. Meir Ya'ari of Hashomer Hatzair for example suggested sending Jewish physicians to Russia, and Tabenkin suggested that Jewish military units "bearing the Zionist national flag" be sent to aid the Red Army.[3]

Because of the above described motives, various Zionist attempts to influence Stalin took place during the War years. The main points of contact between Zionist politicians and Soviet diplomats were London and Washington, but meetings also took place in the Middle East. A senior Soviet diplomat, contacted by Zionist politicians was Ivan Maisky, Russia's envoy to England. He met several times with Chaim Weizmann, President of the World Zionist Organization and David Ben Gurion, Chairman of the Jewish Agency Executive. The Zionist leaders and Maisky realized that the measure of Soviet-Zionist cooperation would depend on the readiness of Zionist leaders to induce Jewish public opinion to support Soviet wartime policy objectives. Ben Gurion, at a meeting with Maisky in October 1941, pointed out that the Histadrut Labor Union in Palestine (dominated by Mapai) had good connections with the Jewish Labor movement in America. Maisky, for his part, made it clear that U.S. Jewry's support for the USSR was a central consideration of Soviet war propaganda. In a memo submitted to Maisky, Ben Gurion strongly emphasized the joint interests of the Yishuv and World Jewry. Soviet Ambassador in Washington Konstantin Umanskii, hinted quite openly during an encounter with representatives of Jewish and Zionist organizations that the future Soviet stand on Palestine would depend on wartime Jewish attitudes towards Russia.[4] Zionist leaders also established contacts with Maxim Litvinov, Umanskii's successor. Both Weizmann and Ben Gurion met Litvinov, but it was Goldmann of the WJC who remained the top Zionist contact with Soviet diplomats.

While the chief Soviet objective in 1941–1943 was to gain Jewish and Zionist support for the Soviet war effort and for Soviet wartime policies, the latter part of the War witnessed a growing Soviet interest in the future of the Middle East. Maisky's visit to Palestine in early October 1943 was a reflection of this interest. It was explicitly on his own initiative that he met with the leaders of the Yishuv and acquired information on Palestine. The Soviets apparently hoped that his mission would help them in formulating their postwar policies in regard to the region. Ben Gurion and Golda Meyerson (later Meir) both of whom spoke with Maisky, regarded him as the leading Soviet foreign office expert on Jewish and Zionist affairs and evaluated his mission to Palestine as of "top value." Maisky's report, to his superiors in Moscow on the Yishuv and its potentialities helped formulate a favorable attitude to Zionist objectives in Palestine.[5] A year later, Ben Gurion was warmly received by communist politicians in Rumania and Bulgaria, and Soviet diplomats in the U.S. told Goldmann that the USSR viewed favorably the emigration of Jews from the Balkans to Palestine. It was also around that time that Umanskii, now Soviet Ambassador to Mexico told the Jewish Telegraphic Agency that the Soviet Union was adopting a favorable attitude toward Zionism.[6]

Representatives of Yishuv institutions, political parties and voluntary public organizations also met with minor Soviet diplomats stationed in the Middle East. Thus, quite close contacts were established between Soviet diplomats and leftist elements within Hashomer Hatzair. Members of Hashomer Hatzair's Department of International Relations met with and submitted reports to Soviet diplomats.[7] The divergence of views, in regard to the nature of the Soviet regime and its attitudes to Jews and Zionism, resulted in bitter debates and accusations within Zionist-Socialist circles. Meir Ya'ari, Yaakov Hazan and particularly Yaakov Riftin (all of Hashomer Hatzair), accused Mapai of anti-Soviet behavior. *Mishmar,* Hashomer Hatzair's mouthpiece in Palestine, published pro-Soviet views and propaganda almost indiscriminately.[8]

The V League

Jewish Communism was always a marginal movement in Palestine. Communist and Soviet stands during the periods of unrest in 1929 and 1936, the growing Arabization of the Communist Party and its increasing support for Arab nationalism, discouraged Jewish communists and led to a split between the Arab and Jewish branches of the Party. Jewish communists played a less prominent part in Palestine than in the U.S. in the founding and running of pro-Soviet fronts (such fronts began to emerge in Palestine in the 1920's). One such organization, was the League Against Imperialism, a branch of the international League of Oppressed People, founded in the mid-twenties and chaired by Albert Einstein. In Palestine, it was supported mainly by the Left Poalei Zion. Another front organization, MOPR (an organization for rendering assistance to arrested and exiled communists), succeeded in enlisting the support of some outstanding liberal Jewish intellectuals such as Dr. Judah Magnes, President of the Hebrew University. Ihud discussion clubs formed in the mid-twenties, enjoyed some backing within Gedud Ha-Avodah and Hashomer Hatzair.[9] The events in Spain in the 1930's led to the emergence of yet another front, the ANTIFA (Antifascist League), which was organized and supported by Left Poalei Zion. It seems that a major obstacle to the implementation of the popular front and unity principles by the various front organizations in Palestine was the Zionist issue. It constituted a dividing line between the communists and the majority of the Yishuv. The Molotov-Ribbentrop Agreement was also counterproductive to front-type activities among Palestinian Jews.

The volte face in the war situation in summer 1941 resulted in a change of heart. The August 1941 Soviet-Jewish Appeal evoked an immediate emotional response within the Yishuv. Hashomer Hatzair sent a message of support to Soviet Jews, proclaiming ". . . Jews of the Soviet Union . . . your brothers in Palestine hail your heroic resistance to Nazism."[10] Weizmann reported to Maisky in London on the positive response of the Jewish Agency. On September 28th, the Voice of Jerusalem broadcast an official message from representatives of Palestine Jewry to Soviet Jews. Among the speakers were Menahem Usishkin, the senior Russian-born Zionist leader; Chief Rabbi of Palestine, Dr. J. A. Herzog; President of the Jewish National Council (Vaad Leumi), Yitzhak Ben Zvi; Berl Katznelson, prominent leader of the Labor Movement and Chief Editor of *Davar;* the poet, Shaul Tschernikhovsky, and the leading lady of the Habimah theatre, Hana Rovina. The tone of the speeches, some delivered in Russian, was highly emotional. Most of the speakers, like an overwhelming majority of the Yishuv leadership at that time were of Russian origin, and the mere prospect of falling barriers and reunification with Russian Jewry was very exciting to them.

In early October, the powerful Histadrut (Labor Federation) announced an Aid to Russia Campaign to collect medical supplies for the Soviet Army. Soon after, a Public Committee to Aid the USSR in its War against Fascism was established. It was organized and supported mostly by radical socialists and liberal intellectuals. A key man behind the scenes at this time was Shlomo Tsirulnikov, a leftist, non-Zionist socialist, previously active in the ANTIFA. During the latter part of the thirties, influenced by the events in Spain, he became indiscriminately pro-Soviet. Russia's war against Nazi Germany confirmed his loyalty and dedication to the USSR. It is difficult to establish whether he was, in fact, a crypto-communist as some of his wartime colleagues maintain, but he was undeniably a dedicated fellow-traveler. Tsirulnikov seemed to perform in Palestine a function similar to that of B. Z. Goldberg in America. Another member of the "Public Committee" was Arnold Zweig, the German-Jewish writer who settled in Palestine after Hitler's rise to power. Zweig, a onetime Zionist who in time started to lean towards Communism, lived in Haifa, detached from the cultural life of the Yishuv. Although not a Party member, he was always ready to lend his support to Soviet and communist causes, and it was, therefore, only natural that he cooperated fully with Tsirulnikov.

The initial, group started to extend the basis of its public support during the first months of 1942 and in May of that year changed its name to the League for Victory, (or as it was to be known The V League). Its Chairman, Shlomo Kaplansky, a well-known public figure and Director of the Technion (Israel Institute of Technology), was a moderate Socialist-Zionist of Russian origin. He was the founder of Poalei Zion in Austria and performed various functions within the World Zionist Movement. Kaplansky became increasingly radical during the War, left Mapai and later joined Mapam. (The United Workers' Party—a left-wing Zionist party founded by Hashomer Hatzair). L. Tarnopoler, a veteran of Gedud Ha-Avodah and a leading member of the left Poalei Zion, became the League's secretary. Among the supporters were socialists of all shades of opinion, such as Dr. Avigdor Mandelberg, a former Menshevik and Israel and Mania Shochat, both founders of the para-military Hashomer organization, and well known public figures in the Yishuv. The communists within the League were not too happy about the continuous diversification of the League's political base, fearing that they stood to lose their influence and control. There were also continuous arguments about the prime objectives of the League. Whereas the Communists and radical socialists stressed pro-Soviet activities exclusively, the moderates pressed for a Zionist-oriented policy. The eventual inclusion of representatives of all the political parties belonging to the Histadrut, in the V League in June 1942, finally determined the nature of that organization. Unlike the Committee of Jewish Writers in the U.S. and similar pro-Soviet wartime fronts elsewhere, the V League formulated a balanced policy vis-à-vis the USSR. It saw its two basic objectives as support for the USSR in its struggle against Nazi Germany, and efforts to shape favorable Soviet attitudes toward Zionism. Still, some elements within the League considered themselves bound only by the Soviet-supporting paragraph. In spite of the differences of opinion and frictions, which became part-and-parcel of the League's existence, the fact that a wide spectrum of political forces was represented within it, enhanced its weight and significance. Histadrut support and the involvement of influential public figures increased its popularity. During the first year of its existence, the League succeeded in enlisting twenty-thousand members and established one hundred local branches, an achievement unmatched by any corresponding Jewish organization.[11]

The highlight of the League's activities was its August 1942 convention in Jerusalem attended by 250 delegates from all over Palestine. It was also the first time that Soviet officials took part in a public event sponsored by the Yishuv. In fact, this Soviet visit could be described as a mission. Though Mikhailov and Petrenko, the First Secretary and Press Attache of the Soviet Embassy in Turkey arrived as official guests of the League, they also met representatives of various Yishuv institutions. Their number one contact man in Palestine seemed to be Tsirulnikov, with whom they conferred and whose advice they sought.[12] As a loyal fellow-traveler with good connections, he was apparently preferred by the Soviets to local communists, who were isolated from and mistrusted by the Yishuv. The Soviet objective in this case was twofold: to mobilize maximum political and public support for Soviet war interests and to collect information on Palestine. The Mikhailov-Petrenko visit was the first Soviet fact-finding mission to this area during the War, and their report to the Soviet Foreign Ministry was later instrumental in formulating Soviet policies for the Middle East.[13] Though they responded noncommitally to the requests and pleas of their Jewish hosts concerning Soviet Jews and Jewish war refugees in the USSR, the two diplomats stated explicitly in private conversations with Tsirulnikov that the Soviet government did not wish any interference in its internal affairs. Mikhailov and Petrenko were enthusiastically received in the various localities which they visited, especially in Hashomer Hatzair communal settlements. Meir Ya'ari, chief ideologue of the movement, in a lengthy speech at Kibbutz Maabarot, stressed short and long-term common interests and goals for his movement and Soviet Russia.[14] The Soviet guests were also warmly received by the liberal philosopher and theologian Martin Buber.

Another Soviet attempt to collect information on Palestine and the Yishuv took place a few months later in the winter of 1942/43. Samuel Volkovich, a Jewish journalist from Poland, who apparently enjoyed some measure of Soviet confidence, was entrusted by the Soviets with the task of investigating the situation within the Yishuv; he was to meet with its leadership and to report his findings to the USSR. Volkovich, who had been active in the anti-Nazi Movement in Poland in the 1930's and affiliated with the Bund, was among those Jewish refugees from Poland who were detained by the Soviets in 1939 and released in the fall of 1941. After his release he settled in Kuibyshev, the temporary seat of Soviet government offices and foreign embassies, and acted as representative of the American Federation of Polish Jews at the Polish Embassy. He also served as correspondent of the Jewish Telegraphic Agency and the Palestinian Hebrew daily *Haaretz*. Volkovich met with members of the Jewish Antifascist Committee, which was being organized in Kuibyshev, and maintained contact with the Soviet Foreign Ministry and Lozovskii. He also met with such political and cultural Soviet personalities as Korniichuk, Wasilewska and Ehrenburg. Meetings and discussions with Soviet officials convinced Volkovich that the Jewish Yishuv in Palestine was considered by the Soviets as an influential factor in the shaping of world Jewish public opinion. Volkovich left the USSR and flew to Teheran aboard a Soviet military aircraft in November 1942, and a few weeks later arrived in Palestine. There he presented himself as a semi-official "go-between" whose services were sought by the Soviets and should also be appreciated by Yishuv leaders. Though initially there was some mistrust toward him he did succeed in meeting with a number of Jewish Agency officials. In February, 1943, Volkovich met with Yitzhak Rabinovich, head of the Jewish Agency's Russian Bureau and together they drafted a report to be delivered by Volkovich to the Soviet authorities. This memo suggested, among other things, that a meeting be arranged between Yishuv representatives and representatives of the JAC. Volkovich himself did not return to the USSR (he was no longer sure of his special status, after the severing of Soviet-Polish diplomatic relations in the spring of 1943). However, he succeeded in sending his report with Henry Shapiro, an American journalist who passed through Palestine on his way back to Russia and who was himself on friendly terms with Lozovskii.[15]

The Mikhailov-Petrenko visit was the first in a series of contacts between the V League in Palestine and Soviet diplomats in neighboring countries. It should be recalled that the Soviets did not maintain a diplomatic outpost in Palestine at that time, and the League was used, at least partially, in lieu of a formal mission. For example, it assisted Soviet trade officials on missions to Palestine. In addition to Mikhailov, who persisted in his Palestinian contacts, A. Sultanov, First Secretary of the Soviet Legation in Cairo, also became involved in Soviet activities within the Yishuv. Though basically an expert on Arab affairs (he was a Moslem from the Caucasus and a graduate of the Institute of Oriental Studies in Moscow), he gradually familiarized himself with Jewish and Zionist aspects of the Middle Eastern situation. It is possible that the Soviets chose Sultanov as chief liaison with the League. If so, he performed a function similar to that of Evgenii Kisselev, Soviet Consul-General in New York. Mikhailov and Sultanov visited Palestine in the spring of 1944 and met leaders of the V league. They were concerned about the intensification of pro-Soviet propaganda in Palestine and its financing, and way of maintaining regular contacts between the League and Soviet diplomats in the area. Sultanov also met Jewish Agency representatives, including Ben Gurion, and seemed eager to learn as much as possible. In his encounters with Yishuv leaders, he hinted openly that Soviet attitudes toward the Jewish question and the Middle East after the War would depend on Jewish support for Soviet interests. Another Soviet diplomat, the Consul in Beirut, M. N. Agronov, approached the League's Secretary, Tarnopoler, and inquired about the Haganah. Tsirulnikov, who held extensive discussions with Sultanov and other Soviet diplomats, gained the impression that public opinion and especially American Jewish attitudes were of great weight in Soviet eyes and that the Russians considered the relatively small Jewish community of Palestine an extremely influential element in this respect.[16]

Direct contacts between V League representatives and Soviet officials also took place in Teheran. From this main junction of Allied
diplomacy during the War, emissaries of various Yishuv institutions
tried to establish both official and clandestine contacts with Jews
inside the Soviet Union. Military ambulances and medical equipment
were delivered to the Soviets by V League missions to Teheran in April
and December of 1943 and in November 1944. These missions were
made up of representatives of the various components of the League,
and as such reflected differences of opinion and purpose; some
members were concerned primarily with Jewish and Zionist objectives,
while others went out of their way to stress the ideological affinity of
the Yishuv with Communist Russia. It was pointed out to the Russians
time and time again that the Yishuv in Palestine could be useful to the
Soviet Union if Zionist objectives were supported by the USSR. The
two top Soviet contacts of the League delegates in Teheran were
Ambassador Smirnov and the head of the Soviet Red Cross mission in
Teheran, Dr. Baraian. The latter's official position was apparently a
cover for a much more substantial political appointment. Baraian, like
most Soviet diplomats who met with representatives of the Yishuv,
showed keen interest in the military potential of the Yishuv. Another
Soviet diplomat in Teheran quoted Georgii Malenkov as saying that
"the Soviet Union will have to heal the wounds of the long-suffering
Jewish people," apparently hinting at Soviet support for Zionist objectives after the War. At the same time, Soviet official announcements
presented the Soviet stand in a much less definite manner. Thus, when
a Soviet daily published in Teheran reported on one of the V League
"ambulance missions," it deleted those passages from a V League
representative's speech which dealt with Zionism.[17]

The V League and the JAC

The fact that the V League represented Jewish national and Zionist
interests, resulted in a complex and, at times, uneasy relationship with
the Jewish Antifascist Committee. Contacts between the two organizations were already established in the early summer of 1942, when the
newly-founded League, sent greetings to the first JAC Plenum. It was
perhaps no accident that the reply from Russia was addressed to
Arnold Zweig, a representative of the strongly pro-Soviet faction in the
League. Then, a few months later, on the occasion of the first national

V League convention, the Soviet Jewish Committee sent a cable of greetings abounding in Jewish national and cultural references.[18] At the same time, however, there was no Soviet response to the League's invitation to JAC representatives to participate in its August 1942 convention. The Mikhailov-Petrenko Report must have mentioned that the League and other Yishuv institutions considered the Jewish Committee in Russia to be the representative body of Soviet Jewry, and were eager to establish direct contacts with it. Some information on the Yishuv's war effort, such as a report of the "ambulance mission" to Teheran, and pictures of Palestinian-Jewish soldiers in the British Army, were published in *Eynikayt* in 1942 and early 1943. In September 1942, *Eynikayt* praised Palestinian Jews for their immediate response to the August 1941 Soviet-Jewish Appeal, and in February 1943, it published Weizmann's greetings to the Second JAC Plenary Session. Shakhno Epshteyn, in his report to the Session, mentioned the encounter of Soviet diplomats (Mikhailov and Petrenko) with the Yishuv, and pointed out that Palestinian Jews were among the first to respond to Soviet calls for assistance.[19] At the same time, however, any direct reference to the League's efforts to gain Soviet support for the Zionist cause was strictly censored inside Russia. Thus, when *Eynikayt* published the League's platform, its "Zionist-oriented" clause was omitted. V League protests to the JAC on this matter went unanswered, as did a request that a Committee representative be sent to Palestine.[20]

The problematic relationship between the JAC and the Yishuv was also reflected in the unsuccessful attempts to have Mikhoels and Fefer visit Palestine during their mission abroad. Although they stopped over in Lydda airport, no arrangements were made to actually meet with Palestinian Jews. The first invitation to Mikhoels and Fefer to visit Palestine was extended by Dr. Goldmann during his speech at the July 8th 1943 Polo Grounds rally honoring the JAC leaders. Two weeks later, during a meeting of Mikhoels and Fefer with Dr. Weizmann, the possibility of such a visit was mentioned again. Weizmann, after a three-hour highly emotional encounter, could only report vaguely that "Soviet Jews hope to establish permanent contacts with Jews in other countries."[21]

Another attempt of a semi-official nature, was made in early August 1943, by Israel Meriminsky (later Merom), a Histadrut representative in the U.S.. Meriminsky, whose task, among other things, was to foster relations with pro-Soviet circles in the U.S. invited Mikhoels and Fefer to come to Palestine. An exchange of cables between Meriminsky and his superiors at the Histadrut indicated that personal contacts with Mikhoels were highly desired in Histadrut and V League circles. Meriminsky met Mikhoels in a New York hospital where the latter was convalescing; (his arm had been accidentally broken at a Chicago mass rally). As at his meeting with Weizmann, Mikhoels was extremely moved by his direct encounter with a representative of the Yishuv. Meriminsky reported that, while Mikhoels clearly indicated his personal feelings in regard to Palestinian Jewry, he kept hinting that neither he nor his Committee made the important decisions. Mikhoels repeated several times in the course of the conversation that he was a "messenger only" and that the JAC was already "doing more than it could."[22] He advised to send an official invitation to Moscow and to contact Soviet diplomats in the U.S. A number of official invitations were then sent to the JAC by the V. League urging JAC representatives to visit Palestine to participate in the presentation of V League ambulances to the Red Army in Teheran, planned for December 1943. One of the League's messages even suggested that a V League national conference be convened on the occasion of a Mikhoels-Fefer visit to Palestine. Another invitation was sent while the JAC representatives were visiting England. The JAC's final reply stated that Mikhoels and Fefer were being recalled urgently from their mission abroad to participate in the reorganization of Committee activities inside Russia. The question of their visit to Palestine would be decided only after their return to Moscow.[25] When the two JAC representatives were asked by a journalist, during a stopover in Cairo on their way home, about a possible visit to Palestine, their somewhat strange reaction was: "We would have been glad to visit Palestine . . ., however, we did not receive an invitation to do so . . ."[24] The League's protestation to the JAC concerning this reply never received a satisfactory explanation.

It is difficult to pinpoint any particular reason for the misunderstanding. In the late summer and early fall of 1943, the JAC was indeed being reorganized as a result of its transfer from Kuibyshev to Moscow and was busy planning its activities in light of the liberation of the Western Soviet territories. At the same time, however, Mikhoels and Fefer were allowed to spend a number of weeks in England, and a short visit to Palestine could not really have interfered too much with their schedule. One possible explanation is that the invitations extended by the Histadrut and the V League were belated and not entirely sincere, since some Zionist politicians did not really wish to see

JAC representatives visit in Palestine. An article in *Mishmar* (Hashomer Hatzair's mouthpiece,) entitled "Double Bookkeeping" accused Mapai's counterpart in the U.S. of hostile attitudes toward the Mikhoels-Fefer Mission there and blamed Mapai politics in Palestine for their failure to arrange the visit.[25] When the affair is considered in the context of Soviet apprehensions about direct contacts between Soviet and World Jewry, it seems quite natural that an encounter between JAC leaders and the overwhelmingly Zionist Yishuv was not welcome by the Soviets. It may also be that such a visit had indeed been contemplated at the outset of the Mikhoels-Fefer mission, but that information reaching Moscow about the highly emotional welcome they had received in the U.S., with its obvious national overtones, served to deter the JAC.

Another flare-up in the relations between the V League and the JAC occurred in the spring of 1944, around the time of the April meeting of the JAC in Moscow. The League made one more attempt at direct contact and tried to obtain an invitation to the Conference. The JAC advised the League to request visas from the Soviet Embassy in Turkey, but to no avail. The possibilities that overseas Jewish delegations might attend the JAC April 1944 Conference was also raised by the British Section of the World Jewish Congress, with similar result.[26] The Soviet attitude towards the moderate socialist parties in the Yishuv was becoming increasingly critical at this time and was echoed in JAC circles. Epshteyn, chief political watchdog of the Committee, criticized *Davar* (the Histadrut and Mapai newspaper) for its opinions on Soviet Jewry. He even went so far as to accuse it of cooperation with the hated American Jewish *Forward*. He also attacked the publication of a book on Soviet Jews by the *Davar* Publishing House[27] Another step of the continuously deteriorating relationship between the JAC and the League was the JAC's treatment of the League message to the JAC April 1944 Conference. Although the message was signed by David Remez (Mapai representative in the V League), *Eynikayt* arbitrarily added the signatures of such loyal fellow-travelers as Zweig and Tsirulnikov. The League, of course, protested and again without receiving a satisfactory response.[28] It now became increasingly apparent that the Soviets were dissatisfied with the stand taken on Soviet-related issues of the moderate socialist publications of the Yishuv. An additional warning came from the Jewish Press Agency of the JAC. In a cable, this time to *Mishmar,* in early August 1944, the JAC accused *Davar* of hypocrisy, and stated that it would not send

Davar any more material.[29] These incidents clearly indicated that from now on JAC contacts with the Yishuv would be limited to loyal pro-Soviet elements only. In late September 1944 came the final blow: a JAC telegram to the V League stated: "The activities of your League do not correspond with its initial objectives. The (JAC) Committee Presidium is, therefore, questioning the continuation of contacts . . ." The League responded: "In two years of correspondence you never made remarks or offered constructive suggestions regarding our activities. Therefore, we do not understand your (current) criticism, and above all the manner in which it was published . . ." Once more the League suggested that a JAC representative be sent to Palestine.[30] The deteriorating relations between the two organizations also resulted in growing tension within the V League. Pro-Soviet members fully supporting the JAC's criticism, demanded complete acquiescence in Soviet demands.[31]

It seems strange that shortly after this exchange of telegrams, an article entitled "The Rebirth of a Nation" was published by Shakhno Epshteyn in *Eynikayt*. In it, Epshteyn approved of the idea of Palestine as a homeland for those war-stricken Jews who would choose to emigrate there. At the same time, however, he left no room for doubt that this solution was not meant for Russian Jews, whose problems had been solved by the Soviet regime.[32] Diplomatic contacts between the USSR and Zionist politicians also continued in a satisfactory manner. Even a delegation of the V League itself, then visiting Teheran, was warmly received by its Soviet hosts, who claimed to know nothing about the embarrassing exchange of telegrams.[33] The only explanation for this seemingly self-contradictory Soviet behavior is, the clearcut Soviet differentiation between foreign-policy considerations and the Jewish problem inside the USSR. This assumption alone can explain why the JAC-V League relationship was deteriorating at a time when Soviet diplomatic contacts with the Yishuv and Zionist organizations continued.

7

POSTWAR YEARS

Soviet Propaganda and the Jews

The growing tensions between the USSR and the West in the postwar years, and the onset of the Cold War did not diminish the significance of Soviet overseas propaganda, although some of its ideological concepts changed. Whereas during the War Soviet propaganda usually perceived the world as "vertically" divided into "good" and "evil" states and societies (i.e. the Allies vs. the Axis Powers), its postwar approach was increasingly "horizontal", depicting progressive and peaceloving versus reactionary and warmongering sectors *within* each state and society in the West.[1] The progressive elements were envisaged as supporting Soviet views and checking the policies of their respective governments.

Since Jewish elements in the West were considered particularly receptive to Soviet postwar propaganda, the Soviets were very careful about the image of Soviet treatment of the Jewish minority in the USSR. A Soviet official who joined the USSR Embassy in Ottawa in the summer of 1945 told his colleagues that "The secrecy of this action (i.e. the discriminatory employment policies towards Soviet Jews— S.R.) is prompted by a desire not to alienate the loyalty of those Jews abroad who espouse our cause either as Communists or supporters of various "Aid-to-Russia" plans."[2] Soviet officials abroad did their best to encourage positive Jewish attitudes towards the USSR[3] and the Jewish Antifascist Committee continued functioning as an instrument of Soviet foreign propaganda. Progaganda tactics abroad, and especially the necessity to fight anti-Soviet stands in the U.S., were discussed at a JAC Presidium meeting shortly before the War ended.[4]

Soviet Yiddish broadcasts to North America were expanded considerably as late as 1947. Around that time Fefer cabled Meisel of the IKUF
in New York and asked him "(to) send all (Jewish American) periodical publications regularly . . . so that (the JAC) would be able to react
on time . . ."[5] The pro-Soviet propaganda of the JAC centered around
both Jewish and general issues. The Soviets never tired of repeating
that the USSR had been the principal saviour of European Jewry
during the War and the only country fighting antisemitism. Soviet
support for Jewish culture inside Russia was also emphasized. The
JAC was exploited as a platform for criticism of antisemitism in the
West. A special meeting of the JAC Presidium discussed the issue of
antisemitism in England and published a protest addressed to the British Trade Unions.[6] As for the general issues, a central propaganda
theme in JAC's *Eynikayt* was ongoing Soviet criticism of the Polish
Government in London. An appeal signed by the JAC, in connection
with the events in Greece was published in *Pravda.* Using contemporary Soviet propaganda phraseology, it appealed to "progressive-
minded Jewish organizations" abroad on behalf of the "Jewish
community" in the USSR.[7]

The U.S. remained the main target of Soviet Jewish-oriented propaganda. Cold-war objectives began to replace wartime themes. Jewish
and non-Jewish anti-Soviet elements in America were constantly
attacked and condemned in *Eynikayt.* Fefer and Ehrenburg stood out
as the most venomous critics of American politics and the American
way of life. Even Markish, who did not usually participate in
Eynikayt's propaganda campaigns was now forced to toe the line.[8]
Religion was also exploited in order to foster pro-Soviet attitudes.
Archbishop Alexei of Yaroslavl', who visited the U.S. in early 1946
met Rabbi Israel Goldstein and assured him that there was religious
freedom in Soviet Russia. Rabbi Shliefer of Moscow corresponded
with the JCRWR and praised it for assisting in "further rapproche-
ment among the peoples of the Soviet Union and the U.S."[9] Pro-Soviet
American Jewish organizations were continuously encouraged by the
Soviets to maintain contacts with the USSR and its Jewish Committee.
Thus, when Russian War Relief officials visited the USSR after the
War, Mikhoels and Fefer expressed their hope "for the continuing
good work of the Jewish Council for Russian War Relief."[10] Louis
Levine of the JCRWR visited Russia in 1946 and met, inter alia, with
Mikhoels. The JAC also maintained its contact with IKUF. Postwar
IKUF activities and conferences were warmly welcomed by *Eynikayt*

however, despite repeated invitations, no representative of the Committee ever attended those events. The Committee of Jewish Writers
and B. Z. Goldberg maintained their exceptionally close connection
with the USSR and the JAC. Goldberg himself was granted the unusual honour of spending almost half a year in the Soviet Union as an
official guest of the Jewish Antifascist Committee.

Goldberg and Novick in Russia

B. Z. Goldberg came to Moscow on January 11, 1946 after visiting
war-stricken Poland, and the next day *Eynikayt* announced the arrival
of "the famous writer, journalist and prominent public figure."
Mikhoels introduced him to the audience and actors of his theatre on
the 13th, and on the 14th a special meeting of the JAC Presidium was
convened to welcome the important guest from abroad. Mikhoels told
the Committee's leadership that Goldberg, more than any other person, had contributed to the "consolidation of progressive forces within
American Jewry" and expressed his appreciation of the welcome he
and Fefer had received in the U.S. back in 1943.[11] Shortly afterwards,
Mikhoels accompanied Goldberg on an official visit to the ailing President of the USSR, Mikhail Kalinin. Among the issued raised by
Goldberg during this meeting were Jewish settlement in Birobidzhan
and in Palestine.[12] A few days later, Goldberg, accompanied by Fefer,
started his "tour" of Jewish communities in postwar Russia, with a
visit to the Baltic republics and Belorussia. Both in Latvia and in
Lithuania, he was received by high-ranking Soviet government officials, as well as by local Jewish and non-Jewish writers. Goldberg
visited Riga, Vilna, Kovno and Minsk, and everywhere, he was
shown Jewish cultural institutions which had started to function again
after the War. Goldberg found mixed emotions in those places—hope
as well as apprehension. While in Kiev he was taken to Babi Yar and
told that a monument to commemorate its victims would soon be
erected there. He also visited such towns as Lvov and Brod in the
Western Ukraine. According to Goldberg, his "touring" circuit was a
carefully and cautiously-arranged affair. He was always accompanied
by JAC functionaries such as Fefer or Shpigelglas. The official Soviet
propaganda aim was, of course, to impress favorably a popular Jewish
journalist who would share his attitudes with his readers and audiences
back in the U.S. But certain specific though covert Jewish interests of

the JAC were also involved. Though Fefer was usually very careful not to turn the "tour" into a distinctly Jewish affair, he seemed to be interested in impressing local Soviet officials with the importance of the Jewish factor in Soviet foreign policy.[13] Some JAC leaders also hoped to use Goldberg as a harbinger of a positive Soviet stand in regard to reviving Jewish activities in postwar USSR. Whether this meant Birobidzhan or the Crimea was not clear. The people around the Committee appeared to be awaiting "good news from the Kremlin," which Goldberg was expected to announce abroad.[14] Goldberg was under the impression that, in spite of postwar difficulties, the JAC was vitally important for Soviet Jewry and its leadership of the Jewish community was taken for granted by numerous Soviet Jews.[15] At a special farewell meeting at the JAC in early June, he was told again how important he was to Soviet aims abroad. Goldberg must have left with the feeling that his visit had achieved a number of significant goals both in the field of Jewish culture inside the USSR and in regard to cooperation between Soviet and World Jewry. He had reached an agreement with the JAC leadership, for a number of joint JAC-Writers' Committee projects. One of them was to be a literary almanac whose editorial board was to include Fefer, Mikhoels, Bergelson, Halkin, Kvitko, and Lina Shtern. The publication of a book on Jewish heroism during the War, was also planned, its editorial board including inter alia Mikhoels, Grossman, Markish, Kushnirov, Bregman and Gonor. The possibility of a visit to America by the Moscow Jewish Theatre was also discussed.[16]

Goldberg tried in his own way to influence Soviet stands and policies vis-à-vis the Jewish Antifascist Committee. Thus, he attempted to convince Lozovskii, that it would be in the Soviet interest to transform that body from a narrowly-defined "Antifascist" Committee into a central organization of Soviet Jews. In a cautiously written letter to Lozovskii on the eve of his departure, Goldberg stated: "I wonder if you fully appreciate the strategic position the Jews occupy in the sphere of public opinion in all parts of the world . . . Here is where the Jewish Antifascist Committee can be of great service." He suggested "two lines of action," i.e. in order to gain more prestige and influence in the West, the Committee should become involved in all phases of Jewish life inside the USSR and it should also establish closer, direct contacts with Jewish communities abroad.[17] We do not know with which members of the JAC leadership he discussed the matter. However, Mikhoel's daughter testified to the fact that her father considered

Goldberg's visit extremely important and that when Goldberg came to visit Mikhoels privately, the two men conversed in great secrecy.[18] There was also a distinctly personal angle to Goldberg's visit. He was honored and feted, not only as the head of a useful pro-Soviet front in the U.S. but also as the son-in-law of Shalom Aleichem, one of the most popular authors in the Soviet Union. On the eve of Goldberg's departure for the USSR, his wife, (Shalom Aleichem's daughter) sent a warmly-worded letter to the government of the Ukrainian Republic, in which she thanked them profoundly for naming the Kiev Yiddish Theatre after her father.[19] Shalom Aleichem's death was commemorated in the spring of 1946 in most major Jewish population centers throughout the USSR. The Moscow meeting took place in one of the most prestigious public places—the Trade Union Hall of Columns. In his reply to the speakers, Goldberg announced that his father-in-law had never considered America his true home and always hoped to return to Russia.[20]

Goldberg apparently returned from the Soviet Union with an ambiguous outlook. Officially and publicly he pronounced nothing but praise. The articles he sent to the *Tog* from Russia were admiring as were his reports at public meetings after his return. During a reception organized by Ambijan, of which he was Vice-President, Goldberg told his audience about Kalinin's promise that Birobidzhan would become a Soviet-Jewish republic in the not too distant future. He also denied finding any traces of antisemitism in the USSR.[21] In a propaganda booklet *Soviet Union: Friend or Foe,* Goldberg defended the Soviet Union and its general and Jewish policies. At the same time he revealed confidentially, that not all was rosy. He admitted that antisemitism was on the rise and that the survival of Soviet-Jewish culture was endangered. His feeling about the situation seemed to be that despite, and perhaps even because of the prevailing circumstances inside the USSR, only continuous contacts with the world Jewish community could act as a deterrent.[22] In a message to Mikhoels and Fefer sent shortly after his return to New York, Goldberg took great pains to point out that the Jewish man in the street in the U.S. is much friendlier to Soviet Russia than overall American public opinion, a fact which should obviously bolster attempts to continue contacts and cooperation between Soviet and American Jews.[23] One wonders whether this was calculated strategy on Goldberg's part, or whether he made an all-out effort to square the circle, since this was the only way to nurture his beliefs and expectations. Despite of some apprehensions,

Goldberg was apparently convinced that his work and that of the Writers' Committee was extremely important. He wrote to friends from the USSR that "our Committee's work is greatly appreciated . . . (and it) should look to expansion and to great prestige."[24] He must have also considered himself as an extremely important and useful person, who would build bridges between Soviet and world Jewry. Suspicions that Goldberg was a "Red Agent" mounted in Jewish and official American circles. The FBI and the Immigration Service even considered at one time the possibility of revoking his U.S. citizenship.[25]

Another Jewish visitor from the U.S. who followed in Goldberg's footsteps was Paul Novick, Chief Editor of the Communist *Morning Freiheit*. He arrived in Moscow in late September 1946 and left in early January 1947.[26] Novick, (himself Russian-born) had visited the USSR back in the 1920's and 1930's. He was acquainted with some of the leading Soviet journalists and had assisted Shakhno Epshteyn during his last stay in America. Besides his Party assignments, Novick was a leading member of Jewish-American fronts such as the IWO, IKUF, Ambijan and the Writers' Committee. Over the years he maintained an extensive correspondence with Soviet-Yiddish writers, especially Fefer, and when Mikhoels and Fefer visited the U.S. in 1943, he was among their closest associates. He was, thus, no stranger to the JAC leadership when he arrived as a guest of the Committee three years later. The purpose of the visit was apparently to counter anti-Soviet conceptions held by U.S. Jews, especially with regard to postwar antisemitism in the USSR. A number of non-Jewish Soviet personalities participated in a reception in his honour, held at the JAC offices. A Russian war hero, Colonel Linkov; the partisan leader Vershigora; and the Ukrainian writer, Maksim Rylskii, all spoke of friendship among Soviet nationalities.[27] Novick also met with Jewish war heroes such as General Katz, Colonel Vilensky and Paulina Gelman.

Novick's impressions of visits to centers of Jewish population in the USSR were similar to those of B. Z. Goldberg. Like Goldberg, he was approached by local Jews and asked to intervene with the Soviet Government in Jewish matters. While in Kiev, Novick met Yiddish and Ukrainian intellectuals. He was asked to convey the message of Ukrainian-Jewish friendship, and was promised that everything was being done to eliminate the harmful influences of Nazi anti-Semitism in the Ukraine. He was also shown Babi Yar and told about the documentation work on the Holocaust which was being conducted at the

Cabinet of Jewish Culture of the Ukrainian Academy of Sciences.[28] In Minsk he met with local Belorussian writers and with the actors of the Belorussian Jewish Theatre. The message was similar to that presented in Kiev;—Belorussian Soviet authorities were supporting the revival of Jewish culture in their republic.[29] Novick was most moved by his visit to Vilna, where he met with young Jewish survivors and students of the only local Jewish school. Accompanied by the poet Aaron Kushnirov, member of the JAC Presidium and by the local Yiddish poet, Hirsh Osherovich, Novick was also received by the President of the Lithuanian Republic, Iustas Paletskis. A central topic in their discussion was the criticism voiced in the U.S. against the antisemitic excesses of the Lithuanians during the Nazi occupation. Paletskis was clearly anxious to alter this public image because of its impact on general American attitudes towards Soviet Lithuania.[30]

During a farewell meeting at the JAC Novick was asked time and again to present Soviet Russia in a positive light on his return to the U.S. He indeed did not fail his hosts. Even before leaving the USSR, in a conversation with a U.S. Moscow Embassy official, Novick stated that he had encountered no evidence of anti-semitism in postwar Russia.[31] In a series of articles published in *Morning Freiheit* he was full of praise for the USSR. In truth, however Novick sensed that not all was well in regard to Jews and Jewish culture there. The poet Kushnirov, for example, confided in him that he could not have a poem published since it was considered "too pessimistic" by the authorities. A number of requests in various parts of the USSR that he, Novick, intervene with Soviet authorities to revive Jewish culture must also have aroused his apprehensions. Years later he admitted "The feeling was that there was a future . . . That's why I overlooked many things."[32]

Postwar Contacts and Plans

The Palestinian theme played a significant role in Soviet postwar propaganda aimed at Jewish public opinion in the West. Besides projecting Russia's image as the major enemy of Hitler's Germany and the saviour of millions of Jews, Soviet and Communist propaganda increasingly exploited the growing involvement of the USSR in the Middle East to foster pro-Soviet attitudes among Jews. Not only pro-Soviet front organizations but even outright communist groups and personalities spoke out in favor of Zionist demands. A prominent Ameircan-Jewish communist wrote shortly after the War: "A common ground was created for an understanding and for . . . cooperation between the Jewish Yishuv in Palestine . . . and the democratic forces in other countries, including Jewish communities . . ." In early 1946 the CPUSA published a resolution in which support was expressed for "a national homeland for the Jews in Palestine."[33]

In the meantime, the V League in Palestine continued its activities and while its ties with the JAC weakened, contacts with Soviet diplomats continued. Zisling, Remez and Kaplansky met Viktor Kokin, counselor of the Soviet Embassy in London, in the summer of 1945. His suggestions were symptomatic of Soviet postwar considerations regarding the "Jewish link" in Soviet foreign propaganda. He expressed his appreciation for the League and encouraged its future activities. At the same time, his response to a request for direct contacts with the JAC either via a V League delegation to the USSR, or through the participation of JAC representatives in a V League convention in Palestine, was noncommital.[34] Representatives of the V league which in later 1945 changed its name to the Friendship League with the Soviet Union, also met with Soviet diplomats in the Middle East and Eastern Europe. It continued to pursue the twin policy of pro-Soviet public activities and attempts to build up contacts with Soviet Jewry. Kaplansky declared at the founding convention of the Friendship League, that it would continue opposing anti-Soviet propaganda in Palestine on the one hand and would continue its efforts for contacts with Soviet Jewry and the Jewish Antifascist Committee on the other.[35] A last unsuccessful attempt to meet with Soviet Jews was made in the summer of 1947 when the League asked for JAC assistance in securing visas for its representatives to the 30th anniversary celebration of the Bolshevik Revolution.

Another focus of pro-Soviet activities in the Yishuv, besides the League continued to be Hashomer Hatzair. Radical intellectuals connected with Hashomer Hatzair founded a Council for Progressive Culture, which immediately established links with IKUF and the Writers' Committee in the U.S. Hashomer Hatzair "roving emissaries" met on numerous occasions with Soviet diplomats in the Middle East and Europe, who naturally welcomed their pro-Soviet sympathies. However, Hashomer Hatzair attempts to establish direct links with Soviet Jewry never succeeded.[36] B. Z. Goldberg established close ties with Hashomer Hatzair during his stay in Palestine after his Soviet Union

visit. While still in Moscow, he was asked by Hashomer Hatzair's
Mishmar to send it articles about Russia. Goldberg arrived in Palestine
in late August 1946 and was overwhelmed by the reception. He cabled
back to Moscow ". . . because of my visit to the Soviet Union and the
chairmanship of the American Committee (of Writers) . . . I was
received as a sort of unofficial ambassador of the Jewish progressive
movement in America and in the world at large . . ."[37] While in Palestine Goldberg met with such Hashomer Hatzair leaders as Meir Ya'ari
and Yaakov Hazan and established particularly close ties with Yaakov
Riftin, because of their common Russian background and ideological
affinity with the Soviet Union. Goldberg's Committee now advocated
a combination of pro-Soviet with pro-Zionist activities. Thus, it sponsored a number of public events emphasizing friendship and cooperation between the Jewish Yishuv in Palestine and the USSR. The most
impressive was the "Salute to the Jewish State," a mass rally on May
15, 1948.

Another outcome of Goldberg's visit to Palestine was the idea of
founding an international Jewish "progressive" movement based on
the various Jewish wartime antifascist committees. Some of the V
League leaders, had been entertaining such thoughts for some time.
Goldberg's response was extremely enthusiastic. It was agreed that the
first step would be an international conference of all Jewish antifascist
organizations to be held in the summer of 1947. Goldberg then cabled
his friends at the JAC: " . . . The call for such a conference coming
from Palestine, from a League in which *Mapai* is represented and
which acts with the agreement of the Jewish Agency, would greatly
help the work of the Anti-Fascist and Pro-Soviet Committees in various countries, and would even further the organization of new
ones."[38] It is quite obvious that Goldberg's motivation and plans differed from those of Yishuv politicians. After discussions with
Kaplansky, who visited the U.S. in the fall of 1946, Goldberg again
cabled the JAC: "Their [the Palestinian League's] idea is not only to
mobilize public opinion for the Soviet Union, but also to gain a
friendly hearing from these pro-Soviet leagues, and possibly also from
your Committee, for the cause of a Jewish Palestine. However, this
matter can be dealt with in the planning of the agenda for the world
conference."[39] Goldberg also suggested to Mikhoels and Fefer
that a JAC representative meet with a representative of the Writers'
Committee . . ."somewhere in Europe, privately, before the meeting
of the various leagues, so that we can arrive at some understanding on

the general agenda for this meeting." He also urged that a JAC representative participate in the future conference. This idea was further discussed at an informal meeting held during the 22nd Zionist Congress in Basel in December 1946 by representatives of the Friendship League in Palestine, the Writers' Committee, the IKUF, and Jewish personalities from Poland, Rumania, Bulgaria, France, Germany and Switzerland. All supported the idea of JAC participation in the planned conference, and a resolution to this effect was tabled.[40] In early January 1947, Goldberg again cabled the JAC that their reaction "would be highly appreciated." In a letter to Mikhoels and Fefer he wrote that "Both of you would have to participate in the Conference."[41]

Another Jewish organization, which was untiring in its attempts at direct contacts with the Jewish Antifascist Committee in the USSR, obviously for somewhat different reasons, was the World Jewish Congress. When a European Conference of the WJC was being planned in 1946, the JAC was asked to send its representatives. Fefer's reply, in which he inquired about the composition of the conference, left room for some hope.[42] However, in spite of the fact that representatives of Jewish communities in Eastern Europe participated in the Prague European Conference in April 1947, no JAC representatives came. The stand of The Prague Conference and the WJC on issues of interest to the Soviet Union must have been disappointing to the USSR. Soviet criticism was voiced openly in two successive *Eynikayt* articles. The first attacked the "neutral" position adopted by some WJC leaders in regard to East-West relations. The second, although praising Dr. Wise and WJC activities during the War, accused it of not being a really "democratic" organization and of being overinfluenced by the Zionists.[43] A resolution published by the Committee of Polish Jews under Soviet pressure, demanded that "the nature and organizational structure" of the WJC be altered.

The WJC renewed its efforts during the second half of 1947 in connection with the planning of its Montreux Conference. Soviet diplomats were promised explicitly that the Conference's stand vis-à-vis the USSR would be favorable. The JAC indicated indirectly that only if the Soviet Union was granted a major role in the preparation of the agenda would they participate. The official Soviet reply was evasive.[44] In addition, the WJC pursued direct, personal contacts. F. Hollander of the Swedish Section of the WJC met in December 1947 with Grigorii Kheifets, the ex-spy and diplomat who was now acting as

JAC's secretary and watchdog. Hollander learned, somewhat to his surprise, that "the JAC was tremendously well informed about the activity of the World Jewish Congress." Even though Kheifets was openly critical of the Congress he nevertheless maintained that "he could see possibilities (for the JAC) to cooperate or even join the Congress." As for the attacks on the WJC published in *Eynikayt,* Kheifets remarked that "although this article attacked the Congress on some points, it still made it clear that the door was left open."[45] The Montreux Conference which convened in the summer of 1948, further exacerbated WJC-Soviet relations. A number of delegates attacked what they referred to as the pro-Soviet policy of the WJC leadership, while Jewish delegates from Poland and communist delegates from the U.S. were highly critical of U.S. policies and the support they had received from some WJC American delegates. A final blow to whatever relations still existed between the World Jewish Congress, the Soviet Union and the Soviet Jewish Antifascist Committee was delivered by Fefer in an *Eynikayt* article in early October 1948.[48]

Impact of "Zhdanovshchina"

Soviet-Jewish culture was adversely affected by the onset of the Cold War and by the launching of rigidly conservative policies (known as the "Zhdanovshchina"), in the realm of Soviet culture. Andrei Zhdanov, one of Stalin's closest associates at that time and the virtual dictator of the cultural scene in the USSR, was responsible for the August 1946 CPSU Central Committee resolutions on literature and art, which condemned Western influences on Soviet culture. Non-Russian national sentiments tolerated and even encouraged during the War were increasingly attacked in the wake of the August decrees. Party and Government control of literature and publishing, relaxed to some extent during the War was reimposed. The "Zhdanovshchina" seemed to take an anti-Jewish turn in the summer of 1947, when Isaac Nusinov, a leading figure in Soviet-Yiddish culture and a member of the Jewish Antifascist Committee was severely criticized at the 11th Plenum of the Soviet Writers' Union.[47] However, the first salvo in a campaign against Jewish cultural nationalism was fired in *Eynikayt* already in September 1946. Aron Vergelis, the future editor of *Sovetish Heymland,* at that time a young and obscure Yiddish writer, published an attack on Yiddish literary criticism in the USSR. He singled out such outstanding literary figures as I. Nusinov and N. Oyslender for criticism.[48] During the following weeks, Fefer emerged as the principal advocate of the new Party line on Yiddish literature and culture. At a meeting of the Moscow Bureau of Yiddish Writers, he accused Soviet Yiddish writers of preoccupying themselves with such "undesirable" issues as the Holocaust and admiration for the Jewish past instead of dealing with contemporary Soviet achievements. He also attacked the writers David Hofshteyn and Itsik Kipnis by names. On another occasion, Fefer called for a growing political involvement of the Jewish sections of the Soviet Writers' Union.[49] In the postwar years Fefer continued to build himself up as a political figure. During a meeting of the Ukrainian Section of the Writers' Union he was praised not only as a loyal Soviet poet but also as one who contributed to the "consolidation of progressive Jewish forces."[50] Fefer continued to act as chief *Eynikayt* commentator on Jewish affairs abroad. Thus, in late 1946 Fefer discussed the ideological implications of the wartime "unity" principle, a doctrinal cornerstone of JAC's activities. He went out of his way to deny the existence of a national Jewish unity principle and pointed out that the JAC "never spoke of all-encompassing Jewish unity ("klal yisroel" unity)," neither in its appeal to Jews in the West nor during his and Mikhoels' mission abroad. The Committee, according to Fefer, never approved of any kind of "unity," "if it (was) not based on a positive attitude towards the Soviet Union."[51] Mikhoels joined in this political-cultural campaign, relatively late, in the summer of 1947, when he expressed his support for Anna Stelmakh, a Yiddish writer who fully subscribed to Zhdanov-type principles in writing.[52] Throughout 1947 and 1948 *Eynikayt* published criticism and attacks in accordance with Party directives. The Jewish Antifascist Committee and *Eynikayt* wer directly involved in the official cultural campaign. Thus, in early 1948 the editors of *Eynikayt* discussed with Soviet-Jewish composers the implications of the Party line on Jewish music in the USSR.[53] *Eynikayt* also published numerous attacks on Itsik Kipnis, a Yiddish writer from Kiev. Kipnis' short story "Without Giving it a Thought," published in a Polish-Yiddish newspaper in the spring of 1947, was widely criticized in the Soviet Union for its Jewish national motifs, and became a central target for attacks on Jewish nationalism. Fefer was among its most outspoken critics. He also viciously attacked the *Forward,* for defending and praising Kipnis.[54] *Eynikayt* also provided space for a campaign against Der Emes Publishing House, which started in late 1947 and continued throughout the first months of 1948. The Director, Strongin, and Chief Editor, Falkovich, were accused of reverting to traditional Yiddish orthography in the printing of books. Finally, Strongin admitted his mistakes and the Party cell at the Publishing House decided to act in order to "increase the ideological level" of the works published by Der Emes.[53]

The postwar tightening of controls in the sphere of Soviet Jewish culture was accompanied by personal changes at the highest level of the Jewish Antifascist Committee. Already in early 1945, a few months before Shakhno Epshteny's death, Solomon Shpigelglas a Party and Government official and complete outsider to the circle of Yiddish cultural activists on the Committee, was appointed as Deputy Secretary, a post he held until his death in late 1946. Then, in mid 1947, another "outsider," Grigorii Kheifets, was appointed as Assistant Executive Secretary of the Committee. Kheifets seemed to be a man of many talents and careers. A veteran Party member and one-time secretary to Lenin's wife, Nadezhda Krupskaya, he is known to have served during the War in diplomatic and intelligence capacities in the U.S.A. He arrived there in the Fall of 1941 and a few months later was appointed Soviet Vice Consul in San Francisco. Kheifets maintained contacts with the National Council of American Soviet Friendship on the West Coast and it is possible that he functioned there as the major Soviet contact with various pro-Soviet "fronts," (a function performed on the East Coast by Soviet Consul in New York Evgenii Kisselev.) It seems likely that Kheifets' most significant job was that of Chief of Soviet Intelligence on the West Coast. He was known to have maintained contacts with American Communists and communist sympathizers, especially in intellectual and scientific circles.[56] Kheifets apparently left the U.S. a few months after the War and reappeared in mid-1947 as a top JAC official. His high standing at the Committee is indicated by the fact that he was coopted to the Presidium, and that his signature began to appear on official JAC correspondence together with those of Mikhoels and Fefer. He also seems to have been the chief political expert of the Committee. Thus, it was Kheifets who, in late 1947, discussed JAC-WJC relations with F. Hollander of the Swedish Section of the Congress. There are also indications that he dealt with JAC policies regarding Israel. Thus, when a number of Soviet Jews turned to the Committee with a suggestion that it organize assistance to the newly established state, Kheifets advised them to "wait and see."[57] The JAC, as well as similar Soviet war propaganda structures geared to function abroad, were connected from their inception with the Soviet security apparatus. Even Shakhno Epshteyn although active mainly in Jewish culture and journalism, maintained contacts with Soviet security agencies. Kheifets, was apparently a full time employee of those agencies, appointed to serve as watchdog over the JAC, during the crucial last phase of its existence.

The Death of Mikhoels

Increased repressive supervision of Jewish national culture in the USSR was evident from late 1946, but 1948 brought a decisive change for the worse, which started with the death of Mikhoels and ended in the liquidation of the Jewish Antifascist Committee and the imprisonment of its leading members. The evidence at hand though far from conclusive, seems to indicate that Mikhoels' death in January 1948 was a preamble to the liquidation of the Committee in November of that year. The crucial question is, of course, whether Mikhoels died accidentally or was murdered. His last public appearance was on December 27 at a "Mendele Moykher Seforim" literary evening at the Moscow Polytechnic.[58] In early January he left for Minsk, the capital of Belorussia, where he was supposed to review plays and recommend them for Government prizes. Members of his family were under the impression that during the preceding period Mikhoels had been extremely tense and had suffered from anxiety.[59] This was apparently brought on by the general atmosphere of unease in respect to Jewish culture in the USSR, the Committee and its Chairman. For some time he received anonymous threatening letters. Mikhoels was in an agitated and extremely anxious frame of mind when he left Moscow for Minsk.[60]

The most detailed, official account of Mikhoels' death seems to be that of Itsik Fefer, who wrote three weeks later that "a few hours before the tragic accident . . . on Monday January 12th . . . we parted about 6 p.m. In a matter of a few hours, Mikhoels' restless heart stopped beating under the heavy wheels of a truck . . ."[61] This was also the official Soviet version of Mikhoels' death. The unofficial versions varied. According to a U.S. Embassy report from Moscow, "the recent and sudden death of Solomon Mikhailovich Mikhoels . . . has roused a remarkably large crop of rumors . . . The crime may have been perpetrated by common thieves." It went on to say that "the only factors common to all the various stories are that he (Mikhoels) died violently in or near the city of Minsk . . ."[62] According to one source, Lev Sheinin, a high-ranking official of the Prokuratura, (Chief Prosecutors Office) was sent to Minsk to investigate the circumstances of Mikhoels' death, and related years later that the head of the Minsk security police refused to discuss the case with him and that Mikhoels was beaten and tortured before his death.[63] It is known that it took unusually long to prepare Mikhoels' body for burial. Available information on the political and security setup in Minsk throws some light on the case. The chief Party boss in Belorussia at that time, was Nikolai Gusarov, a high ranking Central Committee funtionary who was sent there to carry out a series of purges, aimed especially at local, non-Russian elements. His son described him years later as "a personal representative of Stalin." Gusarov, was also an outspoken critic of Jewish nationalism.[64] It should be remembered that outright and crude antisemitism prevailed in the highest Party circles in Belorussia after its liberation. Pantaleimon Ponomarenko, whom Gusarov replaced as First Party Secretary of the Republic had accused the Jews of "raving nationalism."[65] Fefer's presence on the scene in Minsk, also raises some suspicions. Mikhoels, in a telephone call shortly before his death, told his family in Moscow that he was quite surprised to see Fefer in Minsk. Fefer, strangely enough did not pay a condolence call to Mikhoels' family, after the funeral.[66] Another fact which may be relevant to Fefer's role in the affair, was that he assisted the Soviet Security police in carrying out a search at the offices of the Moscow Jewish Theatre in the fall of 1948.

Besides these items of information we have at least two accounts of persons who were either politically or personally close to Stalin. According to Khrushchev, "Mikhoels was thrown in front of a truck .-. . Stalin did it, or at least it was done on his instructions . . . . ."[67] Stalin's daughter wrote that Mikhoels "had been murdered" and that "Automobile accident was the official version, the cover up suggested by my father when the black deed had been reported to him."[68] Then, Fefer himself told Alec Waterman a Jewish Communist from England who visited Moscow in May 1948, that Mikhoels had been murdered and not killed in an automobile accident.[69] Markish, in a poem commemorating Mikhoels' death hinted quite clearly that it was murder.[70] Ehrenburg remarked in his memoirs that at the time of Mikhoels' funeral he did not suspect a premeditated murder, but that his views changed towards the end of 1948, when numerous arrests of Jewish writers were taking place.[71] A noted specialist on the USSR suggested that Mikhoels' death was indeed an accident or "an ordinary murder covered up as an automobile accident," since "ordinary crimes are not supposed to take place in a socialist society."[72] However, too many sources seem to refute such an explanation.

We may assume, then, that Stalin was behind the decision to murder Mikhoels, either as an initiator or as a "passive" accomplice to a suggestion by somebody else. What was the reason behind such a decision and how was it carried out? It is known that mid-1947 witnessed an intensification of that facet of Zhdanovshchina which condemned non-Russian nationalism in the USSR and cited Jewish nationalism as a prime example of deviation from desired Soviet and Russian attitudes. Mikhoels, as Chairman of the central Jewish institution in the USSR was apparently regarded by Stalin as a supporter of Jewish national sentiments, and his liquidation was supposed to serve as a warning. There is a theory that Stalin acted not via the top security boss-Beria, but via Abakumov, one of Beria's subordinates, appointed in 1947 to lead the Ministry of State Security. Some sources also believe that Beria was not "entrusted" with Mikhoels' murder because of his allegedly favorable attitude to Jews. This argument can be refuted by the fact that Tsanava, who was Beria's representative in Minsk, must have been involved in one way or another in the murder and in its cover up. Beria was indeed involved in the Erlich-Alter Committee scheme, back in 1941, but one should also remember the tragic end of these two Bund leaders. Hence, the most logical link of complicity in the murder of Mikhoels seems to have been: Stalin-Beria-Tsanava, with the possible assistance of Gusarov. Minsk, rather than Moscow was chosen as the locale of the murder. It was sufficiently far from the Capital and its Party leadership was outspokenly antisemitic.

Mikhoels' death and funeral were reported both in the central and local Soviet press and his body lay in state in the Moscow Jewish Theatre building. The participants and speakers at the obsequies represented all spheres of Mikhoels' activities: there was Aleksandr Fadeev, Chairman of the Soviet Writers' Union, Aleksandr Gundorov of the Slav Committee, and, of course, numerous Jewish writers and artists.[73] Among those who came to pay tribute was also Paulina Zhemchuzhina, Molotov's wife. One of the most moving reactions to Mikhoels' death was that of Ehrenburg. In an article in *Eynikayt* he wrote: "Mikhoels could have hidden himself in the world of art, but he didn't do so . . . he died in Minsk, a city which was a witness to the ghetto and to the partisan movement—to the sorrow and to the pride of the Jews. I consider him as one who perished . . . at war, as a soldier."[74] If Stalin had in fact regarded Mikhoels as a focus for Jewish national identification, his views appeared to be substantiated by the thousands of Russia's Jews who passed by the casket.[75]

The Palestinian Issue

The aims of postwar Soviet propaganda which exploited the Palestinian issue were twofold. In emphasizing USSR's support for the partition of Palestine and the establishment of a Jewish State it was aiming both at world wide Jewish public opinion and at those left and "progressive" elements in the U.S. and Europe which were sympathetic to Jewish claims after the War. Soviet propaganda experts intended to exploit the existing Jewish wartime structures, such as the various antifascist committees and leagues, in order to build up a "progressive" Jewish movement. The new Jewish State was apparently expected to play a central role in this movement, both as a center of Jewish population and even more so—as a channel of influence to other Jewish communities. The "progressive" potential of Israel was quite often emphasized in JAC's *Eynikayt.*

Itsik Fefer and Lev Goldberg (a journalist and editor for *Der Emes* Publishing House and *Eynikayt's* "expert" on Zionism and Israel) skillfully used Soviet Middle Eastern policies in order to influence Jewish public opinion abroad. Gromyko's speech at the U.N. favoring a Jewish State in Palestine was exploited extensively to foster pro-Soviet sentiments among Jews.[76] Soviet diplomats in the U.S. closely followed Jewish reactions to Russia's policy on Palestine and reported them to Moscow.[77] Though the Soviet stand on the Palestinian issue was expressed in other Soviet publications, the statements in *Eynikayt,* the only Soviet-Jewish newspaper in the USSR must have had a special meaning for Jewish readers. In May 1948 *Eynikayt* published a JAC cable to Weizmann: "This (the establishment of Israel) is one of the most meaningful events in the history of the Jewish people."[78] Zhits, Acting Editor, wrote in August 1948 that his paper was publishing numerous articles "which expressed the sympathies of the whole Soviet people and also of Soviet Jews for the struggling young State of Israel."[79] September 1948 seemed to bring a new Soviet approach. Lev Goldberg, in a strongly worded article, attacked Zionist and Israeli leaders and their links with the U.S. Dr. Nahum Goldmann, for years a favorite in the Soviet media, suddenly was denoted a traitor to the "progressive" cause.[80] Then, Ehrenburg made everything clear in a *Pravda* article. Zionism and Israel were vilified throughout the article but the most significant message was directed at Soviet Jewry. "They (Soviet Jews) all regard the Soviet Union as their homeland," stated Ehrenburg. "They are not looking toward the Near East."[81] An *Eynikayt* editorial echoed Ehrenburg's ideas.[82] A few weeks later Zhits wrote: "We (Soviet Jews) have our beloved socialist homeland—the Soviet Union." Then he went on to stress the orthodox communist class approach: "Soviet Jews sympathize with the *toilers* of the State of Israel . . . however, these sympathies do not mean that they regard Israel as their homeland."[83]

This harsh and outspoken Soviet negation of ties between Soviet Jewry and the newly established Jewish State coincided with the arrival of the first Israeli diplomats in Moscow. The Israeli Legation opened during the first week of September. Israeli diplomats were warmly welcome at the Moscow Central Synagogue on the 11th, and their visit to the Moscow Yiddish Theatre on the 16th, aroused "enormous excitement."[84] It seems that Ehrenburg's appeal in *Pravda* on September 21 was primarily a warning in the wake of the arrival of the Israelis and their first encounters with Soviet Jews. These were to be followed, in spite of Ehrenburg's warning, by the famous mass demonstration of Moscow Jews around the Central Synagogue during the High Holidays, in early October. The spontaneous Jewish reactions to the arrival of Israeli diplomats in Moscow, in September and early October had been preceded by other manifestations of sympathy. From May 1948 and possibly even from late 1947, following the U.N. resolution on Palestine, Soviet security authorities must have been aware of a "Zionist wave" in the USSR.[85] Soviet Jews, encouraged by official Soviet attitudes toward the emergence of a Jewish state volunteered their services to Israel, as did members of Jewish communities elsewhere. Some prospective Soviet Jewish volunteers directly approached the highest Soviet authorities;[86] others considered it only natural to approach the Jewish Antifascist Committee. The Committee had been the only central Jewish structure in the USSR for a number of years, it specialized in contacts with Jews abroad, and was quite explicit (in *Eynikayt*) in its support of the pro-Zionist Soviet stand. A Kiev Jew wrote in his diary in May 1948 "Rumors have it that our government is undoubtedly assisting the Government of Israel . . . Some say that the Jewish Antifascist Committee in Moscow accepts requests from Jews who wish to emigrate as volunteers to Israel . . ."[87] In a memo written a few months later Mordecai Namir, Counselor of the Israeli Legation in Moscow, reported that he had met a Soviet-Jewish ex-Army officer who had turned to the JAC and suggested that Soviet Jews organize help for Israel. The officer and his friends had been trying to find ways of doing so since May 1948, and he (the officer) was convinced that if it were possible, thousands of Jews would volunteer in Moscow alone.[88] Perets Markish confided to his wife that an impressive number of volunteers' requests, from Moscow and other cities and towns had reached the JAC offices.[89] A Jewish war refugee from Poland who asked the JAC to be allowed to participate as a volunteer in the war for Israel's independence was told that the Committee had received a great number of similar requests.[90] The Committee leaders as well as most Soviet Yiddish writers were extremely careful not to initiate any contacts with the Israelis in Moscow. Any undercurrents of strong national identity with Israel among some Committee members, were well-concealed.[91]

The Fall of the JAC

The Jewish Antifascist Committee was closed down sometime in late November 1948. The last issue of *Eynikayt* was apparently that of November 20th. In early December, Namir cabled the Israeli Foreign Ministry; "The JAC plate was removed from the building." When Israeli diplomats attempted, sometime in December, to subscribe to *Eynikayt* they were told, in a matter of fact manner, that "it had ceased publication, and there were no more subscriptions."[92] Ehrenburg wrote years later: " . . . at the end of 1948 the Jewish Antifascist Committee was dissolved, the newspaper *Eynikayt* closed down . . ."[93] Rumors had it that when the JAC clerical staff arrived one morning at their offices they found dismissal notes on their desks. No details on the actual closing of the JAC offices were ever available. We may assume that both the security apparatus and the Sovinformburo of the Soviet Foreign Ministry were involved. Some sources suggest that Boris N. Ponomarev was personally active in the liquidation of the Committee. Ponomarev, an ex-functionary of the Comintern, and Deputy Director of the prestigious Marx-Engels-Lenin Institute after the War, was appointed Deputy Director of the Sovinformuro in 1946. When Lozovskii was arrested in late 1948 or early 1949, Ponomarev became, Head of the Bureau for a short while. He was also among those Party functionaries who, in 1956, discussed the liquidation of the JAC with Canadian communist leaders.[94]

Analysis of the causes and reasons for the liquidation of the Jewish Antifascist Committee should take both general and specifically Jewish elements into consideration. Nineteen forty eight was a year of extraordinary political turbulence for the USSR. The Truman Doctrine and Marshall Plan on the one hand and the official revival of international Communism through the establishment of the Cominform on the other, were indications of the increasing deterioration in East-West relations. Midsummer 1948 brought the Berlin Crisis and Tito's defection. Anti-Westernism and anti-Americanism in particular now became the main themes of a vast Soviet propaganda campaign against "rootless cosmopolitans" inside the USSR. In order to offset the impact of wartime contacts with Western culture, on certain sections of the Soviet population, and particularly intellectuals, the regime sought to portray the West as decadent and immoral. Jews were chosen to play the villain's role—and were slandered as carriers of the Western cultural "baccilus," endangering the body and mind of Soviet society.[95] They had been involved more highly than any other Soviet nationality in wartime contacts with the West and were now the major victim of the new approach. Moreover, the usefulness of Jewish elements to the Soviet propaganda effort appeared to be on the wane. The Cold War and the campaign against "un-American" elements in the U.S., in particular, had a detrimental effect on pro-Soviet fronts and their activities. It is possible that the fate of the JAC was also linked to personal rivalries within the Soviet ruling elite. Some sources argue that clues should be sought in the Malenkov-Zhdanov controversy. Others suggest that the anti-Jewish campaign and the closing of the JAC were aimed at discrediting Beria, an alleged supporter of Jewish interests and promoter of the Committee. In fact, no sufficient evidence is available to suggest a viable hypothesis regarding such links.

What is certain, however, is that anti-Jewish attitudes and blatant antisemitism intensified in postwar Russia. This was true of considerable sectors of the Soviet population as well as of the top Soviet bureaucracy. Antisemitic gossip and jokes became fashionable within the upper echelons of the Party and the Government. Moreover, Stalin was becoming increasingly suspicious and paranoiac in his later years.[96] He distrusted not only individuals but whole nationalities. Punitive action was taken against whole ethnic minorities during the

War. Stalin's antisemitic prejudices increased throughout the 1940's,
and several people who met with him personally at the time reported
to this effect. He told Polish government officials in 1941 that
Jews were "rotten soldiers."[97] In 1945 he told Roosevelt that Jews
were "profiteers and parasites,"[98] and quite openly boasted to Djilas
in early 1948 about his anti-Jewish attitudes and policies.[99] He also
complained that "the entire older generation (of Soviet Jews) is
contaminated with Zionism," and that "they are teaching the young
people too."[100] Stalin apparently felt Soviet Jewry to be a collective security risk to the regime and to himself. What role could the
JAC have played in Stalin's increasingly paranoiac attitude toward
Soviet Jews?

The Jewish Antifascist Committee did establish during the War contacts with the outside world. Though encouraged and supported by
Soviet propaganda agencies and by Stalin himself at the time, these
contacts were regarded in retrospect as dangerous and treasonous. In
the last few months of Stalin's life the Soviet press was to write openly
about Jewish anti-Soviet links with the West and with the U.S. in
particular. These accusations cited leaders and members of the JAC
such as Solomon Mikhoels, Prof. Miron Vovsi and Dr. Boris Shimelovich. They were accused of receiving orders from U.S. intelligence
via the JDC (Joint American Jewish Distribution Committee),[101] with
which Mikhoels and Fefer had been encouraged to establish contacts
during the War. The public accusations of the early fifties may have
germinated in Stalin's mind already in the late forties. Also significant
was Stalin's view of the JAC's activities on internal Soviet-Jewish
affairs. It was well known to Soviet official circles and to Stalin himself
that the Committee had attempted to perform functions and took
upon itself responsibilities far beyond the initial purpose of its establishment. Mikhoels and other top personalities of the JAC approached
various Soviet authorities, both on matters concerning individual
Jews, and on Jewish cultural and national issues. When top Soviet
Party officials were asked, during a meeting with Canadian communists after Stalin's death, to explain the fate of the JAC, their answer
was: "It (the JAC) became . . . a sort of aid society engaged in securing
jobs and living accommodations for Jews . . . (*Eynikayt*) had done
great damage . . . by constantly exaggerating the role Jews performed
. . . bourgeois nationalist influences had penetrated the Antifascist
Committee."[102] The JAC was apparently regarded by Stalin as a struc-

ture which organized and expressed Jewish national interests, and since he viewed such interests as a security risk to the regime and to himself, it seemed to him a matter of prime importance to wipe out this potentially dangerous organization. [103]

CONCLUSION

The history of the Jewish Antifascist Committee and its contacts with world Jewry sheds light on a unique period in Soviet-Jewish relations, when Soviet Jews were expected and encouraged to act as a "linkage group" with the international environment. They were better equipped than any other Soviet nationality for this task, since the majority of their fellow Jews were dispersed worldwide, especially in the United States, a major target of Soviet propaganda. The organizational pattern, techniques and activities of the Jewish Antifascist Committee were part and parcel of the Soviet wartime propaganda apparatus. However, it differed from other Soviet antifascist committees, including the All-Slav Committee, in that it was the only such structure representing a single Soviet nationality. Stalin apparently considered a specifically Jewish organization to be a particularly useful propaganda instrument. The JAC differed in another sense from its Slav counterpart. Whereas the Slav Committee was of only marginal importance to the Ukrainians and the Belorussians, the Jewish Committee became a focus of national identity for Soviet Jews.

The JAC consisted of a permanent nucleus of leaders and functionaries, assisted by a clerical staff and a larger group of Soviet Jews who were mobilized from time to time for specific functions and activities. For the first time since the Revolution, prominent Soviet Jews of widely diversified backgrounds and professions could meet within a single Jewish framework. Though the wartime plight of the Jews enhanced the sense of national identity and cohesion of the Committee members, there were still differences of opinion. The core group of Yiddish writers shared the common goal of preserving Jewish culture in the USSR but there was occasional rivalry and tension between them. Throughout the Committee's lifetime there were conflicts of views and interests in respect to its objectives. Whereas the regime considered it primarily a tool for Soviet wartime propaganda, Jews in the Soviet Union and abroad tended to regard it as a meaningful representative of Soviet Jewry. Many of the Committee leaders developed a sense of Jewish identity and of commitment to their fellow Soviet Jews. As a result of the somewhat chaotic wartime circumstances and accompanying relaxation of official vigilance, the limits of the Committee's involvement in Jewish Affairs were not always clearly defined. Thus some of the leading members took an active interest in fighting antisemitism in the USSR, and in Jewish culture, settlement and postwar rehabilitation. Some attempted to influence Soviet policies toward Jews, by official requests and appeals and by unofficial intercession.

During the War years the USSR was viewed by Jews abroad as the major victim and main opponent of Hitler's Germany. The image of Soviet Russia as an enemy of social injustice and antisemitism had endured in some liberal and even religious Jewish circles in the West since the 1920's and was skillfully exploited by Soviet wartime propaganda. Soviet propaganda experts nurtured and exploited the image of the USSR as the principal savior of Jews during the War. This was a central theme of Mikhoel's and Fefer's mission to the U.S. The USSR was also not averse to suggestions of Soviet assistance in other Jewish-related matters. Thus, Fefer was allowed to allude to the possible establishment of a Jewish republic in Birobidzhan. Jewish enthusiasm for the USSR was also aroused by Soviet hints to support Jewish claims in Palestine. Stalin was interested in creating the impression that in the wake of the War, permanent contacts between Soviet Jews and world Jewry would be possible. As late as the winter of 1947/48 a leading JAC official hinted that "the door was left open." In fact however, permanent representatives of Western Jewish organizations were never allowed to reside in the USSR and no representatives of Soviet Jewry, were ever allowed to travel abroad after the 1943 Mikhoels-Fefer mission. Still another example of Soviet manipulation of Jewish public opinion was the public flattery of influential Jewish politicians and journalists such as Dr. Nahum Goldmann and B. Z. Goldberg.

Jewish public opinion in the West and particularly in the U.S. applauded Soviet wartime stands and began to believe in the possibility of postwar Soviet-Jewish cooperation. There was however an element of disproportion between premeditated Soviet manipulation of Jewish public opinion and the degree of Jewish reponse. There was also an element of pragmatism bordering on cynicism in attitudes toward the USSR of both some Jewish leaders, and U.S. Government officials; Dr. Goldmann of the WJC and State Department officials did all they could in order to silence anti-Soviet criticism in the wake of the Erlich-Alter Affair. This was of course part and parcel of the overall dilemma of avoidance of criticism of a much needed wartime ally. A point in case was Albert Einstein's ambivalent and complex attitude toward the USSR and Stalin during that period. On the whole, the wartime relations of the USSR and world Jewry were ambiguous. In their opposition to and condemnation of Hitler's Germany they were as one, on other issues, such as direct meaningful contacts between Soviet Jews and world Jewry there were serious conflicts.

The Soviet Union's continued interest in favorable public opinion abroad made the JAC's further existence possible in the immediate postwar years. The prolonged visits to the USSR of the most active American Jewish fellow traveler, B. Z. Goldberg, and the editor of the Yiddish communist *Morgen Freiheit,* Paul Novick in 1946, reflected this interest. Both were official guests of the Jewish Antifascist Committee. The JAC leadership hoped that the Committee was so vital to the regime, that it would become a fixture. However, the very nature of the JAC as a semi-official establishment within the framework of an authoritarian communist regime rendered it inherently vulnerable. An anomaly was apparent in the very essence of the Committee: it's raison d'etre was to be a popular, spontaneous and foreign-oriented organization, which, by its very nature, was anathema to the regime. As a result the Jewish Committee was a motley of writers, artists and scientists supervised by security apparatus watchdogs. Beria himself had a hand in the early attempts to organize a Jewish anti-Hiltertie committee in the USSR. The Soviet Foreign Ministry, whose Sovinformburo supervised JAC activities, was in fact permeated with intelligence and security personnel already on the eve of World War II. Those JAC members who were anxious to turn their Committee into a permanent Soviet Jewish structure, attempted to prove to the authorities that its existence would be beneficial to the regime. The encounters of Mikhoels and Fefer with JDC officials in New York in the summer of 1943, as well as Goldberg's activities during his visit to Russia in 1946 seem to bear out this assumption.

Increasing conservatism and regimentation in postwar USSR and the impact of the Cold War upon Soviet-Western relations rendered the existence of the JAC particularly precarious. The "internaltional-ism" fostered during the War was now anathema to the regime. Russian Jewish relations throughout and after the War were marked by continuous Soviet suspicions. Even when ostensibly supporting Jewish and Zionist objectives abroad, the Soviets were highly sensitive to any impact that such policies might have on the internal Soviet-Jewish scene. The ambivalent perception of Soviet-Jewish relations permitted and even encouraged direct contacts of a diplomatic, political nature while opposing any genuine links between Soviet and Western Jews. Nevertheless some differentiation existed, at least until midway through the War; Mikhoels and Fefer were sent on an official mission to American and British Jews; they were never allowed to visit Palestine. Soviet diplomats met with representatives of Jewish organizations of all shades of opinion, including representatives of the Yishuv in Palestine. However, direct contact between Soviet Jews and Jews abroad was barely tolerated after the Mikhoels-Fefer mission. It is possible that the warm welcome they received in various Jewish communities as well as their own reactions aroused the latent suspicions of the Soviet leadership, which stemmed from a traditional Soviet intolerance and fear of genuine non-Russian nationalism inside the Soviet Union.

The beginning of the end of the JAC could be discerned from the summer of 1946 with the onset of Zhdanov's campaign in the sphere of culture. Vasilii Grossman was still optimistic in the spring of that year about the imminent publication of the Black Book of Nazi atrocities against Jews. JAC leaders made plans with B. Z. Goldberg for future activities and cooperation, before his departure from Moscow, in June 1946. The "Zhdanovshchina" which started in August 1946, soon assumed anti-Jewish overtones, with the Jewish cultural elite centered around the JAC as one of its main targets. Stalin's growing suspicion of Soviet Jewry in the postwar years and the enthusiastic reaction of some Soviet Jews to the emergence of the State of Israel finally sealed the fate of the Committee. The liquidation of the Jewish Antifascist Committee, the subsequent imprisonment of its leading members and the closing of other Soviet Jewish institutions were the tragic consequences of the denial of the status of Soviet Jews as a recognized national minority in the USSR. The "Black Years" of Soviet Jewry commenced.

APPENDIX A

MEMBERS OF THE JEWISH ANTIFASCIST COMMITTEE IN THE YEARS 1941–1948.

Literature

Bergelson, D.
Dobrushin, I.
Ehrenburg, I.
Fefer, I.
Feininberg, E.
Godiner, Sh.
Gordon, E.
Grade, H.
Grossman, V.
Grubian, M.
Halkin, S.
Heler, B.
Hofshtein, D.
Kaganovski, E.
Kahan, A.
Katsovich, L.
Korn, R.
Kovnator, R.
Kushnirov, A.
Kvitko, L.
Levin, H.
Lurie, N.
Markish, P.
Marshak, S.
Nister (Kahanovich, P.)
Notovich, M.

Nusinov, I.
Oislender, N.
Persov, Sh.
Rubin, R.
Sheinin, L.
Shternberg, I.
Sito, F.
Sutskever, A.
Volkenshtein, D.

Theatre/Film

Efros, A.
Eisenstein, S.
Ermler, F.
Gross, I.
Iung, K.
Kaminska, I.
Kapler, A.
Khromenko
Mikhoels, S.
Shteiman, M.
Tairov, A.
Zuskin, B.

Military/Partisan Movement

Bliakhman, L.
Buber, L.

175

Fisanovich, I.
Goldberg, E.
Goldberg, L.
Khazanov, A.
Kats, A.
Kogan, S.
Kreizer, I.
Kuznetsov, E.
Mikhlin, F.
Milner, R.
Turian, P.
Vilenskii, V.
Veprinskii, M.
Volf, E.

Art

Altman, N.
Chaikov, I.
Flier, I.
Gillels, E.
Iofan, B.
Krein, E.
Oistrakh, D.
Pulver, L.
Rabinovich, I.
Reisen, M.
Sabsai, P.
Samosud, S.
Shats
Tishler, A.
Zaks, I.

Government

Baturinskii, D.
Bregman, S.
Briker, V.
Goldmakher, I.
Gubelman, M.
Khaikin
Kheifets, G.
Lishanskaia, L.

Tankilevich, A.
Zilbershtein, B.

Journalism/Editing

Epshteyn, Sh.
Iuzefovich, I.
Riklin, H.
Shpigelglas, Sh.
Strongin, L.
Talmi, L.
Vatenberg, E.
Zaslavskii, D.
Zhits, G.

Administration

Dvorkin, M.
Felhendler, A.
Gonor, L.
Iusim, I.
Nagler, H.
Neimark, S.
Shchupak, D.

Medicine

Bomash
Bukler, P.
Shimelovich, B.
Tsiprinovich, N.
Vovsi, M.

Science

Frumkin, A.
Kapitsa, P.
Shtern, L.

Party

Bakhmutskii, A.
Kushnir, Sh.
Savik, P.

History

Grinberg, Z.
Zilberfarb, M.

Philosophy

Falkovich, E.
Spivak, E.

Law

Shats-Anin, M.

Religion

Shliefer, S.

Unknown

Lukinskii, I.
Shner, I.

APPENDIX B

MEMBERS OF THE JAC PRESIDIUM

1944 Presidium

Bergelson, D.
Bregman, S.
Briker, V.
Epshteyn, Sh.
Fefer, I.
Fisanovich, I.
Frumkin, A.
Gonor, L.
Gubelman, M.
Halkin, S.
Kreizer, I.
Kvitko, L.
Markish, P.
Mikhoels, S.
Nagler, H.
Sheinin, L.
Shimelovich, B.
Shtern, L.
Zuskin, B.

1948 Presidium

Bergelson, D.
Bregman, S.
Fefer, I.
Frumkin, A.
Goldberg, L.
Gonor, L.
Gubelman, M.
Halkin, S.
Iuzefovich, I.
Khaikin, S.
Kheifets, G.
Kreizer, I.
Kvitko, L.
Markish, P.
Sheinin, L.
Shimelovich, B.
Shtern, L.
Tankilevich, A.
Zhits, G.
Zuskin, B.

NOTES

Introduction

1. Major scholarly studies of the history of Soviet Jews during that period are scarce. Among those published, the following should be mentioned: M. Altshuler, *Between Nationalism and Communism; The Evsektsiia in the Soviet Union, 1918–1930,* (Hebrew), Tel Aviv, 1980.

Z. Y. Gitelman, *Jewish Nationality and Soviet Politics; the Jewish Sections of the CPSU, 1917–1930,* Princeton University Press, 1972.

L. Kochan, ed. *The Jews in Soviet Russia Since 1917,* Oxford University Press, 1970.

S. M. Schwartz, *The Jews in the Soviet Union,* Syracuse University Press, 1951.

Kh. Shmeruk, *The Jewish Community and Jewish Agricultural Settlement in Soviet Belorussia,* 1918–1932, Jerusalem, 1961.

2. Scholarly research on attitudes of Jews outside the USSR towards Soviet Russia in the 1920's and 1930's is almost nonexistent, with the exception of Z. Szajkowski, *Jews, Wars and Communism,* New York, 1972.

3. Prof. Kh. Shmeruk pointed out the significance of an in-depth study of the JAC as early as 1960, in his essay on "Jewish Literature in the Soviet Union During and Following the Holocaust Period", *Yad Vashem Studies,* v. 4, 1960, p. 27.

4. Since then several articles dealing with the JAC were published, such as : J. A. Gilboa, "Our Jewish Brethren the World Over; The Story of the Jewish Antifascist Committee", *Bulletin on Soviet and East European Jewish Affairs,* No. 5, May 1970, pp. 78–90.

5. Sh. Redlich, "The Jewish Antifascist Committee in the Soviet Union", *Jewish Social Studies,* v. 31, no. 1, January 1969, pp. 25–36.

6. L. Schapiro, "The Jewish Anti-Fascist Committee and Phases of Soviet Antisemitic Policy During and After World War II". B. Vago and G. L. Mosse,

eds., *Jews and Non-Jews in Eastern Europe 1918–1945,* New York-Toronto-Jerusalem, 1974, pp. 283–300. However, no attempt for a comprehensive study of the JAC has been made.

Chapter 1

1. F. C. Barghoorn, "Propaganda: Tsarist and Soviet". I. J. Lederer, ed., *Russian Foreign Policy; Essays in Historical Perspective.* Yale U.P. 1967 p. 292. For a detailed analysis of Soviet foreign propaganda techniques, see: F. C. Barghoorn, *Soviet Foreign Propaganda,* Princeton U.P. 1964, and, P. Kecskemeti, "The Soviet Approach to International Political Communication", *Public Opinion Quarterly,* V. 10, no. 1 Spring 1956, pp. 299–308. On the contents of Soviet propaganda during World War II see: B. May, *Themes of Soviet War Propaganda,* Yale University Ph.D. Thesis, 1958.

2. Wartime changes in Soviet attitudes towards Church and religion and their role in Soviet foreign policy are discussed in: W. C. Fletcher, *Religion and Soviet Foreign Policy, 1945–1970,* Oxford U.P., 1973. See also: J. S. Curtiss, *The Russian Church and the Soviet State, 1917–1950,* Boston, 1953. Solomon Lozovskii, Soviet Vice Comissar for Foreign Affairs, stated in a press conference "Religion is a private affair for the Soviet citizen in which the State does not interfere", *Information Bulletin,* USSR Embassy, Washington, D.C., October 6, 1941.

3. See for example a message from the Moscow Jewish community, *Information Bulletin, ibid.,* November 21, 1942 and a message from Moslem clergy, *Izvestia,* October 19, 1943.

4. *Jewish Telegraphic Agency News Bulletin,* March 3, 1944. However efforts to send a joing Anglo-American Jewish denominational delegation to the Jewish community of Moscow met with persistent Soviet refusal. An example of Stalin's attempts to manipulate public opinion abroad via religious channels was the Orlemanski affair. In the spring of 1944 an unknown priest of Polish origin from Massachussetts was officially invited to the Soviet Union and granted an audience by Stalin. For details see: A. Rothstein, ed., *Soviet Foreign Policy During the Patriotic War. Documents and Materials,* London, 1943, pp. 78–80 and R. L. Roy, *Communism and Church,* New York, 1960, pp. 172–174. By this maneuver Stalin sought to increase U.S. public support for Soviet policies in the Polish question.

5. "Miting predstavitelei ukrainskogo naroda", *Pravda,* November 28, 1941.

6. See for example: "K ukrainskomu narodu", *Pravda,* January 21, 1942; "K ukrainskomu narodu", *Izvestia,* April 2, 1942; "Vtoroi miting predstavitelei ukrainskogo naroda", *Pravda,* September 5, 1942.

7. "Miting predstavitelei belorusskogo naroda", *Pravda*, January 20, 1942; "Vtoroi miting predstavitelei belorusskogo naroda", *Pravda*, October 1, 1942; "Miting predstavitelei latyshskogo naroda", *Pravda*, March 3, 1942; "Miting predstavitelei estonskogo naroda", *Pravda*, March 24, 1942; "Miting predstavitelei litovskogo naroda", *Izvestia*, April 29, 1942.

8. "Antifashistskii miting predstavitelei narodov severnogo kavkaza", *Pravda*, September 1, 1942; "Antifashistskii miting narodov zakavkaz'ia", *Pravda*, September 6, 1942.

9. "Antifashistskii miting predstavitelei narodov uzbekskoi, kazakhskoi, turkmenskoi, kirgizskoi, tadzhikskoi sovetskikh respublik", *Pravda*, February 21, 1943.

10. During the War various national units were formed in the Soviet Army. See: *Istoriia velikoi otechestvennoi voiny sovetskogo soiuza, 1941–1945*, V. 2, Moscow, 1963, p. 460.

11. These activities are discussed in: A. P. Artem'ev, *Bratskii boevoi soiuz narodov SSSR v velikoi otechestvennoi voine*, Moscow, 1975, pp. 96–103. See also: *Istoriia kommunisticheskoi partii sovetskogo soiuza*, V. 5, Part 1 (1938–1945), Moscow, 1970, pp. 327–328. The only military unit within the Soviet army where Jewish cultural activities were tolerated was the Lithuanian Division, which consisted of a large percentage of Jews. For details see: D. Levin, *They Fought Back: Lithuanian Jewry's Armed Resistance to the Nazis, 1941–1945* (Hebrew), Jerusalem, 1974, pp. 89–104.

12. *To Women the World Over*, Moscow, 1941.

13. *Our Generation in Danger*, New York, 1941. The use of youth organizations in Soviet foreign propaganda is discussed in: R. Cornell, *Youth and Communism: An Historical Analysis of International Communist Youth Movements*. New York: 1965.

14. "Uchenye vsego mira na bor'bu s gitlerizmom", *Pravda*, October 13, 1941. The mobilization of Soviet intellectuals for wartime ideological and propaganda activities is discussed in: V. M. Savel'ev and V. P. Savvin, *Sovetskaia intelligentsiia v velikoi otechestvennoi voine*, Moscow, 1974.

15. Although at these meetings nothing was mentioned about the establishment of permanent structures, subsequent Soviet publications regard the initial meetings of "representatives" as the official beginning of the various committees.

16. The substitution of Party organs by state agencies during the War is discussed in: W. O. McCagg, Jr. *Stalin Embattled, 1943–1948*. Wayne State U.P., 1978. The Sovinformburo and its functions are discussed in: L. Nemzer, *The Structure of Soviet Foreign Propaganda Organization*, University of Chicago Ph.D. Thesis, 1948, pp. 348–360. It is possible that the Bureau, although officially linked with the Commissariat for Foreign Affairs, received its directives also from the Agitation and Propaganda Department of the Central Committee of the CPSU.

17. Stalin's personal interest in Soviet information and propaganda sent abroad was mentioned by both Khrushchev and Ehrenburg. According to Khrushchev; "The Sovinformbureau and its Jewish Antifascist Committee were considered indispensable to the interests of our State, our policies and our Communist Party", *Khrushchev Remembers*, London, 1971, p. 259. See also: I. Ehrenburg, *The War: 1941-1945*. Cleveland and New York, 1964, p. 11. The work performed by the Sovinformburo during the War apparently pleased the Soviet leadership. Its Deputy Director, Lozovskii, was awarded the Order of Lenin in 1944.

18. According to an official history of the CPSU "A. S. Shcherbakov was entrusted by the Central Committee to head the ideological sector of Party work", *Istoriia kommunisticheskoi partii, op. cit.,* p. 405. According to the account, Shcherbakov used to have his direct "supervisors" at the various antifascist committees of the Sovinformburo; this information was relayed to the author by Prof. Sh. Ettinger, based on testimony by B. Mark, a Jewish historian from Poland affiliated with the Jewish Antifascist Committee during the War. It is quite likely that the committees, as agencies which conducted Soviet foreign propaganda were also supervised by Soviet security personnel. It is a fact that Soviet intelligence officers abroad were involved in the activities of pro-Soviet "fronts". The Erlich-Alter affair too suggests that the security apparatus was active in the field of Soviet foreign propaganda. For details see Chapter 2.

19. Report by G. F. Kennan to the Secretary of State, May 11, 1945. NADB 861.44 SHCHERBAKOV, ALEKSANDR S. Khrushchev remembered the man as "one of the most contemptible characters around Stalin during the War", *Khrushchev Remembers, op. cit.,* pp. 171–172, 203–204, 284, 301. According to Ehrenburg, Shcherbakov wasn't too happy with Jewish themes in the author's writings during the war. I. Ehrenburg, *The War, op. cit.,* p. 121. On Shcherbakov's antisemitism see also: H. Smolar, *Where Are You Comrade Sidorov* (Hebrew) Tel Aviv, 1973, pp. 188–189.

20. For an extensive discussion of the use of foreign visitors for Soviet propaganda purposes see: S. R. Margulies, *The Pilgrimage to Russia: The Soviet Union and the Treatment of Foreigners, 1924-1937.* The University of Wisconsin Press, 1968. For a Soviet artist's candid view of this phenomenon see: D. Shostakovich, *Testimony,* S. Volkov, ed., New York, 1979, pp. 198–203.

21. D. Caute, *The Fellow Travelers: A Postscript to the Enlightenment,* New York, 1973, p. 133. The "fellow-traveling" phenomenon is also discussed in: N. Wood, *Communism and British Intellectuals,* Columbia U.P., 1959, in M. Decter, "The Great Deception", O. Jensen, ed., *America and Russia,* New York, 1960, pp. 266–270 and in P. Selznick, *The Organizational Weapon,* New York, 1952. See also: B. S. Morris, "Communist International Front Organizations: Their Nature and Functions", *World Politics,* V. 9, October 1956, pp. 76–87.

22. F. A. Warren, *Liberals and Communism, the "Red Decade" Revisited,* Indiana U.P., 1966, pp. 69, 221–222.

23. S. R. Margulies, *op. cit.,* pp. 34, 41, 60.

24. J. Starobin, *American Communism in Crisis, 1943–1957,* Harvard U.P., 1972, pp. 24–25.

25. N. Wood, *Op. cit., p. 164.*

26. *A. B. Ulam, Stalin: The Man and his Era,* New York, 1973, p. 648.

27. The Council had branches in 35 American cities and established various national committees such as the Committee of Women, Science, Education, Art, Theatre, Religion and Nationalities. It also published a monthly; *Soviet Russia Today,* books and pamphlets.

28. The appeal of the 1942 Congress of American-Soviet Friendship stated that "Any American can support this Congress wholeheartedly, regardless of what his position may be on Soviet or American domestic issues . . .", *Salute to Our Russian Ally,* New York, 1942, p. 12.

29. For this and similar contacts see: FBI Reports on the National Council of American-Soviet Friendship, January 31, 1944 and NADB 811.00B NATIONAL COUNCIL OF AMERICAN SOVIET FRIENDSHIP, INC/7.

30. FBI Report on the National Council of American-Soviet Friendship, August 28, 1944.

31. The American-Russian Institute for Cultural Relations, established in the 1930's acted mainly in the cultural and educational fields and was probably controlled by VOKS, from whom it received most of its materials. The Institute used to send Soviet information and propaganda to various U.S. publications, show Soviet films, prepare radio programs on the USSR, hold seminars and exhibits and also run a Speakers Bureau.

32. For Stalin's statements on the significance of the Slav movement see: H. Kohn, *Pan Slavism: Its History and Ideology,* New York, 1960, p. 292; E. J. Rozek, *Allied Wartime Diplomacy: A Pattern in Poland,* New York, 1958, p. 93; *Slaviane,* 5/1945, p. 8 and 10/1946, p. 10. The importance of the Slav element in Soviet war propaganda was also reflected in official Party slogans. Thus, the appeal to "Brother Slavs" was the 12th among 54 Party slogans published on the eve of the Revolution Anniversary in November 1944.

33. A leading figure in the Polish branch of the Slav movement summarized its concept as that of ". . . an additional element in the . . defense activity (of the USSR)". H. Batowski, *Wspolpraca Slowianska,* Warsaw 1946, p. 85. As for similarities between the Slav and the Jewish propaganda campaigns, both started in August 1941 and identical techniques were used in both cases. Not much was heard about both between the fall of 1941 and early spring of 1942, apparently due to the relocation of Soviet government offices from Moscow to Kuibyshev and to organizational difficulties. *Slaviane* and *Einikayt,* publications of the Slav and Jewish committees respectively, started to appear in June 1942. Even the principal slogans used in both campaigns were identical;

"Brother Jews" and "Brother Slavs". The inner structure of both committees was also very much alike.

34. One of them, A. Lavrent'ev, a veteran Soviet diplomat, served after the war as Ambassador to Yugoslavia. T. Gorbunov, the Belorussian editor of *Slaviane,* was later appointed as Secretary for Propaganda of the Belorussian Party CC. Among the few Party officials affiliated with the Committee was A. N. Shelepin, a Secretary of the Komsomol CC, and a future head of the KGB.

35. M Djilas, *Conversations with Stalin,* New York, 1962, pp. 25–27.

36. For Beria's involvement in the Erlich-Alter plan for an Anti-Hilterite Committee in the period September–November 1941, see Chapter 2. The closest counterpart of Mochalov on the Jewish committee was apparently Shakhno Epshteyn. Grigorii Kheifets, the last Secretary of the Jewish Committee, served as Soviet diplomat and intelligence agent in the U.S. prior to his appointment to the JAC.

37. An additional center of Pro-Soviet Slav activities in North America was Canada. Slav propaganda was also initiated in South America. Slav activities in the Middle East were institutionalized as late as 1944. Organizational and operative techniques in those regions were similar to those used by the American Slav Congress.

38. There is no comprehensive history of the American Slav Congress. Some information can be found in: L. L. Gerson, *The Hyphenate in Recent American Politics and Diplomacy,* University of Kansas Press, 1964, pp. 162–177 and in: E.J.P. Pawlowski, *Pan-Slavism During World War II,* Georgetown University Ph.D. Thesis, 1968.

39. G. F. Kennan to the Secretary of State, January 24, 1946. NADB 811.00B/1-2446 and L. A. Steinhardt to the Secretary of State, January 30, 1946. NADB 811.00B/1-3046. See also L. L. Gerson, *ibid.,* pp. 175–176.

40. Pirinsky was imprisoned in the late forties when the AMSC was listed as an anti-American subversive agency. He was later deported from the U.S. and settled in Bulgaria where he continued to be active in public affairs. Another leading figure of the AMSC, Louis Adamic, a leftist writer, is believed to have committed suicide after the War.

41. L. F. Budenz, *This is My Story,* New York, 1947, p. 237. It could be assumed that the most loyal pro-Soviet members of "front organizations" consulted with each other in "closed" circles both on intra-organizational and inter-organizational levels. One such confidential consultation was held, for example, in February 1946 with the participation of members of the AMSC, RWR and the IWO. OSS Report, NA RG. 226, no. 40831, U.S. National Archives, Washington, D.C.

42. R. B. Levering, *American Opinion and the Russian Alliance, 1939–1945,* The University of North Carolina Press, 1976, p. 202.

Chapter 2

1. The history of the Bund in Poland is discussed in: B. K. Johnpoll, *The Politics of Futility: The General Jewish Workers Bund of Poland, 1917–1943.* Cornell U.P., 1967. Henryk Erlich and Wiktor Alter were quite familiar with Russia and the Bolsheviks from earlier experiences. Erlich, a veteran Social-Democrat, was a member of the Petrograd Soviet in 1917. Stalin and other Soviet leaders of his generation must have been personally aware of Erlich's Menshevik and Bundish attitudes. Alter was also a veteran of the socialist movement. He was arrested twice by the Bolsheviks, in 1918 and in 1921.

2. E. Nowogrodsky to W. Wasilewska, March 20, 1940, E/A, Bund; B. Long to Mrs. E. Roosevelt, January 29, 1942, NADB 861.00/11927.

3. H. Erlich to E. Nowogrodsky, September 27, 1941, quoted in *Henryk Erlich un Victor Alter,* New York, 1951, pp. 184–185.

4. Information on the imprisonment of Erlich and Alter and on the period from September/October 1939 to September 1941 is based on letters sent abroad by Erlich and on reports by persons who met with Erlich and Alter during their arrest and after their release, as published in *Henryk Erlich un Victor Alter, ibid.,* pp. 13–169. The date of the death sentences, quoted in an official Soviet letter, was August 1941, see: M. Litvinov to W. Green, February 23, 1943, NADB 861.00/11986. The somewhat conflicting information on the dates of their release is from the aforementioned letter by Erlich and from the messages nos. 16 and 17 sent by S. Kot, Polish ambassador to the USSR, to the Polish Foreign Minister in London, September 16, 1941, IHS, A. 7. 53/2. If the latter is correct, then, at least in Erlich's case, there was a discrepancy of 2–3 days between his release and his appearance at the Polish Embassy. An Inturist invoice sent to the Polish Embassy in April 1943, gave explicit dates for Erlich's and Alter's occupancy in the Metropol Hotel in Moscow. The registration date for both was listed as September 13, 1941, message no. 173 from the Polish Embassy in the USSR to the Polish President and Prime Minister in London, April 15, 1943, IHS, P.R.M. 102/2.

5. British Foreign Office to British Embassy, USSR, July 26, 1941, FO 371 26756 3245 and Polish Embassy, USSR to Soviet Ministry of Foreign Affairs, March 7, 1942, PGHI, container 585.

6. A. Clark, *Barbarossa: The Russian-German Conflict, 1941–1945,* New York, 1965, p. 141. For additional details of the military situation at that time see: J. Erickson, *The Road To Stalingrad: Stalin's War With Germany,* vol. I, New York, 1975, chapter 5.

7. R. E. Sherwood, *Roosevelt and Hopkins: An Intimate History,* New York, 1948, pp. 327–344. See also I. Ehrenburg, *The War, 1941–1945,* Cleveland & New York, 1964, p. 11.

8. W. S. Churchill, *The Second World War, vol. 3: The Grand Alliance,* Boston, 1950, pp. 462–463.

9. J. Armstrong, *The Politics of Totalitarianism*, New York, 1961, pp. 131–132 and A. Ulam, *Stalin: The Man and His Era*, New York, 1973, pp. 553–554. For additional details on the atmosphere which prevailed in Moscow in mid-October 41 see Steinhardt's messages to the Secretary of State, October 15, 1941, NADB 701.0061/58, October 26, 1941 NADB 740.0011 EUR. WAR 1939/16119 and October 28, 1941, NADB, 740.001 EUR. WAR 1939/16219. The urgency of the situation, although muted, was conveyed by Molotov in his conversation with Steinhardt in Kuibyshev, on October 22, Steinhardt to the President, October 22, 1941, NADB 740.001 EUR. WAR 1939/16074.

10. On Beria's various functions during the war see: J. Armstrong, *ibid.*, pp. 133–134; R. Hingley, *The Russian Secret Police*, New York, 1970, pp. 186–193; T. Wittlin, *Commissar: The Life and Death of Lavrenty Pavlovich Beria*, New York, 1972, pp. 294–299, 314–315. Wittlin, more than other authors, emphasizes Beria's role in Soviet foreign policy, considering him as both chief of foreign intelligence and of foreign propaganda. B. Nikolaevsky argued that Beria's influence in the sphere of Soviet foreign policy dated back to the eve of the War. B. I. Nikolaevsky, *Power and the Soviet Elite*, New York, 1966, p. 124. One of Beria's closest associates, a veteran Chekist, V. Dekanozov was Soviet Ambassador to Germany until June 1941, and Deputy Commissar for Foreign Affairs from 1939. The Commissariat for Foreign Affairs became infiltrated up to its highest level by security personnel already in the late thirties. See: T. J. Uldricks, "The Impact of The Great Purge on the Peoples' Commissariat of Foreign Affairs", *Slavic Review* vol. 36, no. 2, June 1977, pp. 187–204. The fact that Soviet intelligence officers abroad were involved in the activities of pro-Soviet fronts, seems also to point to Beria's role in Soviet foreign propaganda.

11. Memo of a conference of General W. Anders with Colonel Evstingneev, November 11, 1941, IHS, K.G.A. 17/17. On Volkovyskii's involvement in Soviet-Polish relations see also *Documents on Polish Soviet Relations*, vol. 1, London, 1961, pp. 201, 240, 295. Volkovyskii was, according to L. Blit, one of the most influential men in the Soviet Ministry of Internal Affairs at that time, see: *The Case of Henryk Erlich and Victor Alter*, London, 1943, p. 12. On Zhukov's and Fedotov's roles in the planning of the Jewish committee see: S. Kot to W. Sikorski, October 10, 1941, S. Kot, *Conversations with the Kremlin and Dispatches from Russia*, New York, Toronto, 1963, p. 60.

12. Memo by Erlich and Alter to the Polish Embassy, USSR, October 10, 1941, IHS Kol. 25/24.

13. *Erlich un Alter, op. cit.*, pp. 106–107. Volkovyskii, who was Jewish, was anxious to show Erlich and Alter the little Yiddish he knew. Another Jewish NKVD officer, who assisted Volkovyskii as liaison with the Bundist leaders was Khazanovich.

14. Kot to the Polish Minister of Foreign Affairs, London, November 8, 1941, S. Kot, *Conversations, op. cit.*, p. 102. See also *Erlich un Alter, ibid.*,

p. 185 and the author's interview with A. Fajnzylber, New York, August 3, 1976, Oral History Division, Institute of Contemporary Jewry, Hebrew University, no. 17(93). The NKVD, for example, offered its assistance in forwarding abroad Erlich and Alter's mail.

15. Interview with A. Fajnzylber, *ibid.*

16. See draft of Erlich and Alter's plan for the future Jewish Anti-Hitlerite Committee, E/A, Bund; Memo by Erlich and Alter to the Polish Embassy, USSR, October 10, 1941, IHS Kol. 25/24; *Erlich un Alter, op. cit.*, p. 107. For the first Soviet announcement on the formation of the various antifascist committees see: *Information Bulletin*, Soviet Embassy, Washington, April 25, 1942. The presidium of the committee planned by Erlich and Alter was to consist of a chairman-Erlich, deputy chairman-Mikhoels and secretary-Alter, *The Case of . . . , op. cit.*, p. 13. Volkovyskii asked Erlich and Alter to model their planned committee on a similar Slav committee established in Moscow, "Ostatnie ich tygodnie", *Robotnik Polski*, London, April 15, 1943.

17. The appeals by Erlich and Alter to Stalin and Beria were first published in *Unzer tsayt*, New York, July 1943, pp. 26–30 and reprinted in *Erlich un Alter, ibid.*, pp. 188–195. The term "initiative group" (initsiativnaia gruppa) was also used in regard to early Soviet attempts for organizing the Slav committee, *Slaviane*, no. 9 September 1944, p. 38. Certain details, not included in the Erlich-Alter letter to Stalin, were mentioned in its earlier drafts. In a paragraph dealing with the future membership of the committee, the following names were listed: H. Shreiber, a lawyer representing Cracow, Sh. Goldman, a Yiddish cultural activist from Bialystok and K. Einojgler, a lawyer from Lwow. In the paragraph dealing with establishing contacts with the U.S. and England, the following were mentioned: D. Dubinsky, S. Hillman, N. Thomas, A. Cahan, W. Citrine and H. Dalton, E/A Bund. Most of them were politically close to and personally known by Erlich and Alter. For the full text of the "Appeal to the Jewish Masses in Poland" see: *Erlich un Alter, ibid.*, pp. 196–197.

18. H. Erlich to E. Nowogrodsky, *Erlich un Alter, ibid.*, p. 186.

19. Erlich and Alter to the Polish Embassy, USSR, October 10, 1941, IHS, Kol. 25/24.

20. *Kultura*, Paris, December 1961, p. 118. Alter also told another Bundist, released from a Soviet prison at the end of September, that since the situation was extremely grave, the Soviets needed them (the Bundists), interview with A. Fajnzylber, *op. cit.* The critical Soviet conditions in the first months of the War evoked hopes for a general amnesty in the USSR. In Solzhenitsyn's words: ". . . the course of the War was at the very start such, that it might very likely have led to the breakdown of the entire Archipelago", A. I. Solzhenitsyn, *The Gulag Archipelago, 1918–1956: An Experiment in Literary Investigation*, parts 3–4, New York, 1975, p. 130. A report from the U.S. Embassy in the USSR, quoting a "reliable Soviet source", stated that ". . . .the amnesty . . . will affect hundreds of thousands, if not millions, of convicts throughout the

Soviet Union", Thurston to the Secretary of State, January 23, 1942, NADB 861.00/11924. However, to quote Solzhenitsyn again, "It turned out that all the scare had been for nothing, that everything was standing firm", *ibid.,* p. 133.

21. This declaration was submitted personally to Kot on September 24, 1941 and was published in *Unzer tsayt,* New York, October 1943, pp. 37–38.

22. Kot's reply note, October 3, 1941, S/1, YIVO.

23. F. Lowery to R. Makins, December 20, 1941 and December 23, 1941, PRO. FO 371 26780 3213.

24. Kot to Sikorski, October 10, 1941, S. Kot, *Listy z Rosji do Gen. Sikorskiego,* London, 1956, p. 128.

25. For more details on Jews in the Polish Army see: S. Redlich, "Jews in General Anders' Army in the Soviet Union, 1941–1942", *Soviet Jewish Affairs,* no. 2 November 1971, pp. 90–98 and I. Gutman, "Jews in Anders' Army in the Soviet Union", Yad Vashem Studies [Hebrew], vol. 12, Jerusalem, 1977, pp. 171–213.

26. K. Pruszynski, "Dwaj ludzie" (Two People), *Nowa Polska,* London, April 25, 1943, p. 306. See also E. J. Rozek, *Allied Wartime Diplomacy: A Pattern in Poland,* New York, 1958, p. 99.

27. They did suggest, however, that an Office for Jewish Affairs be established at the Polish Army Headquarters, memo on a meeting between General Anders and representatives of Polish Jews in the USSR. Kuibyshev, October 24, 1941, Schwarzbart Collection, Yad Vashem Archives, Jerusalem, Document no. 1326.

28. In a letter written to the Polish Foreign Ministry in London, Kot asserted that "The Jewish organizations should be guided in such a way that public opinion in England and the U.S. would concern itself with the situation that had developed because of the Soviet Government's ambition to achieve a one sided solution to the question of Eastern Poland", S. Kot, *Listy . . . op. cit.,* pp. 331–333.

29. K. Pruszynski, *op. cit.,* pp. 306–307.

30. Polish Embassy, USSR to the British Government, May 5, 1942, PRO. FO 371 31084 6767 and S. Kot, *Conversations, op. cit.,* p. 57. See also: *Erlich un Alter, op. cit.,* p. 109. The plans for their departure abroad were never finalized. Although Erlich had been suggested for membership in the Polish National Council in London, he was interested in travelling to North America where his closest relations resided at that time. Relatives and friends of the two in the U.S. and England started procedures for obtaining them entrance visas. As for Alter's appointment to office inside the USSR, although the Soviet authorities were notified of his planned tour in mid–November, they never replied. Polish Embassy, USSR to the Soviet Ministry of Foreign Affairs, December 8, 1941, PGHI, container 585.

31. F. Lowery to R. Makins, *op. cit.* Erlich and Alter were also known to British and other socialists as leading members of the Second International.

32. W. Citrine, *Two Careers*, London, 1967, pp. 106–107. Sir Walter Citrine, who visited the USSR in 1925 and 1935, was quite critical of the Soviet regime, however, during the War, not unlike other critics of Soviet Russia, he preferred to stress alliance and cooperation. The Alter episode was not mentioned at all in Citrine's account of his 1941 visit to Russia, published during the War.

33. Erlich and Alter to Stafford Cripps, November 13, 1941, PRO. FO 371 26780 3213. Stafford Cripps, a convert to socialism and a laborite, advocated friendly relations with the Soviet Union, and during the period 1939–1941 urged for British rapprochement with the USSR. He was sent to Moscow as ambassador en route in June 1940 and remained there until January 1942. It is very likely that Erlich and Alter told Cripps, as Alter told Citrine, about the treatment they received in Soviet Russia, both before and after their release.

34. E/A, Bund.

35. V. Grosman, "Mord un rehabilitatsye", *Unzer shtime*, Paris, December 28, 1956.

36. J. Erickson, *The Road to Stalingrad, op. cit.,* Chapter 7, especially pp. 266–267. See also: A. Clark, *Barbarossa, op. cit.,* p. 179. For the fact that Soviet military preparations for a counterattack started in late November 1941 see: L. P. Alisova "Kontrnastuplenie Sovetskikh Voysk Severozapadneie Moskvy", *Voprosy Istorii,* December 1978, pp. 28–29. It is also possible that Stalin received definite information on the impending Japanese attack on Pearl Harbor, which meant the direct involvement of the U.S. in the War.

37. B. I. Nikolaevsky, *Power and the Soviet Elite, op. cit.,* pp. 134–136.

38. A. Vyshinskii, Soviet Deputy Commissar for Foreign Affairs, stated clearly that the decision to rearrest Erlich and Alter had been taken by Soviet central authorities, Vyshinskii to Kot, December 6, 1941, S. Kot, *Conversations, op. cit.,* p. 160. A Polish Embassy official, who kept calling Vyshinskii, was told after a few evasive answers, that the arrest had been carried out upon a direct command from Moscow, *Erlich un Alter, op. cit.,* p. 114. Beria and his associates made it clear all along that the green light for activating the Erlich-Alter plan can come from Stalin only, *Erlich un Alter, ibid.,* p. 111 and "Ostatnie ich tygodnie", *op. cit.*

39. *Erlich un Alter, ibid.,* p. 107. See also: Polish Embassy, USSR to the Soviet Ministry of Foreign Affairs, December 8, 1941, PGHI, container no. 585. Kot, in his protest against the second arrest of Erlich and Alter explicitly accused the NKVD of not issuing such documents to the two Bundists, in order to use it as a threat, memo entitled "The Erlich-Alter Affair" (Polish), PEWHI, container no. 108.

40. A. Fajnzylber, "14 yor nokhn sovyetish mord", *Unzer shtime,* Paris, January 19, 1956.

41. For a more detailed discussion of the citizenship question see my unpublished doctoral dissertation: Sh. Redlich, *The Jews Under Soviet Rule During World War II,* New York University, 1968, pp. 76–79 and J. Litvak, "The

Question of the Citizenship of Former Polish Jews in the Soviet Union (1941–1943)", *Behinot,* vol. 7, 1976, pp. 85–100.

42. For a report on the "Kozlowski Affair" see: F. Savory to R. Makins, December 20, 1941, PRO. FO 371 26780 3213.

43. J. Czapski, *Na Nieludzkiej Ziemi,* Paris, 1949, pp. 103–106 and *Polish Telegraphic Agency Bulletin,* Jerusalem, March 16, 1943, p. 7, PGHI, container no. 132. See also: *Erlich un Alter, op. cit.,* pp. 112–113.

44. L. S. Dawidowicz, "Two of Stalin's Victims", *Commentary,* December 1951, p. 615. The Union of Polish Patriots, a nucleus of an alternative Soviet-controlled Polish government, made its first public appearance in late November and early December 1941. This was probably meant to coincide with Sikorski's visit to the USSR.

45. For a sample of Bundist accusations against Mikhoels, see memo no. 410 by Raczynski to the Polish Embassy in Washington, June 1943, PGHI, container no. 700. See also *Polish Telegraphic Agency Bulletin, op. cit.,* p. 8. Mikhoels shunned any discussion of Erlich's and Alter's fate, and seemed uncomfortable when enquiries about them were made during his visit to the U.S.A. in 1943, verbal communication by Prof. A. Erlich, New York.

46. K. Pruszynski, "Two People", *op. cit.,* pp. 305–306. Stalin on the one hand, and Sikorski and Anders on the other, unanimously agreed, for example, that Jews were as a rule poor soldiers, S. Kot, *Conversations . . . , op. cit.,* p. 153. For additional details, see: S. Redlich, "Jews in General Anders' Army", *op. cit.,* p. 93. It would be interesting to quote in this context a U.S. State Department note which stated that Erlich and Alter, "although Polish Nationals, are personae non gratae to the Polish Government", J. H. Keely to B. Long, 15 January 1942, NADB 861.00/11926.

47. Report by H. Shapiro to the American Jewish Committee, 5 June 1944, Waldman Archive, American Jewish Committee, New York, and report by S. Kot, 3 October 1941, S/I, YIVO.

48. K. Pruszynski, "Two People", *op. cit.*

49. Kot's conversations with Vyshinsky, 6 December 1941, S. Kot, *Conversations . . . , op. cit.,* pp. 159–160.

50. Appeal by Blit, Fajnzylber and Oler, 9 December 1941, S/I, YIVO.

51. A. Cahan to U.S. Embassy, USSR, 17 December 1941, E/A, Bund; Dickerson to the Secretary of State, 19 December 1941, NADB 861.00/1192½; Workmen's Circle to the Secretary of State, 19 December 1941, NADB 861.00/11925½. For documentation on the JLC attempts, see JLC Archives, New York.

52. "The Erlich-Alter Affair", *op. cit.,* p. 6.

53. Soviet Ministry of Foreign Affairs to Polish Embassy, USSR, 26 January 1942, PGHI, container no. 585.

54. "The Erlich-Alter Affair", *op. cit.,* p. 5; L. Blit, *The Case . . . op. cit.,* p. 14; Thurston to the Secretary of State, 20 January 1942, NADB 861.00/11931½ *Morgen Freiheit,* New York, 27 February 1943; M. Litvinov to

W. Green, 23 February 1943; NADB 861.00/11986. Litvinov's communication stated that ". . . . they were rearrested and in December 1942, sentenced once more to capital punishment. . . ." The facts surrounding the arrest as well as some non-Soviet communist sources suggest December 1941 as the date of execution. It is possible that the date mentioned in Litvinov's letter was a calculated falsification meant to justify the delay in the official Soviet admission of Erlich's and Alter's death.

55. Soviet Ministry of Foreign Affairs to Polish Embassy, USSR, 12 April 1942, "The Erlich-Alter Affair", *op. cit.,* p. 9. See also Soviet Ministry of Foreign Affairs to Polish Embassy, USSR, 16 March 1942, PHGI, container no. 585.

56. Kot's conversation with Vyshinsky, 2 June 1942, S. Kot, *Conversations . . . , op. cit.,* pp. 245–246.

57. W. Green to B. Long, 12 January 1942; J. H. Keeley to B. Long, 15 January 1942 and B. Long to W. Green, 16 January 1942, all in NADB 861.00/11926; Thurston to the Secretary of State, 20 January 1942; B. Long to W. Green, 27 January 1942, both in NADB 861.00/11931½.

58. A. Erlich to Mrs. E. Roosevelt, 24 December 1941; F.D.R. to B. Long, 28 January 1942; B. Long to Mrs. E. Roosevelt, 29 January 1942, all in NADB 861.00/11927; S. Rosen, the White House, to the JLC, 19 June 1942, JLC Archives, New York.

59. N. Thomas to H. Hopkins, 4 September 1942, NADB 861.00/11958; H. Hopkins to N. Thomas, 1 October 1942, E/A, Bund; N. Thomas to A. Berle, 5 September 1942 and A. Berle to N. Thomas, 15 September 1942, both in NADB 861.00/11957. The Erlich-Alter affair confirmed Thomas' growing disillusionment with Stalin and his regime, W. A. Swanberg, *Norman Thomas: The Last Idealist,* New York, 1976, p. 282.

60. J. Gliksman and A. Fajnzylber to W. Willkie, 16 September 1942, PEWHI, container no. 73; *New York Times,* 5 March 1943.

61. Polish National Council meeting, 7 May 1942, Schwarzbart; Shmuel (Artur) Zygelboym to A. Erlich, 10 September 1942, and R. Niebuhr to S. Cripps, 26 February 1942, both in E/A, Bund; British Foreign Office minutes. 3 February 1943, PRO. FO 371 34563 3207; *Soviet Jewish Affairs,* vol. 3, no. 1, 1973, p. 106.

62. S. Mikolajczyk, *The Rape of Poland: Pattern of Soviet Aggression,* New York, 1948, pp. 24–25.

63. M. Litvinov to W. Green, 23 February 1943, *op. cit.*

64. *Forward,* 27 February 1943; Tsivyon (B. Z. Hoffman), "Tsayt notitsn" (Daily Notices), *Forward,* 3 March 1943; R. Abramovich, "Di tsvey sotsyalistishe martirer Erlich un Alter" (The Two Socialist Martyrs Erlich and Alter), *Forward,* 3 March 1943. Abramovich's son, a volunteer in the Spanish Civil War, had apparently been killed there by Soviet security agents.

65. "Alter hot geholfn di poylishe fashistn shikn mikh in turme" (Alter Helped the Polish Fascists to Send Me to Prison), *Morgen Freiheit,* 16 April

1943; A. Shields, "Worker Tells of Alter-Erlich", *The Daily Worker*, 22 April 1943; A. Chapman, "PM and the Erlich-Alter Case", *Morgen Freiheit*, 20 March 1943; editorial, *Morgen Freihert*, 30 March 1943.

66. *New York Times*, 31 March 1943. When Senator Mead sought the advice of the State Department on his participation in the rally, he was told that his criticism should be constructive, conversation between J. M. Mead and A. Berle, 29 March 1943. NADB 861.00/11988. An internatonal socialist memorial meeting was also held in London on 28 March.

67. *The Daily Worker*, 4 April 1943. The U.S. Communist Party also published a pamphlet. J. Starobin, *The True Story of Erlich and Alter*, New York, 1943.

68. *Morgen Freiheit*, 5 and 6 April 1943.

69. P. Murray of the CIO received telegrams demanding that Carrey's appearance be called off, and La Guardia was pressured to suppress the meeting. Organisers of a memorial meeting in Chicago were intimidated by telephone calls and a meeting in Mexico City was disrupted by local communists.

70. "How Erlich-Alter Case Affects U.S.-Soviet Relations", *PM Daily Picture Magazine*, 18 March 1943. Among the reactions to the Erlich-Alter issue were some with anti-Semitic overtones. Thus a letter to Senator J. F. Guffey stated that ". . . there is an international group . . . sufficiently powerful to use our State Department" and warned, referring to Erlich and Alter as "agitators" and "trouble makers", "against the international element being expelled from Europe and seeking haven in the U.S.", A. B. Gosman to J. F. Guffey, 5 March 1943, NADB 861.00/11990.

71. J. Brainin, "The Erlich-Alter Plot", *New Currents*, 1, no. 2, April 1943, pp. 15–16; "Di Erlich un Alter tragedye", *Der Tog*, 16 March 1943.

72. A. Einstein, "Open Letter on American-Soviet Friendship", *New York Times*, 18 May 1943; *The Ghetto Speaks*, 1 July 1943.

73. O. Lange to E. Nowogrodsky, 1 March 1943, E/A, Bund; S. Arski to the Bund, 26 February 1943, E/A, Bund; "Poles Score Soviet Charge", *PM Daily Picture Magazine*, 5 March 1943. Stefan Arski, in an article published in Poland after the 20th Congress of the CPSU, called for the rehabilitation of the two Bund leaders, claiming they were victims of the Beria system of terror. No steps were ever taken either in Poland or the USSR to implement this request, S. Arski, "W sprawie rehabilitacji H. Erlicha i W. Altera" (On the Rehabilitation of Erlich and Alter), *Zycie Warszawy*, 11 December 1956. B. Mark, the Polish-Jewish historian and Director of the Jewish Historical Institute in Warsaw, also mentioned Erlich and Alter as being Beria's victims, B. Mark, "Tsvishn lebn un toyt" (Between Life and Death). *1961 IKUF Almanakh* New York, 1961, p. 80.

74. J. Ciechanowski to the Polish Foreign Minister, 8 April 1943, and M. Kwapiszewski to the Polish Foreign Minister, 12 April 1943, both in PEWHI, container no. 78. For an example of Polish efforts to influence the U.S. press, see J. Stout, "Capital Comment", *New Leader*, 6 March 1943. The Polish

NOTES   193

Government-in-Exile also disseminated the news about the execution of Erlich and Alter via the underground radio in Nazi-occupied Poland. Bundists in the Warsaw ghetto were shocked. It was a severe blow for them to hear that the Soviet Union, an ally in the war against Hitler, had executed two outstanding Bund leaders. Illegal socialist publications, both Polish and Jewish, carried articles commemorating Erlich and Alter. B. Goldstein, *The Stars Bear Witness*, New York, 1949, p. 175.

75. Interview with Hersz Smolar, Institute of Contemporary Jewry, Hebrew University, no. 20(93).

76. Beginning in March 1943, *Eynikayt* for the first time attacked Jewish circles in the U.S.A. who were critical of the USSR, "Ofene diburim" (Plain Words), *Eynikayt*, 15 March 1943; S. Mikhoels, "Obzogn zikh fun zey" (Let us renounce them), *ibid.*, 25 March 1943; and *Eynikayt's* editorial of 25 March 1943.

77. B. Z. Goldberg, "Ten Years Later", *Israel Horizons*, vol. 10, no. 8, October 1962, pp. 14–20. For a detailed discussion of the Mikhoels-Fefer missions see chapter 5.

Chapter 3

1. Participants and speakers at these meetings were referred to as "representatives" of various nationalities although they were never elected by any constituency or even organization. A JAC official when asked how his Committee's members were elected, stated that they were "representatives from Jewish organizations as well as prominent Soviet Jews." Report by F. Hollander of the WJC Swedish Section on his meeting with Grigorii Kheifets, January 2, 1948, WJC, New York, USSR files, no. 38. Invitations to participate in JAC public affairs were issued on a personal basis. One such invitation stated "The Jewish Antifascist Committee in the USSR invites you to come to Moscow (to participate) in the 3rd meeting of representatives of the Jewish people." Telegram by Sh. Mikhoels and Sh. Epshteyn to J. Rubinstein, March 16, 1944, in author's possession.

2. *Khrushchev Remembers*, London, 1971, p. 259. For an evaluation of Khrushchev's memoirs on the JAC see: Z. Ben Shlomo, "The Khrushchev Apocrypha" *Soviet Jewish Affairs*, no. 1, June 1971, pp. 52–75.

3. *Information Bulletin*, USSR Embassy, Washington, D.C., April 25, 1942.

4. The November 1938 meetings were reported in *Pravda* and *Izvestiia* of November 28, 1938 and in *Der Shtern* (Kiev), Nov. 28 and 29, 1938.

5. Short accounts of the August 1941 meeting were published in *Pravda*, August 25, 1941, pp. 3–4 and *Krasnaia Zvezda*, August 26, p. 3. See also: V. Lidin, *Liudi i Vstrechi*, Moscow, 1961, p. 206. The speeches and appeals

were published in *Brider yidn fun der gantser velt,* Moscow, 1941. A publication of the Soviet Embassy in the U.S. described the Jewish meeting in a highly
exaggerated manner as a "meeting (of) representatives of Jewish communities
throughout the world." *Information Bulletin,* USSR Embassy, Washington,
D.C., August 26, 1941. An English version of the speeches was distributed in
the U.S. as early as August 27. The Jewish appeal was broadcast by radio
Moscow in several languages, *Haarets,* August 29, 1941.

6. See: Yiddishe Kultur, No. 9, September 1942, p. 31, and No. 6, June
1942, pp. 5–6.

7. There is a number of contradictory statements by leading JAC members
on the foundation date of the Committee. Mikhoels, stated that the Committee
"was formed during the first week of the Nazi attack." Minutes of a meeting at
the Central Jewish Committee of Mexico, Mexico City, August 18, 1943.
PRO, FO 371.33988.3168. According to Shakhno Epshteyn "The JAC . . .
had been founded shortly after the first anifascist radio meeting." *Eynikayt,*
June 17, 1942. On another occasion Epshteyn explained that "Although the
Committee was founded shortly after the first Moscow meeting . . . of August
24, 1941, it actually began functioning only in February 1942." In May 1942
Fefer told a Polish-Jewish journalist in the USSR that "the establishing of the
JAC is continuing." *Haarets,* May 24, 1942. When David Bergelson discussed
the JAC in June 1942, he remarked that "until now it has all been preparation"
Eynikayt, June 17, 1942.

8. The meeting was reported in: *Tsveyter antifashistisher miting fun di
forshteyer funem yiddishn folk,* Moscow, 1942. Short accounts appeared in the
daily Soviet press. See: *Pravda,* May 25, 1942 and *Krasnaia Zvezda,* May 26,
1942.

9. *Eynikayt,* June 17, 1942.

10. These meetings were reported in *Eynikayt,* June 28, 1942; July 25, 1942,
September 15, 1942. Similar activities took place in the Kuibyshev region, in
Sverdlovsk, Vologda, Iaroslav, Bashkiria and in the Cherkessian Autonomous
Republic. See: *Eynikayt,* July 25, 1942.

11. Sh. Epshteyn, "Erev dem tsveytn plenum," *Eynikayt,* February 7, 1943.

12. A report on the second plenary session of the JAC was published in
Eynikayt, March 15, 1943.

13. The first issue of *Eynikayt* was published on June 17, 1942, but already a
few weeks earlier the Soviet press mentioned the new Yiddish publication and
its editor, Shakhno Epshteyn. See: *Pravda,* May 25, 1942. For a discussion of
Eynikayt's contents see: A. Greenbaum "Jewish National Consciousness in
Soviet Publications in the *Eynikayt* Period," *Studies on the Holocaust,* v. 1,
Tel Aviv, 1978, pp. 213–221.

14. Sh. Epshteyn in his report to the second plenary session of the JAC.
Eynikayt, March 15, 1943. See also: Sz. Kaczerginski, *Tsvishn hamer un serp,*
Paris, 1949, p. 54.

15. For examples see: *Eynikayt*, October 25, 1942; November 25, 1943; February 24, 1944.

16. *Eynikayt*, February 7, 1943. R. A. Davies, *Odyssey Through Hell*, New York, 1946, p. 152. U.S. Embassy Report. NADB 861.00/1-1348.

17. I. Fefer in *Eynikayt*, July 25, 1942 and M. Itkovich, *Eynikayt*, August 25, 1942. See also: letter by former students of a Jewish school in Dvinsk, Latvia, *Eynikayt*, March 22, 1945. For examples of correspondence from Jewish soldiers in the Red Army Lithuanian Division which was predominantly Jewish during its early stages, see: *Eynikayt*, February 7, 1943. September 30, 1943, April 12, 1945, July 14, 1945.

18. I. Fefer in *Eynikayt*, February 7, 1943 and M. Itkovich in *Eynikayt*, August 25, 1942.

19. *Evreiskii narod v bor'be protiv fashizma*, Moscow, 1945, p. 86.

20. Report by B. Z. Goldberg to *Der Tog*, n.d. (1946), B. Z. Goldberg Papers, Dropsie University, Philadelphia.

21. An examination of the *Eynikayt* in the years 1942–1945 revealed that the number of reporters whose names appeared in the newspaper items increased from 9 to 95 during the above period. It is possible that *Eynikayt* had even more reporters than that, but that some materials were only sent abroad. About a third of the reporters listed were military ones, reporting from all parts of the Nazi-Soviet front. There were also non-Jews among *Eynikayt*'s reporters such as Tychina, Ryl'skii, Paustovskii and Korniichuk.

22. *Eynikayt*, March 15, 1943.

23. The man was Naftali Hertz Cohen, a Jewish writer from Rumania who spent the War years in the Soviet Union. See file no. E-44/1a, Yad Vashem Archives, Jerusalem.

24. *Eynikayt*, March 15, 1943.

25. Report by Rabbi Hager, Teheran, September 10, 1942, File S6/3564, Central Zionist Archives, Jerusalem.

26. For example: *Eynikayt*, May 1 and 27, 1943.

27. L. Arkin, *Eynikayt*, December 23, 1943.

28. B. Z. Goldberg, *The Jewish Problem in the Soviet Union; Analysis and Solution*, New York, 1961, p. 64 and B. Z. Goldberg, "A bazukh in yiddishn antifashistishn komitet," *Eynikayt* (New York), April 1946, p. 22.

29. JAC to the American Committee of Jewish Writers, Artists and Scientists, October 22, 1943. ACJWAS files.

30. *Eynikayt*, February 7, 1943. For a discussion of Yiddish literature and publications in the USSR during the War see: Ch. Szmeruk, "Yiddish Publications in the USSR From the Late Thirties to 1948," *Yad Vashem Studies*, vol. 4, 1960, pp. 5–39 and Ch. Shmeruk, "Yiddish Literature in the USSR," L. Kochan, ed., *The Jews in Soviet Russia Since 1917*, Oxford University Press, 1970, pp. 261–266.

31. See for example: D. Bergelson, in *Eynikayt*, February 7, 1943.

32. JAC to ACJWAS, March 3, 1944, ACJWAS Files and *Eynikayt,* March 30, 1944.

33. Sh. Epshteyn in *Eynikayt,* March 30, 1944; *Tog,* April 2, 1944.

34. R. A. Davies, *op. cit.,* p. 146.

35. The proceedings of the April 1944 Meeting were published in *Evreiskii narod, op. cit.* For discussion of the speeches see: L. Boim, "Od al ha'vaad ha'antifashisti bivrit hamoetsot," *International Problems,* Tel Aviv, June 1971, pp. 19–33.

36. *Pravda,* April 5, 1944.

37. *Evreiskii narod, op. cit.*

38. *Eynikayt,* April 13, 1944.

39. For details see: *Evreiskii narod, op. cit.* and *Eynikayt,* August 24, 1944.

40. The deportation of the Crimean Tatars and the subsequent fate of the Crimean Autonomous Republic is discussed in: R. Conquest, *The Nation Killers,* London, 1972 and A. M. Nekrich, *The Punished Peoples: The Deportation and Fate of Soviet Minorities at the End of the Second World War,* New York, 1978.

41. I. Emiot, *Der birobidzhaner inyen,* Rochester, 1960, p. 7. J. Rubinstein, *Megiles rusland,* New York, 1960, pp. 215–216; Interview with Joseph Rubinstein, no. 2(93); Y. Ianasovich, *Mit yiddishe shrayber in rusland,* Buenos Aires, 1959, p. 256.

42. H. Vaynroykh, *Blut oyf der zun,* New York, 1956, pp. 10–11; A. Sutskever, "Mit Shloyme Mikhoels," *Di goldene keyt,* No. 43, 1962, p. 159.

43. *Khrushchev Remembers,* London, 1971, p. 260.

44. A. Sutskever, "Ilya Ehrenburg—a kapitl zikhroynes fun di yorn 1944–1946," *Di goldene keyt,* no. 61, 1967, p. 32.

45. *Khrushchev Remembers,* p. 260.

46. Interview with B. Z. Goldberg, New York, 1967; Interview with Esther Markish, no. 5(93).

47. Interview with J. Rubinstein no. 2(93); Interview with H. Smoliar, no. 20(93).

48. Interview with J. Rubinstein, no. 2(93).

49. Y. Bauer, *My Brothers' Keepers; A History of the American Jewish Joint Distribution Committee, 1929-1939,* Philadelphia, 1974, pp. 60–61, 69.

50. J. N. Rosenberg to the JDC Emergency Administrative Committee, August 8, 1944; P. Baerwald to P. Mikhailov, April 20, 1945; P. Mikhailov to P. Baerwald, October 10, 1945, JDC Archives, New York.

51. *Eynikayt,* September 28, 1944; D. Bergelson to A. Sutskever, September 4, 1944, quoted in *Di goldene keyt,* no. 7, 1951, p. 223.

52. A. Sutskever, "Ilya Ehrenburg—a kapitl zikhroynes," p. 33; B. Z. Goldberg, *The Jewish Problem,* p. 92.

53. Interview with J. Rubinstein, no. 2(93) and A. Sutskever, "Ilya Ehrenburg—a kapitl zikhroynes," ibid. For Ehrenburg's criticism against the plan see: Sh. L. Schneiderman, *Ilya Ehrenburg,* New York, 1968, p. 36.

54. Interview with Esther Markish, no. 5(93).

55. I. Emiot, Memoirs. Manuscript in the Archives of the Centre for Research and Documentation of East European Jewry, Hebrew University, Jerusalem.

56. *Khrushchev Remembers*, p. 260; J. B. Salsberg, "Talks With Soviet Leaders On The Jewish Question," *Jewish Life*, February 1957, p. 40.

57. I. Emiot's, Memoirs, p. 12.

58. See, R. Conquest, *Power and Policy in the USSR; The Struggle for Stalin's Succession 1945-1960*, New York, 1967, pp. 438–439; L. Schapiro, "The Jewish Antifascist Committee and Phases of Soviet Antisemitic Policy During and After World War II," B. Vago and G. Mosse, eds., *Jews and Non-Jews in Eastern Europe, 1918-1945*, New York, 1974, p. 293.

59. For a discussion of Jewish settlement in Birobidzhan after the War see: J. Lvavi, *The Jewish Colonization in Birobijan*, Jerusalem, 1965, pp. 68–70.

60. See for example: *Eynikayt;* July 25, August 25, December 17, 1942.

61. Among them were I. Emiot, Der Nister, Sh. Gordon, I. Liumkis, A. Kahan and M. Lev.

62. For further details see: *Eynikayt*, April 9 and 16, 1946, January 1, 1947; February 27, 1947; May 24, 1947. JAC attitudes towards Birobidzhan are also discussed in J. Kerler, "Baym onhayb funem sof," S. L. Schneiderman, ed., *Tsuzamen zamlbukh*, Jerusalem, 1974, pp. 88–89, 100–103.

63. I. Emiot, *Der birobidzhaner inyen*, Rochester, 1960, passim and his Memoirs, *op. cit.*

64. For details on Der Nister's involvement in Birobidzhan see: *Eynikayt*, July 8, 1947; August 30, 1947; November 1, 1947. See also: I. Emiot, "Der Nister in Birobidzhan," *Di Goldene Keyt*, no. 43, 1962, pp. 77–83 and Kh. Shmeruk, "Der Nister, Hayav ve-Yezira-to," Der Nister, *Ha-Nazzir ve-ha-Geddiyah*, Jerusalem, 1963, pp. 16–17.

65. B. Z. Goldberg to S. Mikhoels and I. Fefer, October 17, 1946, B. Z. Goldberg Papers.

66. I. Fefer, "Vegn Birobidzhan un nokh epes," *Dos Naye Lebn*, October 24, 1948.

67. I. Fefer to B. Z. Goldberg, August 8, 1944, Goldberg Papers; R. A. Davies, *Odyssey Through Hell, op. cit.*, pp. 137–138; B. Z. Goldberg to *Tog*, n.d., Goldberg Papers, B. Z. Goldberg, *The Jewish Problem in the Soviet Union, op. cit.*, pp. 59, 77–80 and Interview with J. Kerler, no. 9(93).

68. For details see Chapter 4.

69. R. A. Davies, *ibid.*, pp. 149–152; B. Z. Goldberg to *Tog*, n.d., Goldberg Papers; *Eynikayt*, June 22, 1944, November 19, 1946, September 21, 1944 and November 1, 1945.

70. R. A. Davies, *ibid.*, pp. 203–209; See also: D. Dragunskii, *V kontse voiny*, Tbilisi, 1968, pp. 161, 190, 208.

71. *Eynikayt*, March 24, 1945.

72. For details on the book *Partisan Friendship* (Partizanskaia druzhba) see: B. West, ed., *Hem hayu rabim,* Tel Aviv, 1968. For Ehrenburg's remarks about the *Red Book* see: *Morning Freiheit,* December 3, 1947. Shakhno Epshteyn, JAC Secretary was planning at one time to write a book on the contribution of Soviet Jews to the armed struggle against the Nazis, *Eynikayt,* July 5, 1942.

73. JAC to the Writers' Committee, April 21, 1944, ACJWAS Files; *Eynikayt,* June 15, 1944 and August 24, 1944; R. Korchak, *Lehavot baefer,* Merhavia, 1965, p. 303. The JAC was also collecting information on the Jewish population inside the non-occupied parts of the USSR, see: L. Zinger, *Dos ufgerikhte folk,* Moscow, 1948, p. 63.

74. Interview with Eliezer Lidovsky no. 62(4); *Eynikayt,* March 22, 1945; April 23 and 24, 1946.

75. See for example: *Eynikayt,* March 17, 1945.

76. For details see: Interview with E. Lidovsky, no. 62(4); Sh. Kaczerginsky *Tsvishn hamer un serp, op. cit.;* B. Z. Goldberg, *The Jewish Problem, op. cit.,* pp. 61–63; Hersh Smoliar sought Fefer's and Epshteyn's advice on the presentation of an appeal to protest anti-Semitism in liberated Belorussia, and they advised him to turn to the highest Party authorities. See: H. Smoliar, "Kabalat ha panim l'partizanim yehudim—zikhronot mi 1944 be' Minsk ha' meshukhreret," *Shvut,* no. 1, 1973, pp. 166–170.

77. *Eynikayt,* October 23, 1945.

78. *Eynikayt,* June 29 and July 6, 1946.

79. It was hoped, for example, that the circulation would increase from 10,000 to 25,000. See: B. Z. Goldberg to *Tog,* n.d., Goldberg Papers; R. A. Davies, *Odyssey Through Hell,* p. 168; Sh. Kaczerginsky, *Tsvishn hamer un serp,* p. 59. For readers' letters see: *Eynikayt,* March 6 and 17, April 10 and June 5, 1945.

80. *Eynikayt,* March 24 and 31, April 12, July 10, October 18, 1945.

81. B. Z. Goldberg to S. Mikhoels, May 14, 1945; B. Z. Goldberg to Sh. Epshteyn, June 1, 1945, FBI Archives; L. Levine to J. N. Rosenberg, December 12, 1945. JDC New York.

82. L. Levine to S. Wise, June 18, 1947, Wise Papers, file 84; FBI Report, April 7, 1948, no. NY 100-63112; FBI memos dated September 29, 1947 and June 9, 1954. For information on the efforts to rebuild the Yiddish printing industry see also: *Eynikayt,* October 10, 1945 and June 8, 1946.

83. *Eynikayt,* March 2, 1946; B. Z. Goldberg to J. Brainin, April 4, 1946, and B. Z. Goldberg to S. Mikhoels and I. Fefer, November 6, 1946, Goldberg Papers.

84. *Eynikayt,* June 18, 1946; B. Z. Goldberg to *Tog,* Goldberg Papers. For a thorough discussion of Jewish publishing in the USSR during and after the War see: Ch. Shmeruk, "Jewish Literature in the Soviet Union During and Following the Holocaust Period," *Yad Vashem Studies,* vol. 4, 1960, pp. 3–72.

85. For a summary of this period see: Shimon Redlich, "The Jews in the Soviet—Annexed Territories, 1939–1941," *Soviet Jewish Affairs*, no. 1, June 1971, pp. 81–90.

86. Ch. Shmeruk, "Yiddish Literature in the USSR," L. Kochan, ed., *The Jews in Soviet Russia Since 1917*, Oxford University Press, 1970, pp. 263–264.

87. See interviews with Rachel Korn, no. 11(93); Joseph Rubinstein, no. 2(93); Ida Kaminska, no. 14(93) and I. Ianosovich, *mit yiddishe shrayber in rusland*, Buenos Aires, 1959, passim.

88. Interview with Esther Mark, no. 7(93).

89. See interviews quoted in footnote 87, and Ianasovich, *op. cit.* For a discussion of the status of Polish Jews in the USSR during the War see: J. Litvak, "The Question of Citizenship of Former Polish Jews in the Soviet Union (1941–1943)," *Behinot*, no. 7, 1976, pp. 85–100.

90. The "Organizing Committee of Polish Jews in the USSR" is discussed in: H. Shlomi, "Reshit ha'Hitargnuth Shel Yehudei Polin be-Milhemet ha-Olam ha-Sheniyah," *Gal-Ed On the History of the Jews in Poland*, Tel Aviv University, 1975, pp. 315–322. See also interview with D. Sfard, no. 6(93).

91. *Eynikayt*, February 22 and March 1, 1945. *Dos Naye Lebn*, April 10, 1945. N. Gris, "Bagegenishn mit fraynt,"*Dos Naye Lebn*, May 10, 1945.

92. *Dos Naye Lebn*, May 20, 1945.

93. See: *Eynikayt*, May 7, 1945; *Biuletyn Zydowskiego Instytutu History-cznego*, no. 51, July–September 1964, pp. 11–12; Ianasovich, *op. cit.*, pp. 315–316; Kaczerginski, *op. cit.*, p. 66; As late as April 1946, Sfard, a leading member of the Organizing Committee delivered a report on Polish Jews at a JAC Presidium meeting. See: *Eynikayt*, April 16, 1946.

94. For details see: Interview with D. Sfard, no. 6(93) and introductory remarks by D. Sfard and H. Smoliar in M. Altshuler, ed., *Soviet Jewry in the Mirror of the Yiddish Press in Poland*, Jerusalem, 1975.

95. *Information Bulletin*, USSR Embassy, Washington, June 2, 1942; *Eynikayt*, December 27, 1942 and September 13, 1945.

96. *Eynikayt*, February 24, 1945. The Cabinet of Jewish Culture of the Ukrainian Academy of Sciences performed a similar function on the local Ukrainian level. It collected, for example, eyewitness accounts of the Babi Yar massacre. See: *Eynikayt*, February 19, 1946.

97. See, for example, the ACJWAS Files.

98. *Eynikayt*, July 27, 1943.

99. *Eynikayt*, September 30, 1943.

100. *N. Goldmann to S. Mikhoels, January 17, 1944; S. Mikhoels to N. Goldmann, January 30, 1944, WJC file, 38.*

101. *Eynikayt*, January 27, 1944; JAC to the Writers' Committee, January 27, 1944, ACJWAS Files.*

102. *Evreiskii narod, op. cit.*, pp. 89–90; S. Mikhoels and Sh. Epshteyn to the Writers' Committee, October 5, 1944, ACJWAS Files.

103. S. Mikhoels, I. Fefer, Sh. Epshteyn to B. Z. Goldberg, October 30, 1944, ACJWAS Files.

104. I. Ehrenburg, *Merder fun felker,* vols. 1–2, Moscow, 1944–1945; *Znamia,* no. 1–2, 1944.

105. For additional details on Ehrenburg see Chapter 4.

106. Mrs. E. Roosevelt to A. Einstein, January 15, 1945, Einstein Microfilms, Princeton University Library, Section II Cl.

107. B. Z. Goldberg to S. Mikhoels and I. Fefer, September 7, 1945; S. Mikhoels, I. Fefer, V. Grossman to B. Z. Goldberg, n.d., B. Z. Goldberg Papers. The English *Black Book* mentioned that a second volume to include materials on Eastern Europe and the Soviet Union, would follow. See: *The Black Book: The Nazi Crime Against the Jewish People,* New York, 1946, p. 305.

108. In the fall of 1945, during the last stages in the preparation of the English version of the Black Book the Writers' Committee mouthpiece wrote that it would open with a preface "by the greatest Jew of our generation," *Eynikayt* (New York), September 1945, p. 21. However, Goldberg, cabled in early 1946 from Moscow that "the preface must be eliminated." See: B. Z. Goldberg to J. Brainin, Goldberg Papers.

109. J. Brainin to S. Mikhoels and I. Fefer, February 19, 1946, ACJWAS Files.

110. *Eynikayt,* January 1, 1946 and May 21, 1946.

111. A copy of the original Russian version of the Black Book (with some parts missing) is deposited at the Yad Vashem Archives, Jerusalem. It has been published recently as *Chernaya Kniga,* comp. and ed. by V. Grossman and I. Ehrenburg, Jerusalem, 1980.

112. For Grossman's introduction see *Chernaya Kniga, ibid.,* pp. 3–6.

113. *Ibid.,* p. 32.

114. I. Ehrenburg, V. Grossman, L. Ozerov, V. Lidin, eds., *Cartea Neagra,* Bucharest, (1947). See also: D. Litani, "Sefer shahor al shoat yehudei brit ha'moatsot" *Yediot Yad Vashem,* no. 23/24, 1960, pp. 24–26.

115. Interview with Sh. Tsirulnikov, no. 21(93).

116. I. Ehrenburg, *Post-War Years, 1945–1954,* Cleveland & New York, 1967, p. 131.

Chapter 4

1. This includes the signatories of the August 1941 appeal which preceded the actual establishment of the Committee. The information was collected primarily from *Brider yidn fun der gantser velt,* Moscow, 1941; *Tsveyter antifashistisher miting fun di forshteyer funem yidishn folk,* Moscow, 1942; *Evreiskii narod v bor'be protiv fashizma,* Moscow, 1945; *Eynikayt,* February

27, 1943, August 24, 1944, May 10, 1945, May 15, 1945; *Eynikayt* (New York), June–July 1945, p. 31. See also the list of JAC members compiled in Y. A. Gilboa, *The Black Year of Soviet Jewry*, Tel Aviv, 1972, pp. 291–293. For a detailed list of names see Appendix A.

2. The term "intellectuals" is used here in the sense of what has been defined as "creative intellectuals," i.e. "scholars, scientists, philosophers, artists, authors, some editors and journalists." See S. M. Lipset and R. B. Dobson, "The Intellectual as Critic and Rebel," S. N. Eisenstadt, and S. R. Graubard, eds., *Intellectuals and Tradition*, New York, 1973, Part 2, pp. 137–138.

3. According to Kaminska's testimony, Mikhoels' attitude towards her was very ambivalent. Although he kept promising her that she would be given the opportunity to act and direct in his theatre, these promises never materialized. I. Kaminska, *My Life, My Theatre*, New York, 1973, pp. 184–190.

4. She was also active in the Antifascist Committee of Soviet Women and in the USSR Society for Cultural Relations with Foreign Countries. Lina Shtern was imprisoned with other members of the JAC after the closing of the Committee in late 1948. She was released and rehabilitated after Stalin's death and died in 1968.

5. Dr. Vovsi was arrested together with a number of Soviet physicians, mostly Jews, in 1952 and charged with premeditated incorrect treatment of Soviet Party and Army leaders. He was released and rehabilitated after Stalin's death and died in 1960.

6. *Eynikayt*, September 5, 1942; D. Bergelson, "Der general Yakov Kreyzer," *Eynikayt*, July 6, 1944.

7. Z. Szajkowski, *Di profesyonele bavegung tsvishn di yiddishe arbeter in frankraykh biz 1914*, Paris, 1937, passim.

8. Lozovskii was involved in collecting information on world Jewish affairs and on the situation in the Middle East, with particular reference to the Jewish Yishuv in Palestine. For details see: Interview with I. Rabinovich by Y. Bar Haim, no. 8(42); Interview with A. Volkovich by Y. Bar-Haim, no. 19(42); Report on a meeting between A. Volkovich and I. Rabinovich, April 1943, Central Zionist Archives, Jerusalem, S 25/488.

9. H. C. Cassidy, *Moscow Deadline 1941–1943*, Boston, 1943, pp. 60–61.

10. P. J. Jaffe, *The Rise and Fall of American Communism*, New York, 1975, pp. 88–90.

11. Mikhoels was fascinated, for example, by the personality of the 18th century scholar and philosopher Solomon Maimon, one of the first East European Jews to transcend the spiritual and intellectual borderline between the Jewish ghetto and the European intellectual community. See: S. M. Mikhoels, *Stat'i, besedy, rechi*, Moscow, 1964, p. 226.

12. N. Mandelshtam, *Hope Against Hope; A Memoir*, New York, 1970, p. 300.

13. Aleksei Tolstoi became a favorite of Stalin in the 1930's and was often invited to the Kremlin. See: Iu. Elagin, *Ukroshchenie iskusstv*, New York,

1952, pp. 139–144. For additional details of Mikhoels' relationship with Tolstoi see S. M. Mikhoels, *Stat'i, op. cit.*, pp. 502, 503, 531–537 and B. Filipov, "Aktery bez grima," *Iunost'*, December, 1964, p. 198.

14. J. Leftwich, *Abraham Sutskever: Partisan Poet*, New York, 1971, p. 88.

15. For details on the Mikhoels-Markish relationship see: S. M. Mikhoels, *Stat'i, op. cit.*, p. 526; I. Ianasovich, *Mit yiddishe shrayber in rusland*, Buenos Aires, 1959, pp. 80–81; Interview with Esther Markish, no. 5(93).

16. I. Fefer, "Tseshmetrn dem yidishn natsyonalizm," *Farmest*, no. 1, 1934, pp. 196–197, quoted by Shmeruk, Kh., "Yiddish Literature in the USSR," L. Kochan, ed., *The Jews in Soviet Russia Since 1917*. Oxford University Press, 1970, p. 257. On the Mikhoels-Fefer relationship see also: Ianasovich, *op. cit.*, and interview with Natalya Vovsi-Mikhoels, no. 10(93).

17. M. Belenkii, "Dermonung vegn Mikhoelsn," *Yiddishe Shriftn*, March 1968, p. 6.

18. For Mikhoels' reactions to the Holocaust see: S. M. Mikhoels, *Stat'i, op. cit.*, pp. 50, 323, 567; M. Belenkii, "Der yiddisher folkstribun in kamf kegn Hitlerism," *Folksshtime*, May 8, 1965; J. Rotboym, "Shloyme Mikhoels," *Folksshtime*, January 15, 1958 and interview with Natalya Vovsi-Mikhoels no. 10(93). Mikhoels was deeply moved by personal tragedies of individual Jews who wrote to him about their sorrows. See: J. Druker, "Bagegenishn mit Mikhoelsn," *Folksshtime*, September 6, 1969.

19. Mikhoels' attitudes toward Sutskever are discussed in J. Leftwich, *op. cit.*, pp. 81–101. For the Lidovski episode see: Interview with Eliezer Lidovski, no. 62(4).

20. S. M. Mikhoels, *Stat'i, op. cit.*, p. 508.

21. V. I. Lidin, *Liudi i vstrechi*, Moscow, 1961, p. 301.

22. A. Sutskever, "Mit Shloyme Mikhoels," *Di goldene keyt*, vol. 43, 1962, p. 165 and interview with Natalya Vovsi-Mikhoels. Officially, of course, Mikhoels was careful in his statements. See for example, S. M. Mikhoels, *Stat'i, op. cit.*, pp. 203, 257.

23. S. Lvov, "Di Birobidzhaner teg," *Dos Naye Lebn*, July 7, 1947; B. Vaysman, *Yoman mahteret ivri mi'brit ha'moatsot*, Ramat Gan, 1973, p. 131 and interview with Natalya Vovsi-Mikhoels, no. 10(93).

24. I. Fefer, "Mikhoels," *Eynikayt* (Moscow), February 5, 1948; A. Sutskever, *op. cit.*, p. 156; J. Sheyn, *Arum moskver yiddishn teater*, Paris, 1964, pp. 192–193; I. Ehrenburg, *The War, 1941–1945*, Cleveland-New York, 1964, p. 125.

25. *Pravda*, January 17, 1948; J. Sheyn, "Poslednie dni Solomona Mikhoelsa," *Grani*, vol. 23, no. 68, 1968, p. 114.

26. For differing opinions on Mikhoels' relationship with Stalin see: L. Leneman, *La Tragedie des Juifs en URSS*, Paris, 1959, pp. 127–131; Interview with Natalya Vovsi-Mikhoels and A. Sutskever, *op. cit.*, pp. 160–162.

27. Epshteyn, was described by a fellow American-Jewish communist, as "a man of two continents." For biographical information on Shakhno Epshteyn

see: M. Kats, "Shakhne Epshteyn," *Yiddishe kultur,* no. 8–9, August–September 1945, pp. 10–13; I. B. Beylin, "Shakhno Epshteyn-zayn lebn," *Eynikayt* (New York), September 1945, pp. 14, 15, 29 and M. Epstein, *The Jew and Communism, 1919–1941,* New York, n.d., pp. 389–394.

28. See: M. Epstein, *ibid.,* p. 391; I. B. Beylin, *ibid.,* p. 29; *Tog,* February 1, 1944.

29. Juliet Stuart Poyntz, a graduate of Barnard College, was on friendly terms with Shakhno Epshteyn from 1916–17. Later she became a prominent member of the American Communist Party. However, after spending some time in the USSR, she grew disappointed with Communism. Poynts was suspected of having written anti-Soviet memoirs exposing Soviet intelligence practices. Epshteyn was used as a decoy to deliver his former friend to a Soviet security squad in New York in June 1937. See: B. Gitlow, *The Whole of Their Lives,* Boston-Los Angeles, 1965, pp. 338–341; M. Epstein, *op. cit.,* pp. 391–393; D. J. Dallin, *Soviet Espionage,* Yale University Press, 1955, p. 416; L. F. Budenz, *This Is My Story,* New York, 1947, p. 263.

30. FBI Reports on B. Z. Goldberg, February 21, 1945 and April 30, 1946.

31. M. Epstein, *op. cit.,* pp. 390–391. According to the author, a one-time leading member of the Jewish faction in the American Communist Party, Shakhno Epshteyn, after being criticized in the Soviet-Jewish press for an article on Stalin, agreed to carry out intelligence assignments abroad in order to prove his personal dedication and loyalty to the regime.

32. In eulogies following Epshteyn's death in 1945 it was stated that "When a large part of the intelligentsia was being internally torn . . . he (Epshteyn) remained always wholesome," E. Vatenberg, in *Eynikayt* (Moscow), July 26, 1945. This eulogy also stated that "the deceased unsparingly exposed the opportunists in our midst." Epshteyn's Party cell secretary admitted that "the Party entrusted him (Epshteyn) more than once with very serious tasks," *Eynikayt* (Moscow), July 24, 1945.

33. A. Sutskever remembered that during his meeting with Solomon Lozovskii, he saw the signature of Shakhno Epshteyn attached to a denunciation of Perets Markish. See: A. Sutskever, "Perets Markish un zayn svive," *Di goldene keyt,* vol. 43, 1962, p. 34. Markish's widow testified that Markish was aware of Epshteyn's denunciations. Interview with Esther Markish, no. 5(93).

34. H. Polyanker, "Mayn fraynt Itsik Fefer," *Sovietish Heimland,* no. 11, November 1979, pp. 138–141.

35. I. Ianasovich, *op. cit.,* pp. 110–112. B. Z. Goldberg's impression was that "Lozovskii was fatherly (to Fefer)." B. Z. Goldberg to J. Brainin, April 14, 1946, B. Z. Goldberg Papers.

36. *Eynikayt* (Moscow), December 27, 1942. An English translation of this poem was published in *New Currents,* vol. 2, no. 1, January 1944, p. 27.

37. I. Fefer, "Soviet Jews Fight," *New Currents,* vol. 2, no. 7, August 1944, pp. 14, 33.

38. Interview with Rachel Korn, no. 11(93).

39. See: Testimonial no. 03-1671, Yad Vashem Archives, Jerusalem; Kh. Shmeruk, ed. *A shpigl oyf a shteyn; An Anthology of Poetry and Prose by Twelve Soviet Yiddish Writers,* Tel Aviv, 1964, p. 766; B. Z. Goldberg, *The Jewish Problem in the Soviet Union; Analysis and Solution,* New York, 1961, p. 60.

40. According to Markish's widow, who spoke to Lina Shtern after her release from prison, Fefer appeared at the closed trial of the JAC leadership in 1952 as a "witness for the prosecution." According to Mrs. Markish, Fefer also assisted V. S. Abakumov, Soviet Minister of State Security, in his preparation of the arrests of leading Jewish personalities, members of the Committee. Fefer apparently submitted to the Soviet authorities letters from Soviet Jews addressed to the JAC, in which wishes for settling in Palestine were expressed. See: E. Markish, *Le Long Retour,* Paris, 1974, pp. 188, 290–292.

41. E. Markish, "The Young Peretz Markish's Russian Songs of Zion," *Shvut,* no. 2, 1974, pp. 181–183.

42. It was probably then that Markish wrote a philosophical poem with highly national overtones. This poem has never been published in the USSR. See: L. Podriadchik, "Unpublished Writings in Soviet Yiddish Literature," *Shvut,* no. 1, 1973, pp. 23-27.

43. See for example his poem "To A Jewish Danseuse," Kh. Shmeruk, ed., *A shpigl oyf a shteyn, op. cit.,* pp. 467–469.

44. I. Ianasovich, *op. cit.,* p. 321.

45. L. Podriadchik, "Unpublished Writings," *op. cit.,* pp. 18–21.

46. Kh. Shmeruk in: Der Nister, *Ha-Nazir ve-ha-Gediyyah,* Merhavyah, 1963, p. 43.

47. Der Nister, "Has," *Eynikayt,* June 29, 1944.

48. Shlomo Perlmutter, a young Jewish partisan, arrived in Moscow as Syenka/Shloymke Oylitski, in the summer of 1944 and met there with Jewish writers. After Mikhoels' encouragement, Perlmutter wrote an account of the relations between Jews and non-Jews in the partisan units in which he had served. A heavily censored version of this account was published in *Eynikayt* of August 3, 1944. For details of Perlmutter's encounter with Soviet Jewish intellectuals and leaders of the JAC see: Interview with Sh. Perlmutter, 12(93). See also: Kh. Shmeruk in: Der Nister, *Ha'Nazir, op. cit.,* pp. 44, 52. Fefer mentioned this young Jewish partisan in his article "Soviet Jews Fight," *New Currents,* vol. 2, no. 7, August 1944, pp. 14, 33.

49. Interview with E. Lidovski, no. 62(4).

50. I. Ianasovich, *op. cit.,* p. 240.

51. Interview with Rachel Korn, no. 11(93).

52. A. Donat, ed., *Neopalimaia Kupina,* New York University Press, 1973, pp. 319–320. See also his poem "Somewhere in Poland" written in 1915, in which he bewails Jewish suffering and persecution. In this poem Ehrenburg clearly spoke of a Jewish "community of fate," *ibid.,* p. 320.

53. See: T. R. Fyvel, "The Stormy Life of Ilya Ehrenburg," *Encounter*, December 1961, pp. 82–90. For a similar assessment of Ehrenburg's coopera- tion with Soviet intelligence see the testimony of a former Polish Jewish war- time refugee in Russia: A. Zvielli, "Jews of the Koltubianka," *The Jerusalem Post*, August 18, 1978. For a more detailed discussion of Ehrenburg's personal- ity and writings see: M. Friedberg, "Ilya Grigorevich Ehrenburg," Simmonds, G. W., ed., *Soviet Leaders*, New York, 1967, pp. 272–281.

54. I. Ehrenburg, *Merder fun felker*, Moscow 1944–1945, v. 2, p. 4. See also: I. Ehrenburg, *The War, op. cit.*, p. 142. A photograph of Ehrenburg surrounded by Vilna Jewish partisans appeared in *Eynikayt* on July 27, 1944. See, also the testimony of a Jewish partisan-girl a participant in this encounter, no. 831/36 H, Yad Vashem Archives, Jerusalem. According to one source Ehrenburg met in liberated Prague with young Palestinian Jews active in the Brihah. Interview with Shlomo Perlmutter, no. 12(93).

55. *Eynikayt*, July 29, 1947.

56. A. Sutskever, "Ilya Ehrenburg—a kapitl zikhroynes fun di yorn 1944– 1946," *Di goldene keyt*, no. 61, 1967, pp. 22, 30; S. L. Schneiderman, "Ilya Ehrenburg Reconsidered," *Midstream*, vol. 14, no. 8, October 1968, p. 64.

57. For details see: T. Dolzhanskaia, ed., *Na odnoi volne, op. cit.*, pp. 204– 206; B. Choseed, *Reflections of the Soviet Nationalities Policy in Literature: The Jews, 1938–1948*, Columbia University Ph.D. Thesis, 1968, pp. 244, 249; and W. Korey, "Ehrenburg: His Inner Jewish Conflict," *Jewish Frontier*, March 1968, p. 29.

58. This was the main gist of his remarks at the second JAC Plenum. See: *Eynikayt*, March 15, 1943.

59. I. Ehrenburg, "To the Heroes of the Ghetto," *New Currents*, vol. 2, no. 5, May 1944, p. 14. Ehrenburg published in *Eynikayt* a number of articles dealing with Jewish military contribution to the War, see for example: the issues of November 7, 1942, June 25, 1943, July 27, 1944 and November 8, 1944.

60. Ehrenburg's appeals and speeches at the various JAC functions are recorded in: *Brider yidn, op. cit.*, pp. 35–37; *Eynikayt* (Moscow) March 15, 1943; *Evreiskii narod, op. cit.*, pp. 38–41; *Eynikayt*, April 13, January 27, 1944 and January 12, 1946.

61. See: S. L. Schneiderman, *op. cit.*, pp. 60–61.

62. I. Ehrenburg, *Post-War Years, 1945–1954*, Cleveland-New York, 1967, p. 130.

63. H. Smolar, *Heikhan atah haver Sidorov*, Tel Aviv, 1973, pp. 176–179. For additional details see Chapter 3.

64. Ehrenburg was notified about the decision concerning the *Black Book* project by S. Lozovskii, see: A. Sutskever, "Ilya Ehrenburg. ." *op. cit.*, pp. 34– 35. Alexandrov's article was headlined "Comrade Ehrenburg Errs," *Pravda*, April 14, 1945. Ehrenburg's obsession with Nazi crimes became less relevant

now to Soviet policies. Ehrenburg's persistence was even considered obnoxious in some official Soviet circles. See: OSS report, April 21, 1945, National Archives, Washington, D.C., RG 226, XL 8036. See also Chapter 3.

65. For Ehrenburg's derogatory remarks about the JAC see: A. Sutskever, "Ilya Ehrenburg . . ." *op. cit.*, p. 30; Sz. Kaczerginski, *Tsvishn hamer un serp*, Paris, 1949, p. 56 and H. Smolar, *op. cit.*, p. 178.

66. For Ehrenburg's relationship with Mikhoels and Markish see: I. Ehrenburg, *Post-War Years*, *op. cit.*, p. 124; S. L. Schneiderman, *op. cit.*, p. 48; Interview with Natalya Vovsi-Mikhoels, no. 10(93) and with Esther Markish no. 5(93).

67. For details on the Ehrenburg-Sutskever relationship see: J. Leftwich, *op. cit.*, pp. 81–101. Ehrenburg's article entitled "The Triumph of Man" was published in *Pravda* on April 29, 1944.

68. *Eynikayt*, April 20, 1948.

69. At a meeting of Khrushchev with Soviet intellectuals in 1962, Galina Serebriakova, a veteran Bolshevik of Jewish origin and a camp returnee, openly charged Ehrenburg with complicity in the destruction of the JAC leadership. A careful analysis of this incident seems to indicate that her accusations were a rather thinly disguised political maneuver in the then prevailing clash between conservative and liberal intellectuals. For details see: *Khrushchev Remembers: The Last Testament*, Boston-Toronto, 1974, p. 79 and P. Benno, "The Political Aspect," M. Hayward and E. L. Crowley, eds., *Soviet Literature in the Sixties*, New York-London, 1964, pp. 196–197. Khrushchev testified that "Ehrenburg sometimes stood up to Stalin stubbornly," *Khrushchev Remembers, ibid.*, pp. 77–78. Ehrenburg was apparently asked to sign a prepared statement intended for publication in *Pravda*, in which Soviet Jews were advised to leave the urban centers and resettle in the provinces. He refused to do so, sending a personal letter to Stalin, explaining the futility and harm of such a step. See: H. Smolar, *op. cit.*, pp. 192–194 and R. A. Medvedev, *On Stalin and Stalinism*, Oxford U.P., 1979, p. 159.

70. V. Erlich, "The Metamorphoses of Ilya Ehrenburg," *Problems of Communism*, vol. 12, no. 4, July–August 1963, pp. 15–24.

71. For more details on Vassily Grossman see Chapter 3.

72. For details on Shpigelglas and Kotliar see: *Eynikayt*, October 17, 1946, and B. Z. Goldberg, *The Jewish Problem*, *op. cit.*, pp. 73–77. A certain Shpigelglas worked as one of the deputies to the Head of the Foreign Department of NKVD's Chief Administration of State Security in the 1930's. See: R. Conquest, *The Great Terror*, Penguin edition, 1971, p. 139.

Chapter 5

1. For the relationship between Communists and the Jewish community in the U.S. see: M. Epstein, *The Jew and Communism, 1914–1941*, New York,

n.d.; I. Howe, L. Coser, *The American Communist Party, A Critical History*, Boston, 1957; N. Glazer, *The Social Basis of American Communism*, New York, 1961.

2. For differing assessments of the impact of the Molotov-Ribbentrop Pact on Jewish communists in the U.S. see: Howe and Coser, *ibid.*, pp. 401–404; Glazer, *ibid.*, p. 154 and Z. Szajkowski, *Jews, Wars and Communism*, vol. 1, New York, 1972, p. 431.

3. A. Bittelman, *Jewish Unity for Victory*, New York, 1943, pp. 45, 47, 60–62 and same author in *Morning Freiheit*, April 18, 1943.

4. Bittelman, *ibid.*, p. 57.

5. For a discussion of the IWO and the JPFO, see Epstein, *op. cit.*, pp. 151–155; and Glazer, *op. cit.*, pp. 154–155. The JPFO was expelled from the American Jewish Congress in the late forties.

6. For details see: R. Saltzman, "Vi hobn reagirt di amerikaner yidn oyfn ruf fun di sovetishe yidn." *Yiddishe kultur*, no. 10, October 1942, pp. 1–7.

7. For more details about the IKUF see: M. Epstein, *op. cit.*, pp. 324–327 and B. Z. Goldberg, "IKUF un eynikayt," *Yiddishe kultur*, no. 1, January 1943, pp. 8–9.

8. "Bagrisung funem IKUF tsum yiddishn antifashistishn kongres in moskve," *Yiddishe kultur*, no. 5, May 1942, p. 60. The JAC expressed its appreciation of IKUF's work on behalf of the USSR on several occasions. See, for example: *Eynikayt*, September 7, 1944, and I. Fefer, "Vegn zhurnal Yiddishe kultur," *Eynikayt*, May 24, 1945.

9. ICOR and Ambidzhan, for example, collected money for a war project to transfer 30,000 Jewish orphans to Birobidzhan. Both organizations maintained contacts with the JAC and were mentioned favorably in its publication. See: *Eynikayt*, October 6, 1942, December 7, 1944, March 15, 1945 and November 13, 1945. In 1945 ICOR had branches in 50 American cities and was active in raising money for Yiddish cultural purposes in the USSR.

10. Abraham (Abele) Goldberg, who died shortly after wartime pro-Soviet activities were initiated within the American Jewish community, was a Russian-born Yiddish and Hebrew writer. At one time he was a leading Yiddish-Zionist orator. He was also among the founders of the American Jewish Congress.

11. *Tog*, February 28, 1943. For the involvement of B. Z. Goldberg and the Committee of Jewish Writers in the founding of the JCRWR see: memo by M. Perlzweig, April 13, 1942, Wise Papers, file 92 and *New Currents*, vol. 2, no. 4, March 1944, p. 16.

12. Dr. Maurice Perlzweig of the WJC, for example, pointed out "the need for American representation at the distribution end" (e.g. inside the USSR) and worried lest a Jewish aid campaign for the Soviet Union might affect WJC's fund raising adversely. M. Perlzweig to S. Wise, November 17, 1941, Wise Papers file 91. Leading JDC executives argued that the Russian War Relief was just another pro-communist structure and that its Jewish Section

might compete with the JDC. See: minutes of a meeting of the JDC Executive Committee January 27, 1942 and June 9, 1943. JDC Archives.

13. For these and additional details on the JCRWR see: Interview with Dr. Israel Goldstein; Interview with Rabbi Abraham Bik-Shauli, no. 23(93) and the Israel Goldstein Papers, Jerusalem.

14. E. Reznick, "Why I am Fighting," *New Currents*, vol. 1, no. 2, April 1943, pp. 20–21.

15. For the discussion of the "regional" aid concept between Mikhoels, Fefer and JDC executives see: pp. 131–132.

16. Ch. Zhitlovsky, "Di oyfgabn fun dem shrayber un kinstler komitet in der itstiker tsayt," *Yiddishe kultur*, no. 7–8, August 1942, pp. 3–4.

17. B. Z. Goldberg, "In gang fun tog," *Tog*, April 9, 1943. Goldberg wrote these comments at the peak of the discussion on the Erlich-Alter case.

18. *New Currents*, vol. 2, no. 10, December 1944, pp. 10, 33.

19. *Eynikayt* (N.Y.), October 21, 1943, and January 15, 1944.

20. For Zhitlovsky's attitudes towards the USSR during the War see: Ch. Zhitlovsky, *Di idn in sovetnfarband*, New York, 1943 and M. Unger, "Dr. Chaim Zhitlovsky un eynikayt," *Eynikayt* (New York), no. 4, July 1943, pp. 14–15, 26.

21. See, for example: letter by A. Khalatov, (Head of the OGIZ—the Union of State Publishing Houses in the RSFSR) to Shalom Aleichem's widow, Olga Rabinovitz, April 5, 1932 and Olga Rabinovitz to Solomon Lozovskii (Head of the Goslitizdat—the State Publishing House, at that time), November 17, 1938. Goldberg Papers.

22. B. Z. Goldberg to I. V. Stalin, June 3, 1946. Goldberg Papers.

23. See Goldberg Papers. This is also corroborated by Fefer's statement to the poetess Rachel Korn. Interview with R. Korn, no. 11(93).

24. For Goldberg's attitudes towards and impressions of the Soviet Union at that time see: B. Z. Goldberg, *The Jewish Problem in the Soviet Union*, New York, 1961, pp. 3, 23, 32, 40–41.

25. For the Goldberg-Epshteyn relationship and contacts see: *Tog*, February 1, 1941; Report by a *Tog* Committee submitted in connection with Goldberg's "trial," January 23, 1941, Goldberg Papers; U.S. War Department Report, September 22, 1944, case no. 2 S 294934 and FBI Report no. N.Y. 100 63112.

26. Edlin shared Goldberg's views of the Soviet Union. He was a member of several pro-Soviet organizations such as the JCRWR, the Writers' Committee and IKUF. American-Jewish communists, as well as the JAC, appreciated Edlin's friendly stand regarding Soviet Russia. See: *Morning Freiheit*, December 1, and December 25, 1947.

27. For examples of hostile polemics between Goldberg and the *Forward* see: *Tog*, July 11, 14, 20, 1943 and *Forward*, July 21, 1943. One of the *Forward* people even denounced Goldberg to the FBI and accused him of serving as a

Soviet agent. See: Letter to the Director of the FBI, April 4, 1941, FBI Archives, Washington, D.C.

28. See: B. Z. Goldberg to S. Mikhoels and I. Fefer, September 6, 1945. Goldberg Papers.

29. B. Z. Goldberg, "Di psikhopatologyc fun antisovetizm oyf undzer yiddisher gas," *Yiddishe kultur*, no. 2-3, February–March 1942, p. 5.

30. B. Z. Goldberg, "In gang fun tog," *Tog*, July 1, 1943; "Ikh hob dem koved fortsushteln," *Eynikayt* (New York), no. 4, July 1943, pp. 3-4; *Sovetnfarband faynt oder fraynd*, New York, 1948, p. 25.

31. JAC to B. Z. Goldberg, December 27, 1943; I. Fefer to B. Z. Goldberg, August 8, 1944 and S. Mikhoels to B. Z. Goldberg, September 8, 1944. Goldberg Papers.

32. See: M. Epstein's report to the FBI, FBI Archives, Washington, D.C.

33. For details on Joe Brainin see: *Hadoar*, vol. 49, no. 27, May 29, 1970.

34. See, for example, *Tog*, July 4, 1943. For JAC's appreciation of Unger see: I. Fefer, "Vegn zhurnal yiddishe kultur," *Eynikayt*, May 24, 1945.

35. O. Nathan, H. Norden, eds., *Einstein On Peace*, New York, 1960, pp. 204, 234.

36. *Ibid.*, pp. 322–324.

37. R. Clark, *Einstein—the Life and Times*, New York, 1971, p. 588.

38. December 1945. EMC, Section II c/10.

39. A. Einstein to J. M. Proskauer, February 23, 1944, Waldman Archive, American Jewish Committee, New York.

40. For more details see Chapter 2.

41. *Eynikayt*, March 17, 1945.

42. For details on the encounter between Einstein, Mikhoels and Fefer see: *Einstein on Peace, ibid.*, p. 324; Interview with Natalya Vovsi-Mikhoels, no. 10(93); A. Einstein to S. Mikhoels and I. Fefer, summer 1943, EMC Section II c/5; *Eynikayt* (New York) May 1945, p. 25.

43. I. Ehrenburg, *Post-War Years, 1945-1954*, Cleveland, 1967, pp. 72–77.

44. May 12, 1946. EMC Section II c/10.

45. This preface was published separately. See: A. Einstein, "Unpublished Preface to a Black-book," *Essays in Humanism*, New York, 1950, pp. 106–108. For additional details on the "preface incident" see Chapter 3.

46. Einstein's resignation was caused by the Committee's growing involvement in the partisan politics of the Yishuv in Palestine. He also became increasingly disenchanted with Soviet-Jewish policies. When, in 1949, Brainin asked him to sign a refutation of accusations against Soviet antisemitism, Einstein flatly refused. See: EMC Section II c/10.

47. The JAC mission to the U.S. was a typical Soviet wartime propaganda technique. A Soviet student delegation for example spent four months in the U.S. and England during the second half of 1942. See: *Pravda*, January 12, 1943.

210 NOTES

48. *Eynikayt,* August 15, 1942. For details on Soviet propaganda concerning the issue of the Second Front during the spring of 1943, when the Mikhoels-Fefer mission was initiated see: J. R. Hawkes, *Stalin's Diplomatic Offensive: The Politics of the Second Front, 1941–1943,* U. of Illinois Ph.D. Thesis, 1966, pp. 356–410.

49. *Evreiskii narod v bor'be protiv fashizma,* Moscow, 1945, p. 87.

50. Starting in March 1943, JAC's *Eynikayt* came out for the first time with extreme attacks against those Jewish elements in the U.S. which were critical of the Soviet Union. See: "Ofene diburim" *Eynikayt,* March 15, 1943; Sh. Mikhoels, "Opzogn zikh fun zey," *Eynikayt,* March 15, 1943 and the editorial of *Eynikayt,* March 25, 1943.

51. U.S. visas for Mikhoels and Fefer were apparently issued without delay and they weren't asked to register under the Foreign Agents Registration Act, as were later the representatives of the Soviet All Slav Antifascist Committee. At the same time however, Mikhoels and Fefer complained that U.S. authorities were not too helpful in speeding up their voyage to America. We do know that the FBI conducted a "discreet investigation" of the Mikhoels-Fefer visit, with the approval of the Department of State. For details see: *Evrei i evreiskii narod, op. cit.,* p. 110; *Mikhoels, op. cit.,* p. 258; Department of State memo, September 15, 1944, NADB. 860 H.01/9-1544 and Assistant Secretary of State to J. E. Hoover, September 18, 1943, FBI Archives.

52. Interview of Mrs. A. V. Azarkh by E. N. Trifonov, *Jewish Samizdat,* Vol. 12, Jerusalem, 1977, pp. 103–104, and B. Z. Goldberg, "Ten Years Later," *Israel Horizons,* vol. 10, no. 8, October 1962, pp. 14–20.

53. A. Bittelman, *Jewish Unity, op. cit.,* p. 57.

54. *Evreiskii narod, op. cit.,* p. 92.

55. B. Z. Goldberg, "Ten Years Later . . ." *op. cit.,* The Mikhoels-Fefer invitation is also discussed in B. Z. Goldberg, *The Jewish Problem . . . op. cit.,* p. 144 and in F. Sandler, "Organizatsyes far frayntshaft tsvishn Amerike un Sovetnfarband," *Eynikayt* (New York) February 1946, p. 21.

56. Memo on meeting between N. Goldmann and Loy Henderson, May 11, 1943. Z 5/371. General Zionist Archives, Jerusalem.

57. See: *Yiddishe kultur,* no. 6–7, June–July, 1943, pp. 63–65 and *Morning Freiheit,* July 1, 1943.

58. For a discussion of the Mikhoels-Meriminsky encounter, see Chapter 6.

59. M. Chagall, "Mayn ershte bagegenish mit Shloyme Mikhoels," *Yiddishe kultur,* no. 1, 1944, p. 9.

60. *New Currents,* vol. 1, no. 5, August 1943, pp. 14, 15, 22.

61. See: *Pravda,* July 15 and 16, 1943, *Eynikayt,* July 17, 1943. The Mikhoels-Fefer visit was also reported in *Eynikayt* of July 27, August 15, September 9 and 30, 1943.

62. "IKUF Bagegenish mit der sovetish-yiddisher delegatsye," *Yiddishe kultur,* no. 8–9, August–September 1943, pp. 88–90.

63. For a discussion of Abe Cahan, his personality and views see: I. Howe, *World of our Fathers,* New York, 1976, pp. 522–534 and Z. Szajkowski, *op. cit.,* pp. 422–425.

64. For these and additional *Forward* criticism of the Mikhoels-Fefer mission see; *Forward,* June 10 and 24, July 2, 3, 14 and 22, 1943.

65. Leivick who in the 1920's and early 1930's was affiliated with communist circles, openly condemned the execution of Erlich and Alter. Following the April 1944 JAC meeting in Moscow, exaggerated reports of the wording of Fefer's criticism of Leivick reached the U.S. This resulted in a condemnation of Fefer and the JAC by the Y. L. Perets Association of Yiddish Writers in America, which in turn was protested by B. Z. Goldberg's Committee.

66.ˑ Chaim Greenberg was arrested several times in Bolshevik Russia for his Zionist activities. During World War II he served as Head of the American Zionist Emergency Council and was influential in Zionist circles. American Labor Zionists were the only American Zionists to openly condemn the Erlich-Alter execution and the Mikhoels-Fefer mission. B. Z. Goldberg accused the U.S. Labor Zionists of breaking an alleged promise to Weizmann to abstain from attacks against Mikhoels and Fefer. See: B. Z. Goldberg, "Unity-Ten Million Jews," *New Currents,* vol. 2, no. 1, January 1944, p. 12.

67. J. Ciechanowski (Polish Ambassador to the U.S.) to the Polish Foreign Ministry in London, July 22, 1943 and H. Sztark (Polish Consul General in Pittsburgh) to J. Ciechanowski, July 26, 1943, PGHI, container 700.

68. Interview with Mordecai Corona by Moshe Nes-El. no. 1(93). See also: M. Litvinov to I. Kuttler, January 8, 1942 and M. Litvinov to M. Carona, March 4, 1942. Copies in the author's possession.

69. Interview with M. Corona; *Freivelt,* March 1944, p. 10 and February 23, 1945, p. 7. Umanskii, during meetings with representatives of local Jewish organizations, openly expressed his national identity and on one occasion declared that he intended to study Yiddish "a thing he owed to his People and to himself." See: *Freivelt,* February 23, 1945, p. 6.

70. Interview with M. Corona; *Der veg,* August 19, 1943; *Freivelt,* January–February 1945, p. 6.

71. Minutes of an extraordinary meeting of the Central Jewish Committee of Mexico, with Mikhoels and Fefer, PRO FO 371 33988 3168.

72. *Ibid.,* and *Freivelt,* January 1944, p. 24.

73. S. Mikhoels, I. Fefer, "Piat' dnei v Meksike," *Voina i rabochii klass,* no. 4, February 15, 1944, pp. 28–32.

74. Address by Dr. Israel Goldstein, Sept. 19, 1943. Goldstein Papers, File 3304, General Zionist Archives, Jerusalem; M. Kochansky, "Mikhoels," *The Jerusalem Post Magazine,* December 1, 1972, p. 27.

75. *The Jewish Chronicle,* November 26, 1943. For details about Mikhoels' and Fefer's visit to England and Jewish pro-Soviet activities there see: Interview with Prof. Chimen Abramsky, no. 3(93) and with Joseph Leftwich, no. 16(93).

76. *Eynikayt*, January 13, 1944 and March 30, 1944.

77. I. Fefer, "Fun Moskve kayn Moskve," *Eynikayt*, January 13, 1944.

78. O. Litovskii, *Tak i bylo*, Moscow, 1958, p. 161.

79. I. Fefer to B. Z. Goldberg, August 8, 1944. Goldberg Papers.

80. JAC to B. Z. Goldberg, December 27, 1943. Goldberg Papers; *Eynikayt*, January 6 and 13, 1944; I. Ehrenburg, *The War, op. cit.*, pp. 119–120.

81. S. Mikhoels, F. Fefer, "Poezdka v Ameriku" and "Piat' dnei v Meksike," *Voina i rabochii klass*, nos. 1 and 3, February 1944. The article on America was also published in *Eynikayt*, February 18, 1944.

82. Hamilton to Secretary of State, April 29, 1944, NADB 811.00/1070 and interview with Natalya Vovsi-Mikhoels.

83. Z. Szajkowski, *op. cit.*, pp. 378, 612–613; M. Epstein, *The Jew and Communism, 1919–1941*, New York, n.d., p. 321.

84. S. Wise to I. Goldstein, July 10, 1941, Wise Papers, File 84.

85. S. Wise to M. Boraisha, July 7, 1943, Wise Papers, File 90.

86. S. Wise to Mrs. F. Powell, June 25, 1946, Wise Papers, File 84.

87. Wise wrote in 1947 "I am of that larger number of Americans, who believe and pray for peace and friendship between the U.S. and the Soviet Union," S. Wise to J. Brainin, December 30, 1947, Wise Papers, File 84.

88. Interview with Nahum Goldmann, no. 8(93); A. Tartakower to I. Schwarzbart, October 4, 1943, Schwarzbart Collection, Yad Vashem Archives, Jerusalem, File M-2/448; *Haarets*, October 2, 1944.

89. N. Goldmann to the Jewish Agency in Jerusalem, October 28, 1940, General Zionist Archives, Jerusalem, File S/25. 487.

90. Memo by M. Perlzweig to S. Wise and N. Goldmann, July 17, 1941, WJC/R. File 37; letter by M. Perlzweig, July 13, 1941, PRO. F.O. 371, 27128.3225; see also comments by M. Perlzweig published in *Soviet Jewish Affairs*, no. 2, 1973, pp. 76–78.

91. Quoted in Y. Roi, "Soviet Contacts with the Jewish Yishuv in Palestine and with Zionist Leaders during World War II (June 1941–February 1945)," *Shalem*, vol. 1, Jerusalem, 1974, pp. 531–532.

92. *New Currents*, vol. 1, no. 5, August 1943, pp. 14–15. For criticism directed at Goldmann and the WJC by the *Forward* see: *Forward*, July 3, 1943 and July 14, 1943. The Bund accused Goldmann of not being able to grasp the tragedy of Erlich's and Alter's execution in the Soviet Union, *Der Veker*, August 1943, p. 7.

93. Interview with Chimen Abramsky, no. 3(93); *Erveiskii narod, op. cit.*, pp. 87, 97, 92, 122.

94. A. Tartakower to S. Mikhoels and I. Fefer, September 17, 1943, WJC/R, File 38.

95. American Jewish Congress Release, October 13, 1941. See also A. Tartakower to B. Vest, September 28, 1941, Central Zionist Archives, Jerusalem, File S/25/1935.

96. M. Perlzweig to S. Wise, September 25, 1941. Wise Papers, File 91.

97. Gromyko was anxious to learn whether the World Jewish Congress represented "the whole Jewish People." See: Minutes of the meeting between Goldmann and Gromyko, January 12, 1944. WJC/ File 37 and N. Goldmann to Gromyko, January 15, 1944, WJC/ R File 41.

98. *The Jewish Chronicle,* March 17, 1944.

99. JAC to WJC, May 2, 1944. WJC/ R, File 38.

100. S. Mikhoels and Sh. Epshteyn to N. Goldmann, September 5, 1944 and September 25, 1944. WJC/ R, File 38.

101. L. Zelmanovits to the WJC, January 5, 1945, WJC/ R, File 41. See also: Y. Rosenberg, "Meetings with Soviet Jewish Leaders, 1944–1945," *Soviet Jewish Affairs,* vol. 3, no. 1, 1973, pp. 65–70.

102. Y. Bauer, *My Brothers' Keepers: A History of the American Jewish Joint Distribution Committee, 1929–1939,* Philadelphia, 1974, p. 100.

103. *Ibid.,* p. 64.

104. J. N. Rosenberg to the JDC Administrative Committee, August 8, 1944, JDC/ A.

105. J. N. Rosenberg to the JDC Emergency Administrative Committee, August 8, 1944, JDC/ A.

106. P. Baerwald to J. N. Rosenberg, March 30, 1944, JDC/ A.

107. The suggested regions were the Uzbek and Kazakh Republics in Soviet Central Asia and the Volga Region. Memo of a meeting of Mikhoels, Fefer, Baerwald and Rosenberg, September 13, 1943, JDC/ A. B. Z. Goldberg maintained that JDC leaders planned to raise 25 million dollars for this purpose. See: B. Z. Goldberg, *The Jewish Problem in the Soviet Union, op. cit.,* p. 144.

108. Memo of a meeting, September 21, 1943, JDC/ A.

109. Memo of a meeting, September 27, 1943, JDC/ A.

110. S. Mikhoels and I. Fefer to J. N. Rosenberg, January 3, 1944, JDC/ A; According to one source, the JAC leadership discussed the idea of JDC assistance to the Soviet Union with Lozovskii already in the Summer of 1942. See: Interview with S. Volkovich by Y. Bar Haim, no. 19(42).

111. *Evreiskii narod, op. cit.,* pp. 87–88. See also pp. 107–108, 119.

112. E. D. Kisselev to L. Levine, Feb. 15, 1944. Goldstein Papers, File 3305. See also: E. D. Kisselev to the JDC, November 26, 1943, JDC/ A.

Chapter 6

1. For a discussion of pro-Soviet leanings within Hakibbutz Ha-meuhad see: A. Shapira, *Berl Katznelson; A Biography,* Tel Aviv, vol. 2, 1980, pp. 610–618.

2. See: Y. Roi, "Soviet Contacts with the Jewish Yishuv in Palestine and with Zionist Leaders, During World War II (June 1941–February 1945)," *Shalem,* Vol. 1, Jerusalem, 1974, pp. 527, 557, and *Haaretz,* March 15, 1968.

For an attempt to assess Ben Gurion's attitudes towards Russia and Stalin see: Sh. Sandler, "Ben Gurion's Attitude Towards the Soviet Union," *The Jewish Journal of Sociology*, December 1979, pp. 145–160.

3. Quoted in J. Hen-Tov, "Contacts Between Soviet Ambassador Maisky and Zionist Leaders During World War II," *Soviet Jewish Affairs*, vol. 8, no. 1, 1978, p. 55.

4. For details see: David Ben Gurion in *Davar*, February 14, 1964; Y. Roi, "Soviet Contacts," *op. cit.*, and Sh. Redlich, *Contacts Between Eretz Israel and the Soviet Union During World War II* (unpublished paper), Jerusalem, 1960.

5. See: Y. Roi, "Soviet Contacts," *op. cit.*, pp. 565–567; J. Hen-Tov, "Contacts Between Soviet Ambassador Maisky," *op. cit.*, p. 52; A. Cohen, *Israel and the Arab World*, Boston, 1976, p. 198. Maisky, himself half-Jewish, was arrested in early 1953 and probably accused of his "western" and "Jewish" links during the War. Three senior Soviet diplomats (Litvinov, Maisky and Umanskii) who maintained contacts with Jewish and Zionist leaders during the War, were of Jewish origin.

6. Y. Roi, "Soviet Contacts," *op. cit.*, p. 570.

7. Interview with Aharon Cohen and Shlomo Tsirulnikov, no. 21(93).

8. See for example: *Mishmar*, July 21, 1944.

9. See: J. Hen-Tov, *Communism and Zionism in Palestine, The Comintern and the Political Unrest in the 1920's*, Cambridge, 1974, pp. 45–65 and L. Trepper, *Hatizmoret ha'adumah sheli*, Jerusalem 1975, pp. 27–28.

10. *Information Bulletin*, USSR Embassy, Washington, D.C., September 5, 1941.

11. The activities of the V League are discussed in: *Evreistvo Palestiny narodam SSR, Sbornik ligi V*, Tel Aviv, 1943; A. Cohen, *Israel and the Arab World, op. cit.*, pp. 195–200. See also: Interview with L. Tarnopoler by Y. Bar Haim, no. 23(42) and interview with Sh. Tsirulnikov, no. 21(93).

12. Interview with Sh. Tsirulnikov, no. 21(93).

13. See: Memo of a meeting between Samuel Volkovich and Yitzhak Rabinovich, February 1, 1943, ZA File S 25/686.

14. *Evreistvo Palestiny, op. cit.*, pp. 83–88.

15. For details on the "Volkovich Affair" see: Minutes of the Volkovich-Rabinovich Meeting, *op. cit.;* Memo by Y. Rabinovich to M. Shertok, June 25, 1943, ZA File S 6/879; Interview with S. Volkovich by Y. Bar Haim, no. 19(42). Henry Shapiro was a veteran U.S. correspondent in Moscow with access to Soviet officials. In 1944, he suggested to the American Jewish Committee to act as liaison to the Soviet Government. See: D. Adelson to Slawson, May 3, 1944, Waldman Archive, American Jewish Committee, New York.

16. For contacts between the "V League" and Soviet diplomats see: Office of Strategic Studies Report no. 27502, August 5, 1944, National Archives, Washington, D.C., RG 226.43261; Polish Intelligence Report, August 8, 1944, PGHI, container 223; Interviews with A. Cohen, and Sh. Tsirulnikov, no. 21(93).

17. On "V League" missions to Teheran see: *Pravda,* May 2, 1943; A. Cohen, *Im ambulansim le'Teheran,* Merhavia, 1943; J. Riftin, *Bamishmeret,* Tel Aviv, 1978, pp. 56–61 and Sh. Redlich, *Contacts, op. cit.,* pp. 29–30.

18. S. Mikhoels and Sh. Epshteyn to A. Zweig, June 13, 1942 and JAC to "V League," August 23, 1942, V League Collection, Labour Archives, Tel Aviv.

19. *Eynikayt,* September 5, 1942, February 27, 1943 and March 15, 1943.

20. *Eynikayt,* January 27, 1943; V League to JAC, May 11, 1943, V League Collection, Labour Archives.

21. *Der veg* (Mexico), July 24, 1943 and B. Z. Goldberg in *Tog,* July 23, 1943.

22. Interview with Israel Merom (Meriminsky), no. 3(18).

23. The V League's efforts to have Mikhoels and Fefer visit Palestine are discussed in: Sh. Redlich, *Contacts, op. cit.,* pp. 34–35.

24. *Davar,* December 3, 1943.

25. *Mishmar,* October 25, 1943.

26. Interview with L. Tarnopoler by Y. Bar Haim, no. 23(42). See also Chapter 5.

27. See: *Evreiskii narod v borbe protiv fashizma,* Moscow, 1945, pp. 77–78.

28. *Evreiskii narod, op. cit.,* p. 145; Minutes of a V League Secretariat Meeting, September 26, 1944, V League Collection, Labor Archives.

29. *Mishmar,* August 6, 1944. Soviet contacts with the Yishuv in matters of propaganda seemed indeed to shift from the V League to more reliable pro-Soviet structures, such as Hashomer Hatzair's *Mishmar* and particularly the LEPAC (Levant Publishing Company) Information Agency, established in mid-1943. Lepac's future activities were discussed and planned by Tsirulnikov, Mikhailov and Petrenko back in 1942. They agreed on that occasion that a Palestinian structure modelled on B.Z.G.'s committee in America and fully cooperating with the JAC should become a link in the Moscow-New York—Palestine triangle. Unlike the V League, LEPAC acted on strict Soviet directives, but its public base was obviously much narrower.

30. Sh. Mikhoels and Sh. Epshteyn to the V League, September 28, 1944, ZA, file S 25/5298; Minutes of the V League Secretariat, October 25, 1944, Hashomer Hatzair Archives, file 3/40.

31. See leaflet issued by Tsirulnikov and Nehorai, October 31, 1944, Hashomer Hatzair Archives, file 3/40 and interview with A. Cohen.

32. *Eynikayt,* November 8, 1944.

33. See: V League circular, letter, no. 31, January 9, 1945, V League Collection, Labor Archives.

Chapter 7

1. W. O. McCagg, *Stalin Embattled, 1943–1948,* Wayne State U.P., 1978 pp. 164–166 and M. D. Shulman, *Stalin's Foreign Policy Reappraised, New York, 1965, p. 84.*

2. I. Gouzenko, *The Iron Curtain,* New York, 1948, p. 158.

3. See; for example: E. D. Kisselev to I. Goldstein, February 3, 1945, Goldstein Papers, File 3306.

4. *Eynikayt,* March 24, 1945. It was also reported at that meeting that JAC representatives met with representatives of Polish, Czech, Bulgarian and French Jews. Since, besides Ehrenburg, no JAC leaders had gone abroad at that time, these meetings apparently took place in the USSR.

5. I. Fefer and G. Kheifets to N. Meisel, August 22, 1947, Meisel Papers, Kibbutz Alonim, Israel.

6. *Eynikayt,* August 16, 1947; See also G. Kheifets to the WJC, August 27, 1947, WJC/USSR File no. 38.

7. *Pravda,* May 16, 1948.

8. P. Markish, "Der maskarad," *Eynikayt,* October 21, 1948.

9. S. Shliefer to The American Jewish Council to Aid Russian Rehabilitation, June 25, 1947, Wise Papers, File 84.

10. D. Weingard to I. Goldstein, October 4, 1945, Goldstein Papers, File 3306.

11. *Eynikayt,* January 12 and 17, 1946.

12. U.S. Embassy in Moscow to the State Department, January 24, 1946, NADB, 811.9126/1-2446. See also *Eynikayt,* June 4, 1946.

13. For details on Goldberg's "tour" see: *Eynikayt,* January 29, 1946; February 26, 1946; May 4, 1946 and B. Z. Goldberg, *The Jewish Problem in the Soviet Union, Analysis and Solution,* New York, 1961, pp. 77–80.

14. B. Z. Goldberg, *ibid.,* p. 92 and B. Z. Goldberg, "Ten Years Later," *Israel Horizons,* v. 10, no. 8, 1962, p. 18.

15. B. Z. Goldberg to the *Tog,* n.d., Goldberg Papers; B. Z. Goldberg, "A Bazukh in Yidishn Antifashistishn Komitet," *Eynikayt* (New York), April 1946, p. 22.

16. B. Z. Goldberg to J. Brainin, n.d., and B. Z. Goldberg to W. Morris, March 28, 1946, Goldberg Papers.

17. B. Z. Goldberg to S. Lozovskii, June 7, 1946, Goldberg Papers. See also: B. Z. Goldberg "Ten Years Later," *op. cit.*

18. Interview with Natalya Vovsi-Mikhoels, no. 10(93).

19. *Eynikayt,* December 1, 1945.

20. *Eynikayt,* May 25, 1946. On the 1946 Shalom Aleichem celebrations in the USSR see: *Eynikayt,* May 14, 1946; *Dos Naye Lebn,* June 7, 1946 and B. Z. Goldberg, *The Jewish Problem, op. cit.,* pp. 66–68.

21. FBI Report, March 31, 1947, File no. 100-63112; *The New York Times,* February 26, 1948.

22. Interview with Abraham Shenkar, no. 22(93) and FBI Report, April 7, 1948, no. 100-63112.

23. B. Z. Goldberg to S. Mikhoels, and I. Fefer, October 25, 1946, Goldberg Papers.

24. B. Z. Goldberg to J. Brainin, April 4, 1946 and B. Z. Goldberg to J. Brainin, n.d., Goldberg Papers.

25. Immigration and Naturalization Service to J. Edgar Hoover, September 16, 1948, File no. 56204/104, FBI Archives.

26. *Eynikayt* announced that Novick would spend a lengthy period in the USSR and would visit numerous Soviet localities. See: *Eynikayt*, September 26, 1946.

27. *Eynikayt*, October 22, 1946; P. Novick, *Eyrope tsvishn milkhome un sholem*, New York, 1948, pp. 349–354.

28. *Eynikayt*, November 14, 1946 and P. Novick, *ibid.*, pp. 270–272.

29. P. Novick, *Eyrope, op. cit.*, pp. 306–307; Interview with Paul Novick, no. 15(93).

30. P. Novick, *Eyrope, op. cit.*, pp. 322–325 and Interview with Paul Novick, no. 15(93).

31. Smith to Secretary of State, January 15, 1947, NADB 861,00/1-247.

32. Interview with Paul Novick, no. 15(93).

33. See: M. Kats, "Yidishe komunistn un Erets Yisroel," *Eynikayt*, (New York), September 1945, pp. 9–10.

34. M. Zinger, *Shlomo Kaplansky; Hayav u-Foalo*, v. 2, Jerusalem, 1971, pp. 85–87.

35. Sh. Kaplansky, *Hazon ve-Hagshamah*, Merhavyah, 1950, pp. 239–241.

36. Interview with Aharon Cohen.

37. B. Z. Goldberg to S. Mikhoels and I. Fefer, October 8, 1946, Goldberg Papers.

38. *Ibid.*

39. B. Z. Goldberg to S. Mikhoels and I. Fefer, November 27, 1946, Goldberg Papers.

40. *Eynikayt* (New York), February 1947, pp. 12–13.

41. B. Z. Goldberg to S. Mikhoels and I. Fefer, January 2, 1947, ACJWAS Files and B. Z. Goldberg to S. Mikhoels and I. Fefer, January 7, 1947, Goldberg Papers.

42. Sharp to L. Kubowitzki, November 7, 1946, WJC/R, File 38.

43. I. Fefer, "Oyf a shedlikhn veg," *Eynikayt*, July 12, 1947 and L. Goldberg, "Nokh der sesye funem eyropeishn rat funem Yidishn Velt Kongres," *Eynikayt*, July 22, 1947.

44. A. L. Kubowitzki to A. Gromyko, December 9, 1947, WJC/R, File 41; N. Barou to A. L. Kubowitzki, December 5, 1947 and A. L. Kubowitzki to A. Gromyko, December 17, 1947, WJC/R Files, nos. 38 and 41.

45. Report by F. Hollander to N. Goldmann and A. L. Kubowitzki, January 2, 1948, WJC/R, File 38.

46. I. Fefer, "Of di alte pozitsyes," *Eynikayt*, October 1, 1948.

47. For a discussion of the "Zhdanovshchina" and its Jewish implications see: H. Swayze, *Political Control of Literature in the USSR, 1946-1959,*

Harvard U.P., 1962, pp. 32–42 and B. Pinkus, "Soviet Campaigns Against Jewish Nationalism and Cosmopolitism, 1946–1953," *Soviet Jewish Affairs,* vol. 4 no. 2, 1974, pp. 53–72.

48. *Eynikayt,* September 12, 1946.

49. *Eynikayt,* September 21 and December 14, 1946.

50. *Eynikayt,* March 20, 1946.

51. I. Fefer, "Nokhamol vegn eynikayt," *Eynikayt,* December 3, 1946.

52. *Eynikayt,* July 12, 1947.

53. *Eynikayt,* February 17, 1948.

54. *Eynikayt,* August 9, 1947.

55. For details on the campaign against *Der Emes* Publishing House see: *Eynikayt,* December 25, 1947; February 17, 1948; March 25, 1948 and April 6, 1948.

56. See: Report by W. W. Richmond, San Francisco FBI Office, August 28, 1944, FBI Archives, and D. Dallin, *Soviet Espionage,* Yale U.P. 1955, pp. 435, 439, 467, 469. I would like to thank Mr. Arthur Braunstein for his assistance in obtaining information concerning G. Kheifets.

57. On Kheifets' position at the JAC See: Report by F. Hollander to the WJC, January 2, 1948, WJC/R File no. 38; Y. Roi, *The Relations Between the USSR and Israel, 1947–1954,* Hebrew University Ph.D. Thesis, 1972, pp. 209, 224; N. H. Cohen, "Vos hot gefirt tsum antisemitishn oyfbroyz in Sovetn farband un tsu masn shkhites fun yidishe shraybers?" *Tsukunft,* March 1972, p. 95 and interview with Joseph Kerler, no. 9(93).

58. *Eynikayt,* December 30, 1947.

59. Mikhoels, S. M. *Stat'i besedy, rechi,* Moscow, 1964, pp. 512, 535, 537.

60. Interview with Natalya Vovsi-Mikhoels, no. 10(93).

61. I. Fefer, "Mikhoels," *Eynikayt,* February 5, 1948.

62. Smith to Secretary of State, January 27, 1948. NADB 861.00/1-2748.

63. See: The Testimony by Abraham Shifrin. *Hearings Before the U.S. Senate Committee on the Judiciary,* 93rd Congress, First Session, Washington, 1973, Part I, February 1, 1973, pp. 22, 29 and Part II, February 2, 1973, pp. 96–97.

64. For information on Gusarov see: I. Lubachko, *Belorussia Under Soviet Rule, 1917–1957,* The U.P. of Kentucky, 1972, pp. 172–173; V. Gusarov, "Bestiarii", *Novoe Russkoe Slovo,* September 29 and October 14, 1972 and *Sovetskaia Belorussiia,* February 17, 1949.

65. H. Smolar, *Where Are You Comrade Sidorov?,* Tel Aviv, 1973, p. 171.

66. Interview with Natalya Vovsi-Mikhoels, no. 10(93).

67. *Khrushchev Remembers,* London, 1971, p. 262. A Soviet publication during Khrushchev's rule attributed the murder to Beria. See: *Sovetskaia Litva,* January 13, 1963.

68. S. Allilueva, *Only One Year,* New York, 1969, p. 154.

69. Interview with Prof. Chimen Abramsky, no. 3(93).

70. See: Kh. Shmeruk, ed., *A shpigl oyf a shteyn: An Anthology of Poetry and Prose by Twelve Soviet Yiddish Writers*, Tel Aviv, 1964, pp. 508–512.
71. I. Ehrenburg, *Post-War Years: 1945–1954*, Cleveland and New York, 1967, p. 125.
72. A. B. Ulam, *Stalin; the Man and His Era*, New York, 1973, p. 683.
73. *Pravda*, January 14, 15, 16, 17, 1948 and I. Liumkis, "Bam orn," *Eynikayt*, January 17, 1948.
74. *Eynikayt*, January 15, 1948.
75. For more details see Chapter 4. There are also those who believe that the official funeral was no more than a provocation intended to expose Jewish "nationalists."
76. See for example: I. Fefer, "Arum Gromiko's rede vegn palestine," *Eynikayt*, June 19, 1947.
77. Y. Roi, *op. cit.*, p. 108.
78. *Eynikayt*, May 20, 1948.
79. *Eynikayt*, August 19, 1948.
80. L. Goldberg, "Tsvey tsionistishe konferentsn," *Eynikayt*, September 7, 1948.
81. I. Ehrenburg, "Po povodu odnogo pis'ma," *Pravda*, September 21, 1948. See also: I. Ehrenburg, *Post-War Years, op. cit.*, pp. 125–127.
82. *Eynikayt*, September 25, 1948.
83. G. Zhits, "Undzer heymland," *Eynikayt*, October 19, 1948.
84. A. Dagan, *Moscow and Jerusalem*, London-New York-Toronto, 1970, pp. 36–37.
85. A Jew from the town of Mozir in Belorussia told U.S. Embassy officials in Moscow in early January 1948, that about a third of the Jews in his town were Zionists. See: U.S. Moscow Embassy Memo to the Department of State, January 13, 1948. NADB, 861.00/1-1348. See also: J. A. Gilboa "The 1948 Zionist Wave in Moscow," *Soviet Jewish Affairs*, no. 2, 1971, pp. 35–39.
86. See for example, M. Zand's memoirs published in *Maariv*, July 9, 1971.
87. B. Vaisman, *A Hebrew Underground Diary from the Soviet Union* (Hebrew), Ramat Gan, 1973, p. 228.
88. M. Namir, *Israeli Mission to Moscow* (Hebrew), Tel Aviv, 1971, pp. 356–357.
89. Interview with Esther Markish, no. 5(93).
90. Sh. Redlich, ed., *Jews and the Jewish People; Petitions, Letters and Appeals from Soviet Jews*, v. 1, Jerusalem, 1973, p. 323 and *Maariv*, September 19, 1971.
91. For alleged emotional reactions to the emergence of Israel by some JAC members see: B. Vaisman, *op. cit.*, p. 131 and interview with Joseph Kerler, no. 9(93).
92. M. Namir, *op. cit.*, pp. 250–251.
93. I. Ehrenburg, *Post-War Years, op. cit.*, p. 131.
94. *Jewish Life*, February 1957, p. 22.

95. M. D. Shulman, *op. cit.*, pp. 42–43.

96. For a discussion of paranoiac elements in Stalin's personality see: R. C. Tucker, "The Dictator and Totalitarianism," *World Politics,* v. 17, no. 4, July 1965, pp. 535–582.

97. S. Kot, ed., *Conversations With the Kremlin and Dispatches from Russia,* Oxford U.P. 1963, p. 153.

98. C. E. Bohlen, *Witness to History, 1929–1969,* New York, 1973, p. 203.

99. M. Djilas, *Conversations With Stalin,* New York, 1962, p. 154. Djilas arrived in Moscow on January 12th, 1948, on the eve of Mikhoels' murder.

100. S. Allilueva, *Twenty Letters to a Friend,* New York, 1967, p. 196.

101. *Pravda,* January 13, 1953.

102. *Jewish Life,* February 1957, pp. 20, 32.

103. The Fall and Winter of 1948/9 witnessed the liquidation of most of the Jewish institutions which existed in postwar USSR, such as Yiddish journals, theatres, broadcasts and *Der Emes* Publishing House. Following the liquidation of the JAC most of its leading members were arrested in late 1948 and early 1949.

BIBLIOGRAPHY

Bibliographies

Altshuler, M. *Soviet Jewry in the Mirror of the Yiddish Press in Poland: A Bibliography, 1945–1970.* Jerusalem, 1975.

Ben Yosef, A. *Bibliography of Yiddish Publications in the USSR during 1941–1948. Yad Vashem Studies,* vol. 4, pp. 41–72. Jerusalem, 1960.

Braham, R. L. and Hauer, M. M. *Jews in the Communist World: A Bibliography, 1945–1960.* New York, 1961.

Pinkus, B. and Greenbaum, A. A. *Russian Publications on Jews and Judaism in the Soviet Union, 1917–1967: A Bibliography.* Jerusalem, 1970.

Redlich, Sh. "Jews in Russia and the USSR". Horak, S. M., ed. *Guide to the Study of the Soviet Nationalities: Non-Russian Peoples of the USSR.* Littleton, Colo., 1982, pp. 122–149.

Shmeruk, Kh. *Jewish Publications in the Soviet Union, 1917–1960.* Jerusalem, 1961.

Archives

American Jewish Committee Archives. New York.

American Jewish Joint Distribution Committee Archives. New York.

Bund Archives of the Jewish Labor Movement. New York.

Central Zionist Archives. Jerusalem.

Centre for Research and Documentation of East European Jewry. The Hebrew University, Jerusalem.

(Alfred) Einstein Microfilm Collection. Princeton University Library, Princeton, N.J.

221

Federal Bureau of Investigation Archives. U.S. Dept. of Justice, Washington, D.C.
(Ben Zion) Goldberg Papers at the Dropsie University Archives. Philadelphia, Pa.
(Israel) Goldstein Papers. Jerusalem.
Hashomer Hatzair Archives. Kibbutz Giv'at Haviva.
Hoover Institution on War, Revolution and Peace Archives. Stanford University, Stanford, Calif.
Institute of Contemporary Jewry, Oral History Division. The Hebrew University, Jerusalem.
Jewish Labor Committee Archives. New York.
Labor Archives. Tel Aviv.
(Nachman) Meisel Papers. Kibbutz Alonim.
Polish Institute and Sikorski Museum Archives. London.
Public Record Office. London.
U.S. National Archives. Washington, D.C.
(Stephen S.) Wise Papers at the Archives of the American Jewish Historical Society. Brandeis University, Waltham, Mass.
World Jewish Congress Archives. New York.
Yad Vashem Archives. Jerusalem.

Personal Interviews

Abramsky, Chimen
Bik-Shauli, Abraham
Cohen, Aharon
Corona, Mordecai
Fajnzylber, Abraham
Goldberg, Ben Zion
Goldmann, Nahum
Kaminska, Ida
Kerler, Joseph
Korn, Rachel
Leftwich, Joseph
Mark, Esther
Markish, Esther

Merom, Israel
Novick, Paul
Perlmutter, Shlomo
Rubinstein, Joseph
Sfard, David,
Shenkar, Abraham
Smoliar, Hersh
Sorochkin, Elhanan
Trepper, Leib
Tsirulnikov, Shlomo
Vovsi-Mikhoels, Natalya
West, Benjamin

Newspapers, Bulletins and Journals

Daily Worker
Davar
Der Shtern

Der Tog
Der Veg
Der Veker

Dos Naye Lebn
Eynikayt (Moscow)
Eynikayt (New York)
Folksshtime
Forward
Freivelt
Haarets
Hadoar
Information Bulletin (Soviet
  Embassy, Washington, D.C.
Izvestia
Jerusalem Post
Jewish Chronicle
Jewish Telegraphic Agency News
  Bulletin
Krasnaia Zverzda

Kultura
Mishmar
Morgen Freiheit
New Currents
New York Times
Novoe Russkoe Slovo
PM Daily Picture Magazine
Polish Telegraphic Agency Bulletin
Pravda
Robotnik Polski
Slaviane
Sovetskaia Belorussiia
Sovestkaia Litva
Unzer Shtime
Unzer Tsayt
Voprosy Istorri

Books, Pamphlets and Manuscripts

Allilueva, S. *Only One Year*, New York, 1969.
—— *Twenty Letters to a Friend*, New York, 1967.
Armstrong, J. *The Politics of Totalitarianism*, New York, 1961.
Artem'ev, A. P. *Bratskii boevoi soiuz narodov SSSR v velikoi otechestvennoi voine*, Moscow, 1975.
Barghoorn, F. C. *Soviet Foreign Propaganda*, Princeton, U.P., 1964.
Batowski, H. *Wspolpraca slowianska*, Warsaw, 1946.
Bauer, Y. *My Brothers' Keepers: A History of the American Jewish Joint Distribution Committee, 1929–1939, Phila.*, 1974.
Bittelman, A. *Jewish Unity for Victory*, New York, 1943.
Black Book: The Nazi Crime Against the Jewish People, New York, 1946.
Bohlen, C. E. *Witness to History, 1929–1969*, New York, 1973.
Brider yidn fun der gantser velt, Moscow, 1941.
Budenz, L. F. *This Is My Story*, New York, 1947.
Cartea Neagra, Bucharest, 1947.
Case of Henryk Erlich and Victor Alter, London, 1943.
Cassidy, H. C. *Moscow Dateline, 1941–1943, Boston, 1943.*
Caute, D. The Fellow Travelers, New York, 1973.
Choseed, B. *Reflections of the Soviet Nationalities Policy in Literature: The Jews, 1938–1948*, Columbia University, Ph.D. Thesis, 1968.
Churchill, W. S. *The Second World War. Vol. 3: The Grand Alliance*, Boston, 1950.
Citrine, W. *Two Careers*, London, 1967.
Clark, A. *Barbarossa: The Russian-German Conflict, 1941–1945*, New York, 1965.

Clark, R. *Einstein: His Life and Times,* New York, 1971.

Cohen, A. *'Im ambulansim le-Teheran* (With Ambulances to Teheran), Merhavia. 1943.

—— Israel and the Arab World, Boston, 1976.

Conquest, R. *The Nation Killers,* London, 1972.

—— Power and Policy in the USSR: The Struggle for Stalin's Succession, 1945–1960, New York, 1967.

Cornell, R. *Youth and Communism,* New York, 1965.

Coser, L. *The American Communist Party,* Boston, 1957.

Curtiss, J. S. *The Russian Church and the Soviet State, 1917–1950,* Boston, 1953.

Czapski, J. *Na nieludzkiej ziemi,* Paris, 1949.

Dagan, A. *Moscow and Jerusalem,* London, 1970.

Dallin, D. J. *Soviet Espionage,* Yale U.P., 1955.

Davies, R. A. *Odyssey Through Hell,* New York, 1946.

Der Nister (pseud.) *Ha-Nazzir ve-ha-geddiyah* (The Monk and the She-goat), Jerusalem, 1963.

Djilas, M. *Conversations with Stalin,* New York, 1962.

Documents on Polish Soviet Relations, Vol. 1, London, 1961.

Dragunskii, D. *V kontse voiny,* Tbilisi, 1968.

Donat, A., ed. *Neopalimaia kupina,* New York U.P., 1973.

Ehrenburg, I. *Merder fun felker, 2 Vols.,* Moscow, 1944–5.

—— *Post-War Years, 1945–1954,* Cleveland, 1967.

—— *The War, 1941–1945,* Cleveland, 1964.

Einstein on Peace, New York, 1960.

Eisenstadt, S. N. and Graubard, S. R., eds. *Intellectuals and Tradition,* New York, 1973.

Elagin, Iu. *Ukroshchenie iskusstv,* New York, 1952.

Emiot, I. *Der birobidzhaner inyen,* Rochester, 1960.

—— *Memoirs:* Manuscript deposited at the Centre for Research and Documentation of East European Jewry, The Hebrew University, Jerusalem.

Epstein, M. *The Jew and Communism, 1919–1941,* New York, n.d.

Erickson, J. *The Road to Stalingrad: Stalin's War with Germany, Vol. 1,* New York, 1975.

Evreiskii narod v bor'be protiv fashizma, Moscow, 1945.

Evreistvo Palestiny narodam SSSR: Sbornik ligi V, Tel Aviv, 1943.

Fletcher, W. C. *Religion and Soviet Foreign Policy, 1945–1970,* Oxford U.P., 1973.

Gerson, L. L. *The Hyphenate in Recent American Politics and Diplomacy,* University of Kansas P., 1964.

Gilboa, Y. A. *Ha-Shanim ha-shehorot: Yahadut Berit ha-Moatsot, 1939–1953* (The Black Years of Soviet Jewry . . .), Tel Aviv, 1972.

Gitlow, B. *The Whole of Their Lives,* Boston, 1965.

Glazer, N. *The Social Basis of American Communism*, New York, 1961.
Goldberg, B. Z. *Ha-Ba'aya ha-yehudit bi-Vrit ha-Moatsot* (The Jewish Problem in the Soviet Union), Tel Aviv, 1966.
—— *The Jewish Problem in the Soviet Union: Analysis and Solution*, New York, 1961.
—— *Sovetnfarband faynt oder fraynd*, New York, 1948.
Goldstein, B. *The Stars Bear Witness*, New York, 1949.
Gouzenko, I. *The Iron Curtain*, New York, 1948.
Grossman, V. and Ehrenburg, I., eds. *Chernaia kniga*, Jerusalem, 1980.
Hearings before the U.S. Senate Committee on the Judiciary, 93rd Congress, 1st Session, Washington, D.C., 1973.
Hen-Tov, J. *Communism and Zionism in Palestine, the Comintern and the Political Unrest in the 1920's*, Cambridge, Mass., 1974.
Henryk Erlich un Victor Alter, New York, 1951.
Hingley, R. *The Russian Secret Police*, New York, 1970.
Howe, I. *World of Our Fathers*, New York, 1976.
Ianasovich, I. *Mit yiddishe shrayber in Rusland*, Buenos Aires, 1959.
Istoriia kommunististicheskoi partii sovetskogo soiuza, Vol. 5: 1938-1945, Moscow, 1970.
Istoriia velikoi otechestvennoi voiny sovetskogo soiuza, 1941-1945, Vol. 2, Moscow, 1963.
Jaffe, P. J. *The Rise and Fall of American Communism*, New York, 1975.
Jewish Samizdat, Vol. 12, Jerusalem, 1977.
Johnpoll, B. K. *The Politics of Futility: The General Jewish Workers Bund of Poland, 1917-1943*, Cornell, U.P., 1967.
Kaczerginski, Sz. *Tsvishn hamer un serp*, Paris, 1949.
Kaminska, I. *My Life, My Theatre*, New York, 1973.
Kaplansky, Sh. *Hazon ve-hagshamah* (Vision and Implementation), Merhavia, 1950.
Khrushchev Remembers, London, 1971.
Kohn, H. *Pan Slavism: Its History and Ideology*, New York, 1960.
Korchak, R. *Lehavot baefer* (Flames in the Ashes), Merhavia, 1965.
Kot, S. *Conversations with the Kremlin and Dispatches from Russia*, New York, 1963.
—— *Listy z Rosji do Gen. Sikorskiego*, London, 1956.
Leftwich, J. *Abraham Sutskever: Partisan Poet*, New York, 1971.
Leneman, L. *La Tragedie des juifs un URSS*, Paris, 1959.
Levering, R. B. *American Opinion and the Russian Alliance, 1939-1945*, University of North Carolina Press, 1976.
Levin, D. *Lohamim ve-'omdim 'al nafsham: Milhemet yehudei Lita ba-Natsim, 1941-1945* (They Fought Back: Lithuanian Jewry's Armed Resistance to the Nazis, 1941-1945), Jerusalem, 1974.
Lidin, V. *Liudi i vstrechi*, Moscow, 1961.
Litovskii, O. *Tak i bylo*, Moscow, 1958.

Lubachko, I. *Belorussia Under Soviet Rule, 1917–1957,* U.P. of Kentucky, 1972.

Lvavi, J. *Ha-Hityashvut ha-yehudit be-Birobidzhzan* (The Jewish Colonization in Birobijan), Jerusalem, 1965.

Mandelshtam, N. *Hope Against Hope: A Memoir,* New York, 1970.

Markish, E. *Le long retour,* Paris, 1974.

May, B. *Themes of Soviet War Propaganda,* Yale University, Ph.D. Thesis, 1958.

McCagg, W. O. *Stalin Embattled, 1943–1948,* Wayne State U.P., 1978.

Mikhoels, S. M. *Stat'i, besedy, rechi,* Moscow, 1964.

Mikolajczyk, S. *The Rape of Poland: Pattern of Soviet Aggression,* New York, 1948.

Namir, M. *Shlihut be-Moskva* (Mission to Moscow), Tel Aviv, 1971.

Nekrich, A. M. *The Punished Peoples: The Deportation and Fate of Soviet Minorities at the End of the Second World War,* New York, 1978.

Nemzer, L. *The Structure of Soviet Foreign Propaganda Organization,* University of Chicago, Ph.D. Thesis, 1948.

Nikolaevsky, B. I. *Power and the Soviet Elite,* New York, 1966.

Novick, P. *Eyrope tsvishn milhome un sholem,* New York, 1948.

Our Generation in Danger, New York, 1941.

Pawlowski, E.J.P. *Pan-Slavism During World War II,* Georgetown University, Ph.D. Thesis, 1968.

Redlich, Sh. *Ha-Ksharim bein Erets Yisrael u-Vrit ha-Moatsot bi-tkufat milhemet ha-'olam ha-shniya* (Contacts Between Eretz Israel and the Soviet Union During World War II, Jerusalem, 1960 (Unpublished paper).

——, ed. *Jews and the Jewish People: Petitions, Letters and Appeals from Soviet Jews, 2 Vols.,* Jerusalem, 1973.

—— *The Jews Under Soviet Rule During World War II,* New York University, Ph.D. Thesis, 1968.

Riftin, J. *Bamishmeret* (On Guard), Tel Aviv, 1978.

Roi, Y. *The Relations Between the USSR and Israel, 1947–1954,* The Hebrew University, Ph.D. Thesis, 1972.

—— *Soviet Decision Making in Practice: The USSR and Israel, 1947–1954,* New Brunswick, 1980.

Rothstein, A., ed. *Soviet Foreign Policy During the Patriotic War: Documents and Materials,* London, 1943.

Roy, R. L. *Communism and Church,* New York, 1960.

Rozek, E. J. *Allied Wartime Diplomacy: A Pattern in Poland,* New York, 1958.

Rubinstein, J. *Megiles Rusland,* New York, 1960.

Salute to Our Russian Ally, New York, 1942.

Savel'ev, V. M. and Savvin, V. P. *Sovetskaia intelligentsiia v velikoi otechestvennoi voine,* Moscow, 1974.

Schneiderman, Sh. L. *Ilya Ehrenburg,* New York, 1968.

Selznick, P. *The Organizational Weapon*, New York, 1952.

Shapira, A. *Berl Katznelson: Biografiya* (Berl Katznelson: A Biography), Vol. 2, Tel Aviv, 1980.

Shein, J. *Arum moskver yiddishn teater*, Paris, 1964.

Sherwood, R. E. *Roosevelt and Hopkins: An Intimate History*, New York, 1948.

Shmeruk, Kh., ed. *A Shpigl oyf a shteyn: An Anthology of Poetry and Prose by 12 Soviet Yiddish Writers*, Tel Aviv, 1964.

Shulman, M. D. *Stalin's Foreign Policy Reappraised*, New York, 1965.

Smolar, H. *Heikhan atah haver Sidorov?* (Where Are you Comrade Sidorov), Tel Aviv, 1973.

Solzhenitsyn, A. I. *The Gulag Archipelago, 1918–1956, Pts. 3–4*, New York, 1975.

Starobin, J. *American Communism in Crisis, 1943–1957*, Harvard U.P., 1972.
—— *The True Story of Erlich and Alter*, New York, 1943.

Swanberg, W. A. *Norman Thomas: The Last Idealist*, New York, 1976.

Swayze, H. *Political Control of Literature in the USSR, 1946–1959*, Harvard U.P., 1962.

Szajkowski, Z. *Di profesyonale bavegung tsvishn di yiddishe arbeter in frankraykh biz 1914*, Paris, 1937.

To Women the World Over, Moscow, 1941.

Trepper, L. *Ha-Tizmoret ha-adumah sheli* (My Red Orchestra), Jerusalem, 1975.

Tsveyter antifashistisher miting fun di forshteyer funem yiddishn folk, Moscow, 1942.

Ulam, A. *Stalin: The Man and his Era*, New York, 1973.

Vaisman, B. *Yoman mahteret 'ivri mi-Vrit ha-Moatsot* (A Hebrew Underground Diary from the Soviet Union), Ramat Gan, 1973.

Vaynroykh, H. *Blut oyf der zun*, New York, 1956.

Warren, F. A. *Liberals and Communism, the "Red Decade" Revisited*, Indiana U.P., 1966.

West, B., ed. *Hem hayu rabim* (They Were Many), Tel Aviv, 1968.

Wittlin, T. *Commissar: The Life and Death of Lavrenty Pavlovich Beria*, New York, 1972.

Wood, N. *Communism and the British Intellectuals*, Columbia U.P., 1959.

Zhitlovsky, Ch. *Di idn in sovetnfarband*, New York, 1943.

Zinger, L. *Dos ufgerikhte folk*, Moscow, 1948.

Zinger, M. *Shlomo Kaplansky: Hayav u-fo'alo (Shlomo Kaplansky: His Life and Deeds)*, Vol. 2, Jerusalem, 1971.

Articles

Alisova, L. P. "Kontrnastuplenie sovetskikh voysk severozapadneie Moskvy", *Voprosy istorii*, Dec. 1978, pp. 23–38.

Barghoorn, F. C. "Propaganda: Tsarist and Soviet," Lederer, I. J., ed. *Russian Foreign Policy: Essays in Historical Perspective*, Yale U.P., 1967, pp. 279–309.

Belenkii, M. "Dermonung vegn Mikhoelsn", *Yiddishe shriftn*, Mar. 1968.

Ben Shlomo, Z. "The Khrushchev Apocrypha", *Soviet Jewish Affairs*, No. 1, June 1971, pp. 52–75.

Boim, L. "'Od 'al ha'Va'ad ha-Yehudi ha-Antifashisti bi-Vrit ha-Moatsot" (More on the Jewish Antifascist Committee in the Soviet Union), *Ba'ayot Beinleumiyot* (International Problems), Tel Aviv, June 1971, pp. 19–33.

Chagall, M. "Mayn ershte bagegenish mit Shloyme Mikhoels", *Yiddishe Kultur*, No. 1, 1944.

Cohen, N. H. "Vos hot gefirt tsum antisemitishn oyfbroyz in sovetn farband un tsu masn shkhites fun yiddishe shraybers?", *Tsukunft*, Mar. 1971.

Dawidowicz, L. S. "Two of Stalin's Victims", *Commentary*, Dec. 1951.

Decter, M. "The Great Deception", Jensen, O., ed. *America and Russia*, New York, 1960, pp. 266–270.

Einstein, A. "Unpublished Preface to a Black-book", *Essays in Humanism*, New York, 1950.

Erlich, V. "The Metamorphoses of Ilya Ehrenburg", *Problems of Communism*, Vol. 12, No. 4, Jul.–Aug. 1963, pp. 15–24.

Filipov, B. "Aktery bez grima", *Iunost'*, Dec. 1964.

Friedberg, M. "Ilya Grigorevich Ehrenburg", Simmonds, G. W., ed. *Soviet Leaders*, New York, 1967.

Fyvel, T. R. "The Stormy Life of Ilya Ehrenburg", *Encounter*, Dec. 1961, pp. 82–90.

Gilboa, B. Z. "The 1948 Zionist Wave in Moscow", *Soviet Jewish Affairs*, No. 2, 1971, pp. 35–39.

Goldberg, B. Z. "IKUF un Eynikayt", *Yiddishe Kultur*, No. 1, Jan. 1943.

——"Di psikhopatologye fun antisovetizm oyf undzer yiddisher gas", *Yiddishe Kultur*, No. 2–3, Feb.–Mar. 1942.

——"Ten Years Later", *Israel Horizons*, Vol. 10, No. 8, Oct. 1962, pp. 14–20.

Gutman, I. "Yehudim bi-tsva Anders bi-Vrit ha-Moatsot" (Jews in Anders' Army in the Soviet Union), *Yad Vashem Studies*, vol. 12, Jerusalem, 1977, pp. 171–213.

Hen-Tov, J. "Contacts Between Soviet Ambassador Maisky and Zionist Leaders During World War II", *Soviet Jewish Affairs*, Vol. 8, No. 1, 1978.

"IKUF bagegenish mit der sovetish-yiddisher delegatsye", *Yiddishe Kultur*, No. 8–9, Aug.–Sept. 1945, pp. 88–90.

Kats, M. "Shakhne Epshteyn", *Yiddishe kultur*, No. 8–9, Aug.–Sept. 1945, pp. 10–13.

Kecskemeti, P. "The Soviet Approach to International Political Communication", *Public Opinion Quarterly*, Vol. 10, No. 1, Spring 1956.

Kerler, J. "Baym onhayb funem sof", *Tsuzamen zamlbukh*, Jerusalem, 1974, pp. 88–103.

Kochansky, M. "Mikhoels", *Jerusalem Post Magazine,* Dec. 1, 1972.

Korey, W. "Ehrenburg: His Inner Jewish Conflict", *Jewish Frontier,* Mar. 1968.

Litani, D. "Sefer shabor 'al shoat yehudei Brit ha-Moatsot" (Black Book on the Destruction of the Jews of the Soviet Union), *Yediot Yad Vashem,* No. 23/24, 1960, pp. 24–26.

Litvak, J. "Sheelat ha-ezrahut shel yehudim yotsei polin bi-Vrit ha-Moatsot (1941–1943) (The Question of the Citizenship of Former Polish Jews in the Soviet Union, 1941–1943) *Behinot,* vol. 7, 1976, pp. 85–100.

Mark, B. "Tsvishn lebn und toyt", *1961 IKUF almanakh,* New York, 1961.

Markish, E. "Shirei tsiyon be-rusit mi-yemei neurav shel Perets Markish" (The Young Perets Markish's Russian Songs of Zion), *Shvut,* no. 2, 1974, pp. 181–183.

Mikhoels, S. and Fefer, I. "Piat' dnei v Meksike", *Voina i rabochii klass,* No. 4, Feb. 15, 1944, pp. 28–32.

Morris, B. S. "Communist International Front Organizations: Their Nature and Functions", *World Politics,* Vol. 9, Oct. 1956.

Pinkus, B. "Soviet Campaigns Against Jewish Nationalism and Cosmopolitanism, 1946–1953", *Soviet Jewish Affairs,* Vol. 4, No. 2, 1974, pp. 53–72.

Podriadchik, L. "Yetsiort genuzot be-sifrut yiddish ha-sovetit" (Unpublished Writings in Soviet Yiddish Literature), *Shvut,* no. 1, 1973, pp. 23–27.

Polyanker, H. "Mayn fraynt Itsik Fefer", *Sovietish heimland,* No. 11, Nov. 1979.

Pruszynski, K. "Dwaj ludzie", *Nowa Polska,* London, Apr. 25, 1943.

Redlich, Sh. "Jews in General Ander's Army in the Soviet Union, 1941–1942", *Soviet Jewish Affairs,* No. 2, Nov. 1971, pp. 90–98.

——"The Jews in the Soviet-Annexed Territories, 1939–1941", *Soviet Jewish Affairs,* No. 1, June 1971, pp. 81–90.

Roi, Y. "Soviet Contacts with the Jewish Yishuv in Palestine and with Zionist Leaders During World War II (June 1941–Feb. 1945)", *Shalem,* Vol. 1, Jerusalem, 1974.

Rosenberg, Y. "Meetings with Soviet Jewish Leaders, 1944–1945", *Soviet Jewish Affairs,* Vol. 3, No. 1, 1973, pp. 65–70.

Salsberg, J. B. "Talks with Soviet Leaders on the Jewish Question", *Jewish Life,* Feb. 1957.

Saltzman, R. "Vi hobn reagirt di amerikaner yidn oyfn ruf fun di sovetishe yidn", *Yiddishe kultur,* No. 10, Oct. 1942, pp. 1–7.

Sandler, Sh. "Ben Gurion's Attitude Towards the Soviet Union", *Jewish Journal of Sociology,* Dec. 1979, pp. 145–160.

Schapiro, L. "The Jewish Antifascist Committee and Phases of Soviet Antisemitic Policy During and After World War II", Vago, B. and Mosse, G. L., eds. *Jews and Non-Jews in Eastern Europe, 1918–1945,* New York, 1974, pp. 283–300.

Schneiderman, S. L. "Ilya Ehrenburg Reconsidered", *Midstream*, Vol. 14, No. 8, Oct. 1968, pp. 47–67.

Shein, J. "Poslednie dni Solomona Mikhoelsa", *Grani*, Vol. 23, No. 68, 1968, pp. 106–118.

Shlomi, H. "Reshit ha-hitargenut shel yehudei Polin be-milhemet ha-'olam ha-shniyah" (The Beginnings of the Organization of Polish Jewry During World War II), *Gal-'ed On the History of the Jews in Poland*, Tel Aviv University, 1975, pp. 287–331.

Shmeruk, Kh. "Jewish Literature in the Soviet Union During and Following the Holocaust Period", *Yad Vashem Studies*, Vol. 4, 1960, pp. 3–72.

——"Yiddish Literature in the USSR", Kochan, L., ed., *The Jews in Soviet Russia Since 1917*, Oxford U.P., 1970, pp. 232–268.

——"Yiddish publications in the USSR from the Late 30's to 1948", *Yad Vashem Studies*, vol. 4, 1960, pp. 5–39.

Smolar, H. "Kabbalat ha-panim li-partizanim yehudim: zikhronot mi-1944 be-Minsk ha-meshuhreret" (The Reception of Jewish Partisans: Memories from 1944 in Free Minsk), Shvut, No. 1, 1973, pp. 166–170.

Sutskever, A. "Ilya Ehrenburg: A kapitl zikhroynes fun di yorn 1944–1946", *Di goldene keyt*, No. 61, 1967, pp. 21–37.

——"Mit Shloyme Mikhoels", *Di goldene keyt*, No. 43, 1962, pp. 153–169.

Tucker, R. C. "The Dictator and Totalitarianism", *World Politics*, Vol. 17, No. 4, July 1965, pp. 535–582.

Uldricks, T. J. "The Impact of the Great Purge on the Peoples' Commissariat of Foreign Affairs", *Slavic Review*, Vol. 36, No. 2, June 1977, pp. 187–204.

INDEX